THE RAPID CITY
INDIAN SCHOOL

1898–1933

THE RAPID CITY
INDIAN SCHOOL
1898–1933

by

Scott Riney

UNIVERSITY OF OKLAHOMA PRESS : NORMAN

Published with the assistance of the National Endowment for the Humanities, a federal agency which supports the study of such fields as history, philosophy, literature, and language.

Library of Congress Cataloging-in-Publication Data

Riney, Scott, 1965–
     The Rapid City Indian School, 1898–1933 / by Scott Riney.
       p. cm.
     Includes bibliographical references.
     ISBN 978-0-8061-4470-2 (paper)
     1. Rapid City Indian School. 2. Off-reservation boarding schools—South Dakota. 3. Indians of North America—Cultural assimilation.
I. Title.
     E97.6.R35R56   1999
     373.783'93—dc21   99-25821
           CIP

The paper in this book meets the guidelines for permanence and durability of the Committee on Production Guidelines for Book Longevity of the Council on Library Resources, Inc. ∞

CONTENTS

ILLUSTRATIONS

PHOTOGRAPHS

MAPS

TABLES

ACKNOWLEDGMENTS

Many people have aided me in this work. I am deeply indebted to Peter Iverson for his able direction of the dissertation on which this book is based. Peter also encouraged me to move quickly toward publication and introduced me to, among others, John Drayton of the University of Oklahoma Press. To John and Randolph Lewis go my thanks for shepherding me through the processes of manuscript submission and revision. Of those who have read the manuscript, Craig Howe, Brenda Child, and David Wallace Adams were particularly helpful and encouraging in their comments. Special thanks go to my sister, Pamela Riney-Kehrberg, and my parents, Norman and Mary Riney, for their assistance and moral and other support. I also wish to thank Sharon Kahin for transcripts of oral histories collected by the Warm Valley Historical Project, Fort Washakie, Wyoming. Sharon also put me in touch with Alan Trosper, who secured for me an interview with surviving Rapid City student Eva Enos, who was gracious enough to answer the questions of a young man with a tape recorder. My thanks go as well to the staff of the South Dakota Oral History Center, Pierre, South Dakota, for access to materials of the American Indian Research Project; Bill Nelson, for his excellent cartographic work; the staff of the South Dakota

State Historical Society—State Archives, for photographic repro-
ductions; and the staff of the National Archives—Central Plains
Region, Kansas City, Missouri, for their cheerful and able assistance in my research.

THE RAPID CITY
INDIAN SCHOOL,
1898–1933

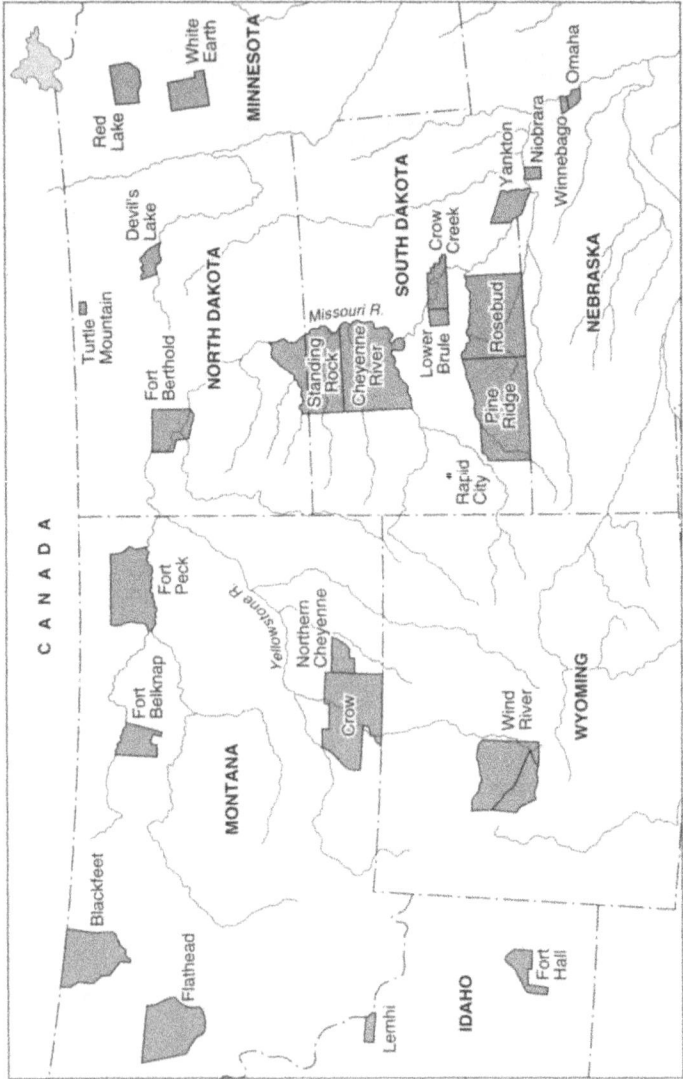

Northern Plains Indian Reservations in 1909

CANADA

MONTANA
Blackfeet
Flathead
Lemhi
Fort Belknap
Fort Peck
Yellowstone R.
Northern Cheyenne
Crow

IDAHO
Fort Hall

WYOMING
Wind River

NORTH DAKOTA
Turtle Mountain
Fort Berthold
Devil's Lake
Standing Rock
Missouri R.
Cheyenne River

SOUTH DAKOTA
Rapid City
Lower Brule
Crow Creek
Pine Ridge
Rosebud
Yankton
Niobrara
Winnebago

NEBRASKA
Omaha

MINNESOTA
Red Lake
White Earth

Introduction

*It did not occur to me at that time that I was going away to
learn the ways of the white man. My idea was that I was
leaving the reservation and going to stay away long enough
to do some brave deed, and then come home again alive. If I
could just do that, then I knew my father would be so proud
of me.*

LUTHER STANDING BEAR
on going to the Carlisle Indian School in 1879
(*My People the Sioux*, 128)

In the fall of 1879, a young Brule Lakota named Ota Kte noticed a
crowd of people around one of the agency buildings at the Spotted
Tail Agency on what is now the Rosebud Reservation in South
Dakota. With his friend Waniyetula, Ota Kte ran to join the crowd
to see what they were looking at. Peering through one of the
building's windows, Ota Kte and Waniyetula saw a room full of
people, several of them white, who tried to lure the boys inside
with sticks of candy.

Unsure what to make of the presence of white people and their
offer of candy, Ota Kte and Waniyetula retreated. When the boys

returned to the window, a mixed-blood interpreter whom they knew came to the door and persuaded them to enter. Inside, they saw with the whites two Santee Sioux boys, dressed in white man's clothing. If they would go east with the white people and "learn the ways of the white man," the interpreter told Ota Kte and Waniyetula, they could dress up like the two Santee boys.[1]

The interpreter's words did not much impress Ota Kte and Waniyetula. They had heard "sweet talk" from government interpreters before. Nor did they entirely trust white people. But to Ota Kte, "the thought of going away with what to us was an enemy, to a place we knew nothing about, just suited me." Ota Kte remembered his father, Mato Najin (Standing Bear), who had many times told his son the value of bravery on the battlefield. It was better to die young on the battlefield, even away from home, than to suffer old age. Yet Mato Najin had made peace with his enemies and no longer fought. Perhaps taking the chance to go east would prove Ota Kte's bravery.[2]

And so Ota Kte, who later took the name Luther Standing Bear, joined the first class to enter the Carlisle Indian School. For Standing Bear, going to a government boarding school in a far-away place was an opportunity to prove his bravery in a world where Lakotas no longer fought Pawnees or the United States Army. In a sense, going to school was a substitute for going to war. In a different sense, for the government, too, the school was a way to continue a conflict by other means. Just three years before Standing Bear made the journey to Carlisle, Pennsylvania, Lakotas and Cheyennes had defeated George Armstrong Custer at the Little Big Horn. With the conclusion of the campaigns that forced Lakotas and Cheyennes back to their reservations or into exile in Canada, the era of warfare on the Northern Plains came to an end.

The end of warfare did not, however, mean the end of conflict or that the United States government would welcome Indians into American life. Instead, the government began a concerted effort to settle the "Indian problem" once and for all by destroying American

Indian tribes and tribal cultures. The focal point of conflict, as always, was land. The large Indian reservations in the trans-Mississippi West, lands guaranteed to tribes when they ceded their territories to the United States, not only were the social, spiritual, and economic bases of tribal life, but were to whites the most visible evidence that Indians still existed within the borders of the United States. Acting on behalf of land-hungry whites, hostile to the continued existence of Indian tribes, Congress forced tribes to sell land on highly unfavorable terms in the 1880s and 1890s.

The largest reservations, and the largest forced sales, were in the Northern Plains. By threatening to seize reservation lands and give nothing in return, congressional delegations badgered the Lakotas into accepting the Great Sioux Agreement of 1889. The agreement took away 11 million acres of Lakota land and broke one large reservation into the five smaller, separate units that are the present Pine Ridge, Rosebud, Lower Brule, Cheyenne River, and Standing Rock Reservations. In return, the government set aside a $1 million trust fund for the Lakotas, but allowed them no say in how the interest income was spent. In 1890, a commission from the Bureau of Indian Affairs (BIA) manipulated Crow tribal politics to get a majority of the tribe's men to consent to the sale of nearly 2 million acres for $900,000, with the money again to be controlled by the BIA.[3] These and other land cessions stripped tribes of much of the land guaranteed them by earlier treaties and gave them in return money to be spent largely by the BIA on its own programs.[4]

Congress and the BIA not only took tribal lands, but tried to destroy tribes altogether by breaking up communal lands and placing them in the hands of individual Indians. The means by which they hoped to achieve this goal was the General Allotment Act of 1887, also known as the Dawes Act, which authorized the survey and division of Indian reservations. After the BIA had assigned a parcel of land (an allotment) to each head of family on a reservation, the "surplus" lands not allotted would be thrown open to white settlement, with the proceeds from land sales going into the reservation funds controlled by the BIA. The ordinary allotment size was 160 acres for family heads, with smaller amounts for minor children. Where land was suitable only for grazing, as on lands covered by the Great Sioux Agreement, the standard allotment was 320 acres. Under the Dawes Act, the BIA would retain control of allotments for twenty-five years as a trustee, during which time the land could not be sold. After twenty-five years, the allottee would receive title to the land and U.S. citizenship.[5]

Under the BIA's definitions at that time, someone who was a citizen was no longer a member of a tribe. Since treaties and other agreements were with the tribes, assigning land and citizenship through the Dawes Act not only would eliminate tribal lands, but would render the treaties moot by removing tribes' membership. In that way, Congress and the BIA hoped to free the federal government of its treaty obligations to American Indians. They hoped, too, that owning property, and being forced to farm their allotments to earn a living, would teach Indians thrift, hard work, responsibility, and other virtues many whites thought Indians lacked. The "Indian problem" would then be solved, for with no reservations, there would be no tribes and no Indians, only new, patriotic citizens scarcely distinguishable from their white neighbors. At the very least, the Dawes Act did much to separate Indians from their land. When John Collier, President Franklin Roosevelt's commissioner of Indian affairs, helped bring allotment to a close in 1934, the Indian land base had shrunk from 138 million acres to 52 million acres. Fragmented landholdings, another legacy of allotment, made Indian utilization of the remaining lands difficult. Fully two-thirds of all Indians were either landless or had too little land to make even a subsistence living.[6]

To facilitate the disappearance of Indians into the population, Congress and the BIA also acted against distinctive Indian religious and social customs. In 1883, commissioner of Indian affairs Hiram Price authorized the creation of special courts on Indian reservations to punish with fines and imprisonment those who participated in dances, giveaway ceremonies, polygamous marriages, or other customs the BIA wished to discourage. Like the Indian police forces on many reservations, the courts were to be staffed by Indian collaborators appointed by Indian agents, with the white officials in charge of each reservation. Though finding men who commanded respect in their communities and yet were pliant enough to follow the agents' orders proved difficult on many reservations, Indian police forces and Courts of Indian Offenses were powerful weapons against Indian religions and social customs. When the Indian police cooperated, Indian agents had both the means and the legal authority to break up dances, stop giveaways, and prevent Indian holy men and women from performing religious rites.[7]

The Indian police also helped Indian agents enforce the attendance of Indian children at white-run schools, either mission schools run by Christian denominations or the BIA's own schools. Boarding schools, particularly those built away from reservations, were the government's most powerful weapon against tribes and tribal cultures. To prevent the transmission of Indian languages, religions, and cultural values from one generation to the next, the BIA took Indian children from their families and enrolled them in government boarding schools for three to five years. Not only was instruction only in English, but the schools forbade the use of tribal languages and the practice of tribal religions and allowed the students little or no contact with their families.[8]

Whether tribes had fought against the United States, as had the Lakotas, or fought for the United States, as had the Crows, the government treated their children as the children of defeated enemies, whose nations were destined to disappear. The principal inspiration for the boarding schools did, in fact, come from experiments with Indian prisoners of war. While in charge of Indian prisoners from the Red River War of 1874–75 at Fort Marion, Florida, U.S. Army Lieutenant Richard Henry Pratt instituted a program of discipline, work, and education that included cutting the prisoners' hair, clothing them in army uniforms, assigning them to manual labor, and schooling them in Christianity and the English language. The prisoners appeared to respond well to Pratt. After their release from Fort Marion, twenty-two volunteered to go with him to the Hampton Normal and Agricultural Institute in Virginia, a school for African-American former slaves and their children run by General Samuel Chapman Armstrong. In 1879, Pratt secured funding from the BIA for a new school, the Carlisle Indian Industrial School in Carlisle, Pennsylvania.[9]

As superintendent of Carlisle from 1879 to 1904, Pratt developed a radical program of assimilative schooling. Students enrolled at Carlisle for a period of years, during which Pratt allowed no home visits. After students arrived, school staff cut their hair short and took away their old clothing and replaced it with uniforms. Pratt organized boys and girls alike into platoons and companies, with student officers, who marched them about campus like so many soldiers. He forbade the use of Indian languages. Children learned Christianity, the English language, and trades, such as tinsmithing or printing. Students spent summers living in the homes of local farmers, in what came to be known as the outing system. Pratt spoke plainly about his goals: "that all the Indian there is in the race should be dead. Kill the Indian, and save the man." Unfortunately, Pratt's school often killed the Indian *and* the man—or child. Between 1881 and 1894, for example, eleven of fifteen children sent to the Carlisle Indian School from the Wind River Reservation in Wyoming either died at school or returned home sick and died soon after.[10]

Thomas Jefferson Morgan, if less bluntly outspoken than Pratt, demonstrated a comparably firm commitment to assimilative schooling as a solution to the "Indian problem." A professional educator, Morgan became commissioner of Indian affairs in 1889. During his four-year tenure, he promoted the idea of universal compulsory education for Indians. Under his leadership, the BIA greatly expanded its schooling program; its most dramatic initiative was the expansion of a network of off-reservation boarding schools. These institutions bore much resemblance to Carlisle, but were not so distant from the western reservations. The BIA had opened twenty-five off-reservation boarding schools by 1898, including schools at Genoa (1884), Nebraska; Fort Shaw (1892), Montana; and Pierre (1891), Flandreau (1893), Chamberlain (1898), and Rapid City (1898), South Dakota (see table 1). The only off-reservation schools built in Plains states after 1898 were at Wahpeton (1908) and Bismarck (1908), North Dakota.[11]

Morgan had great faith in the power of education to bring about the assimilation of Indians. He proclaimed education "to be the medium through which the rising generation of Indians are to be brought into fraternal and harmonious relationship with their white fellow-citizens, and with them enjoy the sweets of refined homes, the delight of social intercourse, the emoluments of commerce and trade, the advantages of travel, together with the pleasures that come from literature, science, and philosophy, and the solace and stimulus afforded by a true religion." By portraying Indian cultures as degraded and backward, utterly useless in a changing world, Morgan was able to cast the government's attacks on the tribes as a positive good that actually benefited Indian children. In "A Plea for the Papoose," he imagined that he could divine the desires and goals of Indian infants and put in their mouths a plea for the gift of civilization, without which they would be lost: "Our only hope is in your civilization, which we cannot adopt unless you give us your Bible, your spelling book, your plow and your ax. Grant us these and teach us how to use them, and then we shall be like you." Lest Indian parents withhold the benefits of civilization from their children, and raise another generation of "barbarians," Morgan strongly supported compulsory education.[12]

Morgan's rhetoric aside, the use of education as a weapon against Indian cultures had predictably adverse effects on Indian children. David Wallace Adams scathingly indicts BIA boarding schools in *Education for Extinction: American Indians and the Boarding*

TABLE 1.

Off-Reservation Boarding Schools and Their Opening Dates

NAME	STATE	DATE OF OPENING
Carlisle	Pennsylvania	1879
Salem	Oregon	1880
Chilocco	Indian Territory	1884
Genoa	Nebraska	1884
Albuquerque	New Mexico	1884
Haskell	Kansas	1884
Grand Junction	Colorado	1886
Santa Fe	New Mexico	1890
Carson	Nevada	1890
Fort Mojave	Arizona	1890
Pierre	South Dakota	1891
Phoenix	Arizona	1891
Fort Lewis	Colorado	1892
Fort Shaw	Montana	1892
Mount Pleasant	Michigan	1893
Tomah	Wisconsin	1893
Pipestone	Minnesota	1893
Flandreau	South Dakota	1893
Wittenberg	Wisconsin	1895
Greenville	California	1895
Morris	Minnesota	1897
Chamberlain	South Dakota	1898
Fort Bidwell	California	1898
Rapid City	South Dakota	1898
Sherman Institute	California	1902
Wahpeton	North Dakota	1908
Bismarck	North Dakota	1908

SOURCE: *Report of the Commissioner of Indian Affairs, 1909, 78.*

School Experience, 1875–1928. In their drive to wipe out Indian tribes as distinct cultural and political entities, he argues, BIA educators did incalculable harm to Indian children. Adams's study is weighted toward the pre-1900 experiences of Indian children. He documents the malnutrition, physical abuse, humiliation, and cultural dislocation many children suffered. Boarding schools did not help Indian children to assimilate into the majority society, which in any case regarded them with suspicion and sometimes outright hostility. Instead, the boarding schools separated children from their parents and cultural heritages and gave them little that was useful. Why teach tinsmithing at Carlisle, for example, when factory-made wares dominated even the reservation markets?[13]

Adams describes the resistance of Indian parents and children to boarding school education, but the thrust of his argument is that the schools victimized Indians. Other works on Indian education lead in different directions. Robert A. Trennert, Jr., more fully develops the evolution of schooling over time in *The Phoenix Indian School: Forced Assimilation in Arizona, 1891–1935*. Studying the implementation of Indian educational policy at the local level, Trennert discusses interactions between the school and its staff and the local Indian and white communities that constrained the school's ability to follow the national policies that Francis Paul Prucha (*The Great Father: The United States Government and American Indians*) describes. Trennert finds an honest attempt to implement well-meaning policies of assimilative education at the Phoenix Indian School (one of the larger and better-funded off-reservation boarding schools) hampered by inadequate funding and the racism prevalent at the time in American society. Problems often had their roots outside the school, in areas beyond the control of school officials.

Another line of inquiry focuses on Indian reactions to boarding schools. Margaret Szasz studies the implications of Indian resistance to assimilative education in *Education and the American Indian: The Road to Self-Determination since 1928*. The BIA began a slow retreat from its policies of forcing Indian assimilation under President

Herbert Hoover's commissioner of Indian affairs, Charles James Rhoads, and assistant commissioner, Joseph Henry Scattergood. In a process that accelerated when John Collier became commissioner of Indian affairs in 1933, Indians began to have more voice in the schooling of their children. Szasz attributes much of the success of the Indian drive for self-determination in the 1960s and 1970s to lessons learned in the 1950s, when Indians tried to defend educational gains made under Collier against renewed pressures for assimilation.

Other works look more directly at Indian experiences with boarding schools. In *They Called It Prairie Light: The Story of the Chilocco Indian School*, K. Tsianina Lomawaima applies a rich collection of alumni oral histories to a case study of the Chilocco, Indian Territory (now Oklahoma), federal Indian boarding school, which her father, Curtis T. Carr, attended. Lomawaima pursues in depth themes of accommodation and resistance among Indian students, arguing that in creating their own cultures within the school Indian students came ultimately to possess it. Sally Hyer uses oral histories and an excellent collection of photographs in *One House, One Voice, One Heart: Native American Education at the Santa Fe Indian School* to claim that Pueblo children at the Santa Fe Indian School not only came to possess the school, but made it a uniquely Pueblo school. In *To Change Them Forever: Indian Education at the Rainy Mountain Boarding School, 1893–1920*, Clyde Ellis makes a somewhat different case for Kiowa responses. The Rainy Mountain Boarding School, a reservation boarding school located in Indian Territory, was comparatively small and badly underfunded. His work is primarily an administrative history, showing Rainy Mountain's evolution through the writings of school superintendents Cora Dunn and James H. McGregor. Ellis does, however, show that Kiowas made the school serve them by using the skills of graduates in the community's fight to resist assimilation.

Brenda J. Child's work is much more oriented toward Indian experiences of boarding school. She brings forth Indian voices from student and parent letters and other archival materials in the records of the Flandreau Indian School (Flandreau, South Dakota) and the Haskell Institute (Lawrence, Kansas) in her University of Iowa Ph.D. dissertation, "A Bitter Lesson: Native Americans and the Government Boarding School Experience, 1890–1940." Child, whose grandmother, Jeanette Jones Auginash, attended Flandreau, finds a more disheartening story of loneliness, deprivation, and loss. Although Child, like Lomawaima and Hyer, emphasizes Indian resistance to assimilative schooling, she places the experiences of Chippewa students in the context of economic and social developments on their reservations in Minnesota. Chippewa families strongly resisted sending their children to boarding schools, but the extreme poverty of their reservations, stripped of much of their land through allotment, forced Indian parents to turn to boarding schools as child care providers of last resort.

Resistance is not the only theme that can be derived from Indian experiences at boarding schools. Devon A. Mihesuah's *Cultivating the Rosebuds: The Education of Women at the Cherokee Female Seminary, 1851–1909* explores issues of race, national identity, and gender at a school controlled not by the BIA, but by the Cherokee Nation. Donal F. Lindsey pursues themes of race from a different perspective in *Indians at Hampton Institute: 1877–1923*. Hampton, an institution originally established to educate African-American former slaves and their children after the Civil War, also schooled a small but significant number of Indian students, whose presence allows Lindsey to throw light on the peculiarities of white prejudices and racial ideologies.

The history of the Rapid City Indian School offers an opportunity to explore in depth the interactions of Indian parents and students with an off-reservation boarding school. Opened in 1898, it was one of the smaller off-reservation schools. Enrollment figures from 1909 allow the school to be ranked with other similar institutions. Rapid City had an enrollment of 232 in 1909, drawn almost entirely from the Pine Ridge, Rosebud, and Cheyenne River

Agencies. Of the other off-reservation schools in South Dakota, Pierre had an enrollment of 162 and Chamberlain of 195. Flandreau, in the eastern part of the state, drew students from both South Dakota and Minnesota, with an enrollment of 411. Fort Shaw, Montana, enrolled 348. In contrast, Carlisle Indian School, in Pennsylvania, had an enrollment of 1,063. The BIA's other major school, the Haskell Institute in Lawrence, Kansas, enrolled 849. The largest of the reservation boarding schools in South Dakota, the Pine Ridge Boarding School, enrolled 244.[14]

The Rapid City Indian School had been constructed in an area of South Dakota west of the Missouri River that was undergoing rapid changes in the first decades of the twentieth century. The Bureau of the Census may have declared the passing of the frontier as a moving line of settlement after the 1890 census; however, the process of white settlement continued for another three decades, as Congress and the BIA pared land from Indian reservations to satisfy white land hunger. The Lakota reservations of western South Dakota quickly fell victim to western promoters and their allies in Congress and the BIA. In 1904, the federal government set off a great rush for land when it held a lottery for 2,412 homesteads carved out of the Rosebud Reservation. In 1907, the government opened the Lower Brule Reservation to settlement. In 1908, more Rosebud land went on the block. Between 1909 and 1915, tracts in the Cheyenne River, Standing Rock, Pine Ridge, and (once again) Rosebud Reservations passed from Indian control to the public domain. Trainloads of non-Indian settlers, most of them white, poured into the region to take advantage of the land offerings. For these people, South Dakota's west river country was "the last great frontier." For South Dakota's Indian population, the loss of land and the influx of white settlers signaled uncertainty about their reservations and their futures.[15]

With the closure of the Chamberlain school in 1909 and Fort Shaw in 1910, Rapid City assumed increasing regional importance. In the 1910s, the school expanded its base of recruitment to include the Wind River Reservation in Wyoming, the Crow, Tongue River (Northern Cheyenne), Fort Peck, and Flathead Reservations in Montana, and the remaining reservations of South Dakota. It remained, however, a predominantly Lakota school: of the 302 students enrolled for the 1921–22 school year, 234 were Lakota, 90 from Pine Ridge. Until 1916, the Rapid City Indian School offered grades four through eight, with occasional enrollments of children in the lower grades. In 1916–17, the school extended its curriculum through grade ten. Exceptional students who wanted to obtain high school educations transferred to the Haskell Institute. The Rapid City Indian School thus occupied an important niche in the educational ladder: not the top rung, but as high as most students would go.[16]

The off-reservation boarding schools that survived John Collier's efforts at consolidation in the 1930s became high schools; Haskell became a junior college. Rapid City met a different fate. For the 1929–30 school year, the BIA converted it to a sanatorium school to educate tubercular students. Rapid City resumed operations as a conventional boarding school in 1930, but lost out to the consolidation process in 1933, when the last of its students transferred and the school closed. In 1939, the BIA opened a full-fledged tuberculosis sanatorium, Sioux Sanatorium, on the old school grounds.

Although it lasted only thirty-five years, the Rapid City Indian School was significant in several ways. Its years of operation encompassed critical changes in reservation life on the Northern Plains. The school also spanned an important era in the history of Indian education, closing as the era of coerced, assimilative schooling came to an end. It took Indian students through formative years of their lives and provided for many the most advanced education they received.

Not all such institutions leave worthwhile archival records. The Rapid City Indian School generated a large volume of documents (some eighty boxes or thirty-nine linear feet), now housed at the

National Archives—Central Plains Region, Kansas City, Missouri. The documents are particularly varied in subject matter, including letters from students and their parents to the school, correspondence with other units within the BIA, and reams of internal correspondence. Reservation records, particularly those of the Pine Ridge Agency and Cheyenne River Agency, contain additional material related to the school. Supplemented by newspaper articles from the *Rapid City Daily Journal* and by oral histories collected by the American Indian Research Project, one of the Doris Duke series of oral history projects, and the Warm Valley Historical Project, from the Wind River country of Wyoming, the documents offer a surprisingly intimate look at the school.

I have chosen to organize my work on the Rapid City Indian School topically, rather than chronologically. A chronological approach would have pushed the work toward a narrative study of the most visible changes over time at the school and in BIA educational policy and limited the questions asked of the evidence. K. Tsianina Lomawaima's work shows the advantages of a topical or thematic approach to the study of off-reservation boarding schools, which allows in-depth analysis of questions beyond policy. Why did students go to the Rapid City Indian School? How well did the school attend to their physical needs? What did it try to teach students? How did students respond? Did the school have functions beyond its educational mission?

Continuing the evolution of the literature of federal Indian boarding schools, I have asked larger questions about the relationships between Indians and the Rapid City Indian School. The works of Lomawaima, Hyer, and Child reveal that Indians did not passively accept the challenges posed to their families and cultures by off-reservation boarding schools. The next question to ask is one of initiative: did Indians go beyond reactive responses to the school? Did they seek it out and initiate interactions? Is the model of action-response, with the school continually impinging on Indian lives and Indians responding, an accurate characterization of relationships at the school? Did Indians approach the school in isolation, or was it only one of many actors on the stage? Finally, and perhaps most importantly, what, if anything, did the Rapid City Indian School have to offer Indians? Could Indians derive any benefits from schooling that the BIA hoped would eliminate them as distinct peoples?

CHAPTER 1

MANY ROADS TO RAPID

On May 17, 1911, Nancy E. Ulargran of Gordon, Nebraska, wrote to the Rapid City Indian School to express her concern about three Indian children in her community. The children's mother had died, and the father, a Potawatomi living in Gordon, could not find a woman to care for them. The father did not want the children separated and asked Ulargran to write the Indian school on his behalf. Could the children, two girls and a boy, be enrolled at the school in the fall?[1]

The enrollment of Indian children in off-reservation boarding schools remains a complex problem in the historical literature. In *Education for Extinction*, David Wallace Adams writes that "[t]he opposition of Indian parents to white schooling was both deeply felt and widespread." Parents were especially reluctant to send their children to boarding schools. Adams details some of the strategies of resistance Indian parents employed: the refusal of individual families or entire communities to enroll children in school, the practice of sending away orphans to fill far-off schools, and the support and shelter given to children who ran away from school. In response, reservation agents withheld rations from resisting families or ordered agency police to round up school-age children.[2]

Case studies of off-reservation boarding schools reveal additional factors. Brenda J. Child emphasizes economic hardship as a
determining factor in the schooling choices of Chippewa families
from the Red Lake Reservation in Minnesota. In "A Bitter Lesson,"
she discusses the ways in which family crises, reservation poverty,
and the catastrophic effects of the Depression forced Chippewa
families to turn to boarding schools for child care. The devastating
effects of poverty played a role equal to the coercion of Indian
agents and reservation police in forcing Red Lake children into
boarding schools.[3]

In *They Called It Prairie Light*, K. Tsianina Lomawaima notes the
effects of the Depression on schooling choices. When hard times
made it difficult to provide for large families, Indian parents turned
to the Chilocco Indian School, in north-central Oklahoma. But
Chilocco represented more than simply a child care provider of last
resort. Indian parents also valued its educational resources. "Invol-
untary recruitment by coercion or starvation was not necessary at
Chilocco in the twentieth century," Lomawaima concludes. "In the
Indian Territory, education was by and large a desired commodity."
Chilocco offered an alternative to public schools, when public
schools would not enroll Indian students. As family members went
to Chilocco, attendance at the school sometimes became a family
tradition.[4]

Adams, Child, and Lomawaima all describe essential elements
of the boarding school experience. Some students attended
unwillingly, taken from their homes by reservation police. Poverty
forced others from their families. And for some students, attendance at an off-reservation boarding school was an opportunity to
gain an education, to meet students from other tribes, or to follow
in the footsteps of other family members. Depending on time and
family or individual circumstances, all of these factors were present
at the Rapid City Indian School. For Indian children from the
reservations of Wyoming, Montana, and western South Dakota,
there were many roads to Rapid.[5]

Luther Standing Bear, Brule Lakota, left the Spotted Tail Agency (later the Rosebud Reservation) for the Carlisle Indian School, in Carlisle, Pennsylvania, in 1879. Neither Standing Bear nor any of the other children in the first class to enter Carlisle knew what to expect from an off-reservation boarding school. Standing Bear at first had no thought of getting an education, but volunteered to go east to show his bravery, for his father had told him that it was better to do a brave deed and die young than to suffer the afflictions of old age. Many of the children expected to be killed by the whites along the way. Indeed, so many died of disease at Carlisle that a bereaved parent threatened Standing Bear with death when he returned to the reservation to recruit more students for the school.[6]

But Standing Bear persisted in recruiting students, and the BIA built more boarding schools. Commissioner of Indian affairs Thomas Jefferson Morgan (1889–93) advocated an integrated system of reservation primary schools, reservation boarding schools, and off-reservation boarding schools, through which children would progress in stages as they learned. An enemy of Indians, who advocated the swift destruction of tribes as political entities and the complete assimilation of Indians as patriotic members of American society, Morgan had little sympathy for Indian parents who showed reluctance to send their children to white schools. He was also aware that the off-reservation boarding schools could be run economically only when at full capacity. Under Morgan, reservation superintendents began the practice of withholding rations from Indian families that refused to send children away to school and used Indian police to seize children from their families.[7]

By 1900, the BIA operated 147 reservation day schools, with 5,000 students; 81 reservation boarding schools, with 9,600 students; and 25 off-reservation boarding schools, with 7,430 students. There were also 32 contract schools, run by independent organizations under contracts providing BIA funding, with 2,800 students; and 22 mission schools unconnected to the BIA, with

1,275 students. A visitor to the Rosebud Reservation in 1904 described Indian education as "compulsory in a way that compels." If a child missed a day of school at a reservation day school, the teacher reported the child's absence to the Indian police, who escorted the child to school the following day.[8]

Indian police played a similar role at the Cheyenne River Reservation, where the combined capacities of a reservation boarding school near the agency, a mission school at Oahe, five reservation day schools, and the nearby Pierre and Rapid City off-reservation boarding schools were sufficient to accommodate the entire school-age population of approximately 650 children. "By the early 1900s," Frederick E. Hoxie declares, "it was almost impossible for a family to avoid sending its children away for an education, the principal goal of which was to separate the children from their traditions and their past."[9]

The Rapid City Indian School was thus part of a larger effort by the BIA to compel the attendance of Indian children at BIA or mission schools.[10] For Luther Standing Bear, there had been only one school and a relatively simple choice: go to Carlisle or stay at home. But by the time the Rapid City Indian School opened in 1898, it had become increasingly difficult for Indian children to avoid white schooling altogether. At the same time, the number of schools increased dramatically. For Indian children and their families, choices became more complex, even as compulsory education dramatically decreased the range of possibilities. Reservation day schools had only the primary grades, often only the first four, and lacked the facilities to offer advanced instruction. Boarding schools offered instruction in the higher grades, but sometimes discouraged the enrollment of children in the fourth grade or lower or children with limited knowledge of English. Would children go to a reservation day school, and stay at home, or would they go away for their schooling? Would they start at a day school and then transfer elsewhere? If children chose to go away for their education, would they stay on the reservation, if not always near their home communities, or would they leave for an off-reservation boarding school? If they stayed on the reservation, would they go to a mission, usually Catholic, school or to a government school? If they left the reservation, would they go to Rapid City or Pierre, Haskell, or Carlisle?

Commissioner Morgan's vision of an integrated, rational system of government Indian schools did not come to pass. Rarely did Indian children go to a reservation day school for their primary education, move to a reservation boarding school for more advanced education, and graduate to an off-reservation boarding school for "industrial education" (a combination of moral and supposedly practical training, discussed in chapter 3) in an orderly progression. No single bureaucratic entity within the BIA coordinated all levels of education. Instead, important elements of Morgan's system fell within the control of separate, often competing jurisdictions within the BIA. Reservation day and boarding schools were within the jurisdiction of reservation superintendents. The off-reservation boarding schools had their own superintendents, each reporting directly to the office in Washington. In 1891, school superintendents became part of the civil service, and civil service reform reached the Indian agencies during the presidency of Theodore Roosevelt. As career civil servants, the superintendents knew that their tenure and advancement in the Indian Service depended on the success (as gauged by enrollments, graduation rates, and other measures of achievement) of their respective institutions.[11]

Rapid City's first two students, Nora and Oscar Ammiott, arrived at the school on September 20, 1898, brought by their father, "a Frenchman," from the Pine Ridge Agency, in South Dakota. Superintendent Ralph P. Collins (see table 2) did not greet the Ammiotts, for he was at Pine Ridge recruiting more students. He recruited twenty-two students from Pine Ridge and shipped them to the school by wagon. A month-long trip to the Shoshone Agency in Wyoming netted only four students, but the agent at the

Cheyenne River Agency, in South Dakota, delivered twenty-two more children to Collins. He took them to the school in wagons driven cross country in cold weather that was hard on the children and the superintendent alike. Such recruiting trips quickly brought the school into conflict with reservation officials. Superintendent Sam B. Davis reported an enrollment of 100 students in 1901 and claimed to have turned away applicants for lack of room. Parental acceptance of the Rapid City Indian School may be at least partially explained by Davis's practice of paying generous travel allowances to parents who brought their children to school. But an enlarged school could easily enroll 300 students, Davis determined, if not for the intransigence of reservation officials, who preferred to keep their own schools filled.[12]

Such bureaucratic jealousies aroused the ire of commissioners of Indian affairs William A. Jones (1897–1904) and Francis Ellington Leupp (1905–9), neither of whom was favorably disposed to off-reservation boarding schools. Jones believed that the number of off-reservation boarding schools was already sufficient for the

TABLE 2.

Superintendents of the Rapid City Indian School

NAME	YEARS OF SERVICE
Ralph P. Collins	1898–1900
Sam B. Davis	1900–1904
Jesse F. House	1904–22
S. A. M. Young	1922–25
Sharon R. Mote	1925–29
Ira C. Nelson	1929–30
S. A. M. Young	1930–32
Raymond E. Staley	1932–33

Source: correspondence of the Rapid City Indian School.

needs of the service, if not excessive. He did not sympathize with their superintendents' efforts to fill the schools to capacity. Jones described a "scramble for pupils among nonreservation schools" that was sometimes "so undignified as to call for drastic measures from this office." To limit competition between off-reservation schools, he assigned a recruiting territory to each school.[13]

Leupp likened the activities of recruiting agents to the African slave trade. Since Congress based appropriations for off-reservation boarding schools on yearly enrollment, at $167 per child, he believed the school superintendents were inclined to fill their schools with little or no regard for the health and welfare of the children. Decrying the "regular system of traffic in these helpless little red people," Leupp forbade outright the practice of sending recruiters to the reservations in 1908. If Indian parents wished to send their children to a nonreservation school, they could apply through their reservation superintendents, who were to respect the parents' wishes. Superintendents of off-reservation schools could send advertising material to reservation families. They could neither send recruiting agents into the field nor pay the transportation expenses of Indian children enrolling in their schools, however, and it was their responsibility to see to it that no child entered an off-reservation school without proper application, including signed forms of parental consent. Leupp supported compulsory education, but he enjoined reservation superintendents from withholding rations or benefits to coerce parents into sending their children to off-reservation schools. The commissioner believed that under these restrictions the system of off-reservation schools would disintegrate by degrees.[14]

Leupp's criticisms of off-reservation boarding schools remained persuasive, for they lent support to a powerful critique of federal Indian policy. Off-reservation boarding schools emerged as places where Indian children, forcibly removed from their families, endured attacks on their persons and cultures at the hands of assimilationist white educators. They stood as stark symbols of the wrongs of racist policies toward Indians. But Leupp's criticisms rested on assumptions about the roles of Indian parents and the nature of the choices before them that deserved closer examination. He assumed that Indian parents, if left alone, would have little reason to send children to off-reservation boarding schools; they sent them only when coerced or tricked into doing so by unscrupulous agents, in whose hands parents, angry and sorrowing as they were, were only so much clay to be molded to the demands of the dominant society. Whether modified through emphasis on parental resistance or on poverty as a motivating factor in parental decisions, elements of Leupp's view persisted in studies of off-reservation boarding schools. The perceptions that Indian parents were reactive, if not wholly passive, and that the off-reservation boarding schools were singularly lacking in appeal guided the discourse on Indian schooling.

Leupp's subsequent experiences as commissioner of Indian affairs suggest flaws in his basic assumptions. He tried to set forth a rational plan of Indian schooling in Education-Administration Circular No. 295, issued May 18, 1909. Indian parents were to be allowed to choose the schools to which they sent their children, "the only requirement being that they place them in some good school and keep them there in regular attendance." In no way did this amount to freedom of choice for Indian parents, for it did not allow them the option of educating their children traditionally, in their own cultures. Leupp believed, however, that allowing Indian parents a modicum of control over their children's schooling prompted an increased interest in education among Indians.[15]

To Leupp's chagrin, Indian parents tended to "overstep the privilege" allowed them, in his opinion, and "disregard the legitimate authority of the Reservation Superintendent by sending to non-reservation schools children of any age and stage of advancement." Leupp believed in a structured system not unlike that proposed by Morgan. He wanted children to go to reservation schools first and preferably to day schools, unless other circumstances, such as distance from a school, forced parents to send their children to reservation boarding schools. The off-reservation schools, expensive to equip and maintain, were for children fourteen or older, who had the maturity and prior schooling necessary to take advantage of the advanced instruction an off-reservation boarding school offered. No children under fourteen were to be transferred to or otherwise enrolled in an off-reservation boarding school without special authority from the Office of the Commissioner. Leupp ordered Circular No. 295 posted conspicuously at school and agency offices, so parents could acquaint themselves with it.[16]

Because Indian parents preferred to keep the children in a family together when at school, the Rapid City Indian School never entirely succeeded in eliminating the lower grades. When the Chamberlain, South Dakota, boarding school closed in 1909, Superintendent Jesse F. House arranged the transfers of former Chamberlain students from the Crow Creek and Lower Brule Reservations to Rapid City. He asked permission from the commissioner of Indian affairs to enroll children under the age of fourteen, for Chamberlain had enrolled whole families of children. To take only the older children would divide the families, to which the parents would not consent. Acting Commissioner F. H. Abbott responded by waiving the age limit for transfers from Chamberlain and allowed House to enroll any child who had an older sibling at Rapid City. The issue came up again in 1910, as House began enrollment processes for fiscal year 1911. House asked commissioner of Indian affairs Robert G. Valentine (1909–12) to lower the age limit for enrollment at Rapid City to twelve and also asked that the limit be removed entirely when necessary to enroll an entire family. "The parents living on these nearby reservations prefer to have all their children in one school," House wrote, "and would not care to send the older children here, and the younger ones to the reservation schools."[17]

As late as 1932, with the BIA closing down the Rapid City Indian School to make way for a tuberculosis sanatorium (Sioux

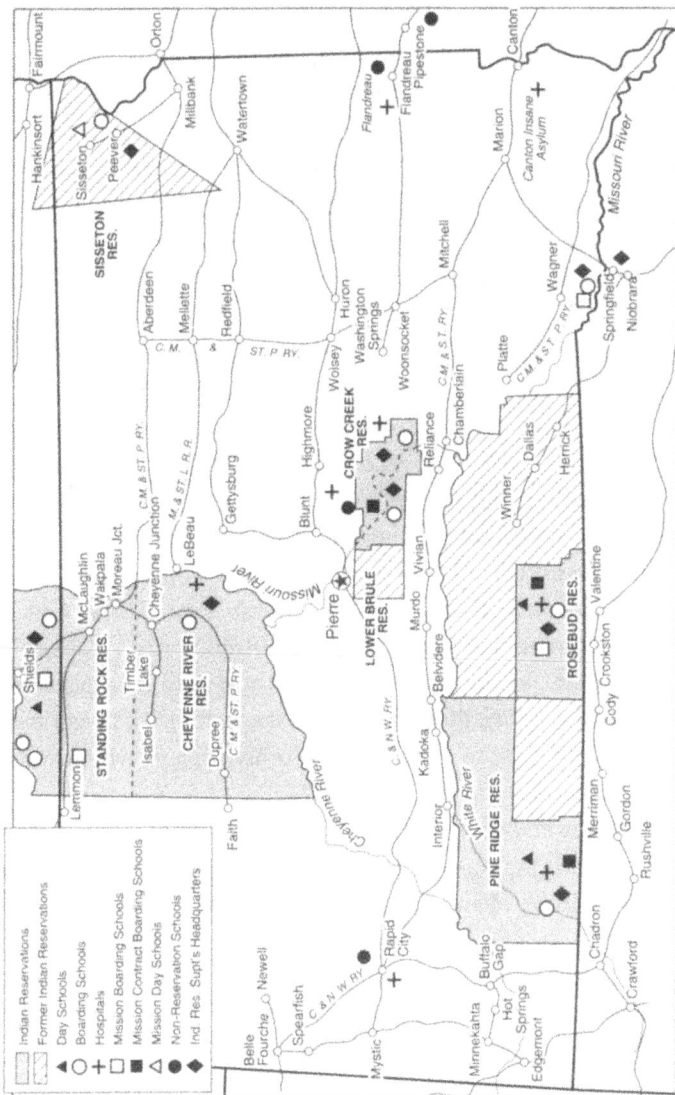

South Dakota Indian Reservations in 1920

Sanatorium or "Sioux San"), the school worked to accommodate the wishes of parents who preferred to keep families together. As part of the consolidation process that preceded the school's closure, the BIA transferred the last of Rapid City's younger pupils, below the fourth grade, to the Pierre, South Dakota, off-reservation boarding school. C. M. Schwandt, school social worker, asked Principal Kirk K. Newport if two of the four children of Moses B. Eagle could be advanced to the fourth grade so they could remain at Rapid City with their two older brothers. The children wanted to stay at the school, and Eagle was "very satisfied with what the school has done for his children. He is confident that they will be safe and for that reason wishes them to remain together." Newport did not think it in the interests of the two younger boys for them to advance to the fourth grade and released the two older boys to the Pierre Indian School so the family could remain together.[18]

The desire of Indian parents to keep families together thus challenged Leupp's assumptions about off-reservation boarding schools. The Rapid City Indian School indeed took in children under a wide range of circumstances. Particularly before Leupp's reforms, it enrolled children under duress. In September 1907, for example, John R. Brennan, agent of the Pine Ridge Agency, authorized the school to round up and enroll thirteen children he believed were "loafing around the town and should be in school." In October 1907, Pine Ridge day school inspector J. J. Duncan asked Rapid City to capture three young women, one of whom was to be enrolled at the school.[19]

As Adams and Child have noted, parents sometimes refused to send their children to off-reservation boarding schools out of fear for the children's health or their very lives. Tuberculosis, measles, and other diseases took a heavy toll, particularly in the early years of the off-reservation schools. Between 1881 and 1894, eleven of fifteen children sent to the Carlisle Indian School from the Wind River Reservation in Wyoming either died at school or returned home sick and died soon after. Of fifty-four children sent from

Wind River to the Genoa Indian School (Genoa, Nebraska), twenty-three died at school or came home to die, and another twelve returned home invalids. Three of the four Wind River children sent to the Santee, Nebraska, school returned home sick and died. Parents had good reason to fear boarding schools, where once-healthy children might be crowded into dormitories and classrooms with students with active, contagious tuberculosis and where medical care was either primitive or wholly absent.[20]

Aware of the risks through bitter experience, parents tried to see that their children went to schools where the children were healthy and kept them out of schools where too many deaths occurred. In 1911, for example, parents of students from the Tongue River Agency in Montana refused to return their children to the Rapid City Indian School at the end of summer vacations. Two Tongue River boys had died the previous year, and the parents feared that more would die over the winter. They were willing to send their children to other off-reservation boarding schools, but not to Rapid City.[21]

Yet parents and children alike sometimes preferred off-reservation boarding schools in general, or the Rapid City Indian School in particular, to other schools. Some found day schools inconvenient or simply inferior to boarding schools. Mrs. Joseph Brown put her two oldest girls in Rapid City because the closest day school on the Pine Ridge reservation, Number 14 Day School, was four miles away and attending school regularly was too great a hardship in winter. Felix Eagle Feather, a Lakota from the Rosebud Reservation and parent of a Rapid City student, told Superintendent House in 1910 that he wished the government would close all the day schools, because the nonreservation schools did more good for the children than day schools did. In 1911, Charlie B. Twiss, a student forced to enroll in a day school as Rapid City tried to transfer out children under the age of fourteen, asked House for permission to return to Rapid City. "I don't want to go to the day school," Twiss wrote. "I could learn nothing so I want to come back." Eva Enos and other Arapaho students from the Wind River Reservation went to Rapid City because they wanted to get away from St. Michael's Mission and try something different.[22]

Parents sometimes complained about the quality of education available at reservation boarding schools or mission schools. In 1910, Nicholas Ruleau applied for his three daughters to enter the Rapid City Indian School. Two of his daughters, Zona and Isabel, had been attending the Holy Rosary Mission at Pine Ridge for three years, and Ruleau complained that "they don't seem to make any progress in their studies." He also wanted to keep all his children at one school. Alfred Black Bear sent his daughter to Rapid City after she ran away from Holy Rosary "because they were always praying" and she wanted to go to a better school. A. Hankaas pulled his two children, a nine-year-old girl and a seven-year-old boy, out of the Rosebud Boarding School and sought their placement at Rapid City, though both were underage. He vowed never to send his children to the Rosebud school again, even if it meant holding them out of school entirely. "I put them there to learn white man way in stead of that they learn how to talk Indian," Hankaas complained. He was also concerned because the Rosebud superintendent turned his children out for the summer before he got to the school to pick them up.[23]

Despite Leupp's hope that the off-reservation boarding schools would disintegrate by degrees, the Rapid City Indian School adapted well to the competitive recruiting environment he created. The yearly routine of recruiting and enrolling students underwent only minor modifications during Leupp's tenure and lasted with few changes until the school's closure in 1933. Recruiting trips to the reservations of Wyoming, Montana, and western South Dakota remained essential to securing students for the school. Leupp's orders shifted the burdens of travel and recruiting back to the school superintendent. During and immediately after his tenure as commissioner of Indian affairs, superintendents had to avoid even the appearance of recruiting. When Superintendent House asked permission in August 1909 to send Rapid City's principal teacher, a Mr. Morrow, to the Tongue River Agency in Montana to return three runaway boys to the school, Acting Commissioner F. H. Abbott refused. It was the "collecting season" on the reservation, and Abbott thought it likely that others in the bureau would consider Morrow's mission merely a thinly disguised recruiting trip.[24]

Superintendent House entered the 1910 recruiting season complaining about the prohibition against using assistants. He had letters from a number of reservation communities indicating interest in the school and thought he could secure full enrollment without difficulty. House intended to do the actual solicitation himself, but believed the work would go better if he had someone else available to arrange for the transportation of the new students, once he had signed them up for the school. Doing the work himself, House thought it took too long to get from place to place. Despite the difficulties, he visited Pine Ridge Agency, Crow Agency, Yankton Agency, and the Rosebud Reservation over a two-week period, passing out 700 school catalogs as well as sending out circular letters to interested students and their families.[25]

House's trip secured 300 students for Rapid City in 1910, some 277 of whom the school enrolled. After physical examinations, the school physician sent home 23 students whose health did not permit their enrollment. House circumvented the restrictions on using assistants by sending out two employees as his "personal representatives," a device that Harvey B. Peairs, supervisor in charge of Indian schools, tacitly approved. One of House's representatives, matron E. O. Stilwell, attended a meeting of Indian parents near Oelrichs, on the Pine Ridge Reservation, where she distributed catalogs and met parents, though without directly enrolling students. The other, Frances Thackery, went to Rosebud at the request of the reservation superintendent, to escort a party of twelve students to the school. House found reservation officials somewhat reluctant to allow students to transfer to Rapid City, but thought there was much more interest in the school among parents and potential students.[26]

In subsequent years, as the controversy over recruitment died down, at least within the BIA, more of the task of recruitment fell on senior employees of the school. Principal George E. Peters spent a week, for example, canvassing the Rosebud Reservation in 1917. He hired teams and buggies when necessary, caught rides with other travelers whenever possible, and told House that the work would go much faster if he had a car. Peters's travels brought him into close contact with students and their families, for he visited them at fairs and in their summer camps. He met old students, who asked him about their grades, and reported "quite a good feeling toward the R.C. school among the Indians." But they moved camp frequently during the summer and were rarely at home, and Peters ran short of money trying to catch up with them. Superintendent House, whose work as supervising superintendent of the Crow Creek, Lower Brule, Rosebud, and Pine Ridge Reservations often took him into the field, suggested that Peters remain at Rosebud Agency and allow the people to come to him. Peters, though, worried about staying ahead of the recruiter from the Pierre Indian School, who was also working the Rosebud.[27]

Superintendent House also sent out Lakota Chauncey Yellow Robe, disciplinarian of the Rapid City Indian School and a graduate of the Carlisle Indian School. Yellow Robe's territory in 1917 was the Sisseton Agency in northeastern South Dakota. Yellow Robe arrived in time for the agency fair, which House had hoped to attend himself, and followed up by going from home to home, a task more easily accomplished at Sisseton than on the Rosebud or other large reservations of South Dakota. Yellow Robe's diligence secured few students, for the children had been "well picked out for the other schools before me and what I have found are too old or too young."[28]

Indian parents sometimes played an active role in the competition between schools and could be quite adept at manipulating the different jurisdictions of the BIA. In December 1918, James H. McGregor, superintendent of the Cheyenne River Reservation in South Dakota, accused House of undermining his authority on the reservation by allowing parents from the Cherry Creek district to enroll underage children at Rapid City. "I am frank to say that I think you are at fault in accepting pupils below the third grade when they go there without any authority from me when I had already informed you that I expected to retain pupils below the 4th grade for the reservation school," McGregor charged. "For you to disregard my policy only makes it harder for me to maintain the discipline that I desire."[29]

Superintendent House tried to placate McGregor, while defending his own actions and those of the Cherry Creek parents. He had no intention of undermining McGregor's authority. He had enrolled pupils from the lower grades, but the children had been brought there by their parents, who invariably said that the enrollment had been approved by the district farmer or other reservation authority. House could not refuse the children, particularly when there were no arrangements made for their return to the reservation. And House was unhappy that McGregor made so few of the older Cheyenne River children available for enrollment at off-reservation schools. Pine Ridge sent a list of sixty-three children eligible to enroll off-reservation; Cheyenne River only sent a list of eight. House had nothing against reservation schools, he told McGregor, but noted that "if you and I were Indians we would not want to feel that we had to continue our children in some of them until they reached the 6th grade."[30]

House attributed McGregor's problems with the Cherry Creek people to reservation politics that predated McGregor's administration. For as long as House had known the Indians of the Cherry Creek country, they had "shown a feeling that the agency authorities were not in sympathy with them." He attributed the tensions in part to the distance of the Cherry Creek district, in the southwestern corner of the vast Cheyenne River Reservation, from the agency and the superintendent's offices. Rapid City was no farther away than the agency, and there were jobs available in Rapid City. Some of the Cherry Creek people could get jobs at what House considered to be very good salaries at any time. Living in Rapid City, Cherry Creek Indians could meet their friends and relatives from other reservations and enjoy contact with a wider world than that available to them at the agency.[31]

As the controversy over enrollment from the Cherry Creek district of the Cheyenne River Reservation demonstrates, reservation boundaries were not absolute barriers. Indian families could, and did, travel off the reservations. Nor were reservations always the centers of community for reservation residents. And contrary to the stereotypes surrounding off-reservation boarding schools, these schools were not necessarily farther from children's homes than the reservation boarding schools. Cherry Creek yields a case in point. For Cherry Creek parents and children, the Rapid City school was more accessible than the reservation boarding school. Whether acting out of frustration with innumerable delays inflicted on them by agency employees, as House implied, or out of a desire to embarrass their reservation superintendent, as McGregor charged, the people of the Cherry Creek district exploited divisions within the BIA to make their own educational choices.[32]

In the 1920s, competition between the off-reservation boarding schools and transfers from reservation to off-reservation boarding schools became somewhat more regularized. C. D. Munro, superintendent of the Cheyenne River Agency in 1922, demonstrated changing attitudes among reservation superintendents toward off-reservation schools when he sent Rapid City's Superintendent S. A. M. Young the names and addresses of students eligible for enrollment in an off-reservation school. Reservation boarding schools facilitated the enrollment of older students in off-reservation boarding schools by hosting the superintendents on their recruiting trips and inviting students to listen to the superintendents and weigh the merits of their schools. Elizabeth Whitehat received such

an invitation in August 1924 from the principal of the Rosebud
Boarding School. Superintendent House, then in charge of the
Flandreau Indian School, Superintendent Young of Rapid City, and
Superintendent Whitlock of the Pierre Indian School planned to
visit the Rosebud Boarding School on August 19, 20, and 21. The
principal of the Rosebud school told Whitehat that the visits of the
three superintendents would be a good opportunity for her to
select her school for the year, if she had not already decided.[33]

The Rapid City Indian School's efforts to recruit pupils, in fact,
could be too successful. In October 1922, Superintendent Young
asked agents of the railroads serving Rapid City to discourage
students from traveling to the school. The school was already more
than full and could accept no more students. Young asked ticket
agents to pass the word along to students who had not yet arrived.
The following year, he asked reservation superintendents to send
no more girls to the school, except by prior arrangement. Unless
some of the girls already in school dropped out, Young could
house no more. While he still had room for a few more boys, he
asked that reservation superintendents inquire before sending out
any who were not already enrolled.[34]

Students enrolled at the Rapid City Indian School for a variety
of reasons. Susie Battle, a Lakota from the Pine Ridge Reservation,
had been impressed by the school catalog. Although the catalogs
changed over the years, they remained a mainstay of the mailings
the school sent to prospective students. Under Superintendent
House, the catalogs constituted lengthy and elaborate documents.
A "Catalog and Synopsis of Courses" from the 1916–17 school year
carried in the inside cover a very formal portrait of House, accompanied by a letter "To Patrons and Those Interested," which drew
attention to the opportunities and advantages offered by the
school. A list of officers and instructors followed, along with a
calendar of the school year. Information on the school and its
location and history, expenses, and detailed descriptions of classes
filled the bulk of the thirty-page document. A picture of the last

graduating class and lists of graduates from previous years rounded out the catalog, which was liberally illustrated with photographs of the school. This feature of the catalog attracted Susie Battle. She obtained the catalog for the 1917–18 year, "saw the pictures of the school and was very much surprised to see it," and decided to go to Rapid City. Later catalogs followed a similar format, with the addition of lists of the previous year's enrollment. Superintendent Young toned down the formality of the document and included more direct advertising pitches. The 1923 catalog noted, among other features, "Better class rooms for boys' industrial work," "A larger school than ever before," and "A better band and orchestra." As an inducement to prompt arrival, the catalog promised "A Good Time the First Week," with a good picture show and a social with refreshments.[35]

Other students enrolled because their parents or relatives had gained employment at the school. Indian employees commonly enrolled their children in the institution. Frank and Lizzie Bullard accepted employment as night watchman and assistant seamstress, respectively, only when assured that Rapid City would enroll their children. Chippewa employee Sophie E. Picard, assistant matron in charge of large boys and herself a graduate of the Mt. Pleasant Indian School and the Haskell Institute, enrolled a cousin at Rapid City. The boy was to learn a trade, and his mother wanted Picard to look after him while he was in school. If Picard, a career employee of the BIA, moved to another school, the mother wanted her to take the boy with her. Superintendent House did not know whether or not the boy's transportation could be paid by the BIA, but he readily agreed to enroll the boy under the conditions suggested by his mother.[36]

Personal acquaintance with school personnel sometimes played a role in decisions about enrollment. The Reverend Sam Rouillard led a Presbyterian congregation on the Pine Ridge Reservation when S. A. M. Young taught school at the nearby No. 5 Day School. When Rouillard sought to enroll his son Isaac and four other boys in an off-reservation boarding school in 1922, he wrote to Young, who was by then superintendent at Rapid City, and reminded him of their acquaintance. Young, who remembered Rouillard quite well, was happy to send him applications for his son and the four other boys.[37]

Acquaintances and friendships between children also brought students to the Rapid City Indian School. Alex Two Two, a Lakota working for a Rapid City cement company, had a daughter, Margaret, attending Rapid City. His niece Alice had always gone to school with Margaret and so asked to be enrolled at Rapid City, too. Lucy Cottier, a former student, asked to be allowed to return to Rapid City in 1910 to enroll in its domestic science program, though she could not see well enough to participate in academic work. Cottier's friends were going back to Rapid City, and she wanted to go with them. Cottier also asked for applications for two of her friends, Julia Allen and Laura Stevens, who wanted to enroll. House made arrangements for Cottier to enroll in the domestic science program as she wished and sent catalogs to Allen and Stevens. He urged Cottier to speak to Allen and Stevens about enrollment and hoped that she would bring them with her when she returned to school.[38]

In times of family crisis, the Rapid City Indian School became a child care provider of last resort for Indian parents. In "A Bitter Lesson," Child argues that Chippewa parents turned to boarding schools in times of family crisis. Poor reservation health conditions resulted in many deaths, and the death of a spouse often left the survivor without adequate resources to care for children. Reservation poverty made it difficult for relatives to take in needy children, and the Chippewa tradition of adopting and providing for orphans within the tribe became impossible to maintain in some cases. Enrolling children in boarding schools meant their separation from family and reservation communities, but ensured that the children would be fed, clothed, and housed, and perhaps provided with an education that would benefit them later in life.[39]

The Rapid City Indian School filled similar needs for families and children from the reservations of Wyoming, Montana, and western South Dakota and surrounding communities. The Indian father on whose behalf Nancy Ulargran wrote Rapid City, a Potawatomi named Tesson, had three children to enroll in school: Mary and Rachel, ages eleven and six, and Peter, age nine. Enrolling the children meant giving them up for long periods, but their separation from their father was not permanent. Enrolled for three-year terms in 1911, all three Tesson children re-enrolled in 1914, leaving the school on December 31, 1917. Enrolling all the children, even at young ages, kept them together, as Tesson wished. They were among other Indian children, too, though they were the only Potawatomis at Rapid.[40]

Mrs. Nick Ruleau enrolled three boys (William, age eleven; Edward, age nine; and Blaine, age seven) in Rapid City in 1922. Recently divorced, Ruleau could not earn a living while caring for her children. The three boys attended the Catholic mission school at Pine Ridge, but she wanted them enrolled for a period of four to five years in a school where they would be cared for the entire year and not sent home for the summers. Even with little room at Rapid City, Superintendent Young sought to find space for the boys. School closed June 2, and he did not expect the boys to arrive until other children were going home for the summer.[41]

The Depression forced a number of families to enroll their children in the Rapid City Indian School. In July 1930, Rapid City resident Julia McGaa asked the Pine Ridge superintendent to permit the enrollment of her seven children in the school. Her husband, Hobert, could not find steady work, and the older children had not gone to public school the preceding year because the McGaas could not feed and clothe them properly. Clothes were also a problem for the Provost family. Josephine Provost sent her children, Grace and Harold, to a public school in Rapid City. The children, particularly Harold, did not like to go to school with white children and skipped school half the time. "I think it is because they cannot dress as they might," Provost said, "but I am the only one working in the family and I really cannot dress them & feed them as I should." Rapid City senior clerk George A. Day, investigating the Provost family's home conditions, learned that Provost's husband, disabled by a back injury and unable in the Depression to find suitable light work, received a $40 per month pension for his service as an army scout. The Provosts paid $35 a month in rent for a house in Rapid City, plus $2.75 for electricity and $1 for water service. Money for food and clothing had to come from Josephine Provost's wages from occasional work as a maid at the Patton Hotel, and Day agreed that it would be better if the children were enrolled at Rapid City. Since the Provosts lived in town, sending the children to the school would not mean sending them any distance away. Provost would not send her children away to school, for the last time she did so, "one came home so nearly dead he only lived four months after he came back."[42]

While the Tesson, Ruleau, McGaa, and Provost families initiated the enrollments of their children in the Rapid City Indian School, reservation officials applied varying degrees of suggestion and coercion to get children from financially strapped homes enrolled at Rapid City. Superintendent C. H. Gensler of the Lower Brule Agency, South Dakota, sent two children of Mrs. Driving Hawk to Rapid City after the death of the father. Gensler knew Rapid City was filled to capacity, yet he asked Superintendent Young to take the children because there was no other way of caring for them. After the death of the children's father, Driving Hawk was left with "quite a large family." The nearest public school was some distance from their home, and Driving Hawk could not, in Gensler's estimation, support the family and keep the children in school. Young found Henry and Alvena Driving Hawk to be bright children and apparently pleased to be enrolled at Rapid City. Despite the crowding at the school, Young promised to find "some nail on which to hang them" and was glad he could be of service to the children and their mother. Whether Gensler forced the children's enrollment at Rapid City or merely facilitated it is unclear.[43]

No such uncertainty surrounded the enrollment of the Matt children. In April 1920, Theodore Sharp, superintendent of the Flathead Agency in western Montana, received permission from commissioner of Indian affairs E. B. Meritt to place the nine children of Jule and Peter Matt in the Rapid City Indian School, if Superintendent House could find room for them. Jule Matt, a mixed-blood resident of the Flathead Reservation, had seven children between the ages of five and twelve. After the death of his wife, his children had been without care and often without food, fuel, or clothing. W. G. Brown, the day school inspector, recommended that the children be removed from their home after two of the girls were found at night in the streets of Ronan (a reservation town 3.5 miles from the Matt home), cold, hungry, and crying. The family's relatives were too poor to take care of the children, and there was a waiting list for admission to the state Orphan's Home. Sharp turned to the Rapid City Indian School for their care. He also wanted the two children of Peter Matt seized and taken to Rapid City. Their father had died in the Montana State Penitentiary at Deer Lodge, and Sharp described their mother as "a vicious woman with a notorious reputation who gives the children no proper care." The children circulated between the mother and their relatives, whom he judged to be too poor to care for them. The Rapid City Indian School enrolled the children on July 1, 1920, ten weeks before regular enrollments began.[44]

Such enrollments were not exceptional, for boarding schools were common destinations for Indian children removed from their homes. In 1924, Superintendent Henry J. McQuigg of the Turtle Mountain Indian Agency, North Dakota, asked Young to enroll three orphans who had been staying with a married sister after the deaths of their parents. The sister lacked the resources to properly care for and educate the children, and a meeting of the Indian judges at Turtle Mountain agreed that McQuigg, acting for the government, should without delay seek the children's placement in a government school. Young, though noting that he "really should not take them, since we are more than full and there are children nearby without school facilities," agreed to make room again and squeeze the children in.[45]

Superintendent McQuigg again asked the Rapid City Indian School to accept Turtle Mountain children in 1926. Eliza Hayes, eleven, an orphan, did not have a home. Indian judges ordered Mary C. and Mary Ann Houle, ages seventeen and fifteen, taken from their home because of the unfitness of their parents to care for them. The judges recommended that all three be placed in an Indian school. Matron Theresa C. Kaufman said she would be glad to take them in, but Superintendent Sharon R. Mote refused to admit the girls, since the school was already over capacity. When Young returned to Rapid City in 1930, he too turned away welfare placements. The school had more than enough students.[46]

When Luther Standing Bear left the Spotted Tail Agency in 1879 for the Carlisle Indian School, his people knew nothing of boarding schools and little of reservation life. Custer's defeat was only three years past, and Sitting Bull's return from Canada still in the future. The distance from the Spotted Tail Agency to Carlisle, Pennsylvania, was almost unimaginably great, whether measured by distance or by culture. It is hardly surprising, then, that Standing Bear and his companions feared falling off the edge of the world, as their train traveled east.

By 1898, schools and Indians had come much closer. The Rapid City Indian School was in country the people of the reservations of Wyoming, Montana, and western South Dakota knew well. If they had not actually traveled near the Black Hills (Rapid City was within the historic territories of the Crows, Lakotas, and Cheyennes), the climate, altitude, and vegetation were still familiar. For some, Rapid City, a town of 1,342 people in 1900 and 5,777 in 1920, was closer than reservation headquarters and reservation schools. More importantly, Indians had a better idea of what to expect from BIA schools. From experience with Carlisle and other off-reservation boarding schools, Indian parents knew the advantages and disadvantages of a boarding school education. As the BIA's campaign for the compulsory education of Indian children made it increasingly difficult to avoid white schooling altogether, Indians responded by making the most of the choices the BIA offered.[47]

Taking advantage of the competition between reservation and off-reservation boarding schools, Indian parents forced the Rapid City Indian School to meet their needs to a greater degree than the BIA had anticipated. Ignoring the BIA's plans for a structured system where only the oldest, most advanced students would study at off-reservation boarding schools, Indian parents forced Rapid City to take children of all ages, so families could stay together. If reservation schools did not provide the education Indian parents wanted for their children, they sent them to Rapid City. In an environment where education was compulsory, but the choice of school left largely open, children enrolled at Rapid City to be with friends, to stay close to relatives, or because its superintendent or catalog made a good impression.

The experiences of the Tesson and Matt children reveal a different side of enrollment at the school. The early twentieth century was a difficult period on western reservations. Forced land sessions and allotment hampered the development of reservation economies at the same time that Congress cut back rations and other assistance. The BIA mounted sustained attacks on Indian religious and social customs, including the giveaway ceremonies that traditionally transferred property to the poor. Tuberculosis and other diseases took a terrible toll on parents and children alike, as families crowded into the tiny, poorly ventilated cabins that the BIA considered more civilized than tents and lodges.

In such a difficult environment, the deaths of spouses, poverty, and social dislocation sometimes left Indian parents and their children with few, if any, choices. Enrollment at Rapid City might bring relief from poverty and instability at home, as students received food, clothing, housing, and warmth in the cold Northern Plains winters. Enrollment meant a chance to enjoy Indian school athletics, to get away from parental discipline and the chores of rural life, to meet other young people and strike up romances. Enrollment might also be a reminder of loss and a representation in wood and stone of the pressures the BIA brought to bear on Indian families.

CHAPTER 2

PROVIDING FOR THE CHILDREN

On October 20, 1922, Superintendent C. H. Gensler of the Lower Brule Reservation, South Dakota, relayed to Rapid City Indian School's Superintendent S. A. M. Young a complaint from the father of a Rapid City student: "George Tompkins, the father of Madeline Tompkins a pupil of your school, was in the office the other day complaining about his daughter Madeline not getting enough to eat at your school, and made the request that the girl be sent home to attend public school." Gensler carefully disclaimed any belief in the complaint and dismissed Tompkins as "a chronic kicker." At the same time, he noted the availability of a public school on Cedar Creek, near the family home, and stated that Madeline could be properly educated in the public school, should Superintendent Young decide to send her home.[1]

Young looked into the matter. He found that Madeline worked in the kitchen and thus could eat all she wanted. "Moreover," he replied, "she tells me that she did not write any such letter [of complaint] to her father. She thinks that Leonard wrote it. As I told you, we have found Leonard to be rather unreasonable. Madeline certainly looks well fed, and the same may be said of Leonard" (apparently her brother). Madeline promised to write to her father to reassure him that she was not hungry.[2]

The exchange between Gensler and Young highlights the importance of nutrition and other elements of care to the mission of the school. As a boarding school, Rapid City was responsible for the welfare of the students in residence. How well it fed and clothed the students and the health care it gave them provided important measures of the school's performance and the staff's competence. Parents took a keen interest in these fundamental and easily observable elements of care. Reservation and school officials respected and felt obliged to address this interest, even when questions came from members of the community that administrators personally disliked. While Rapid City Indian School was vulnerable to budgetary pressures, particularly in the lean years following the post–World War I retrenchment in federal spending, it had achieved acceptable standards of nutrition by the 1910s and continued to improve nutrition through the 1920s, even as restrictions on expenditures limited its ability to clothe students properly. Health care at the school, never good, was insufficient to check such chronic diseases as trachoma and improved little, if any, over the life of the institution.

The dining hall and kitchen emphasized the institutional aspect of life at an Indian boarding school. As a boy growing up in a Lakota lodge circle, Luther Standing Bear ate when hunger and the availability of food coincided. Eating by the clock, and not by his appetite, presented a great trial for him in his first year at the Carlisle Indian School. A federal Indian school attempted to teach students the habits of white society, however arbitrary those habits might be. Rooted in a culture that served food in three structured meals a day, the Rapid City Indian School likewise fed students three times a day. In an institution that prized order yet contained within its walls up to 300 children, all of whom had to be fed, the regularization and regimentation of meals was perhaps inevitable. At the sound of a bell, the entire student body marched into the dining hall, with girls and boys going to their assigned places at separate tables. Once everyone was seated, a detail of students serving as waiters brought out the food. Feeding 250 to 300 children three times daily was no small task. Details of girls helped in the kitchen, and a detail of boys helped the baker make the 150 loaves of bread students consumed daily. The school used 1,500 pounds of flour per week.[3]

Such large total quantities of food did not mean that individual children ate well, for the food was divided among many mouths and was not always well prepared. An Oglala student attending Rapid City from 1904 to 1905, interviewed anonymously by the American Indian Research Project in 1971, compared Rapid City food unfavorably to that available on the Pine Ridge Reservation in South Dakota. On the reservation, families combined government rations with traditional food sources. Every two weeks, the agency (as reservation headquarters were known) issued flour, rice, beans, bacon, sugar, green coffee, and soap as well as fresh beef, issued a hindquarter at a time. Some families jerked their meat, but the student remembered that her father put the family's issue in an ice house, on ice cut from the creek above Porcupine. "Of course, there was a lot of fruit in those days, and they'd dry these cherries and plums and currants and buffalo berries so they always had plenty to eat," she recalled.[4]

Boarding school food, as the informant remembered it, offered insufficient quantity and variety. "All they fed them was meat, boiling meat [beef] at noon and they made gravy out of this in a great big kettle, black kettle . . . And they were allowed for one or two slices of bread, one slice for some. And that's all they'd get for dinner, and maybe they'd get a pie, dried apple pie or prune pie or something on Sundays. And we didn't eat any potatoes, just plain stuff . . . Oatmeal would always be wormy, and they'd give us just a little dish of it. Then they'd give us some kind of a soup that tasted more like sorghum. We got a little dish of that and a slice of bread for breakfast. So the kids used to get pretty hungry."

Hunger led some children to run away. The informant's brother joined other boys in parching corn and baking potatoes in the boiler house, a practice that led to tragedy in 1905 when two older boys, assistant engineers tending the boiler without supervision, let cold water into a hot, almost dry boiler and caused an explosion. The assistants escaped before the explosion blew the boiler through the roof. The informant's brother, baking his potato by the boiler, was blown through three partitions and killed, his body so mutilated and covered by soot as to be beyond recognition. After that, "the government found out how they were feeding us."[5]

Parents also played a role in ensuring that Rapid City students received sufficient food. The divisions in authority between reservation and school superintendents worked to parents' advantage, for they could use reservation superintendents to carry their complaints to school superintendents, who would be obliged to respond to fellow officials of the BIA. In November 1911, for example, Pine Ridge's Superintendent John R. Brennan questioned Superintendent House about the food available to students. Children were telling their parents that they did not have enough to eat, Brennan said, and two children asked to be allowed to return home because they were hungry. House promptly investigated and replied that, except for a few days when children were arriving at the school at the beginning of the term, they had been generously fed. There was more food available than ever before, he claimed, and the new cook provided a greater variety of food than did her predecessors. The correspondence took on a sinister note when House asked Brennan to send him the letters the children had written to their parents or to at least provide the children's names. "I will take no drastic or severe measures with the pupils," he said, "but shall aim to show them that such things are very wrong, and that they should not annoy their parents with these false statements."[6]

The identities and fates of the letter writers are unknown, but the attention turned on the school brought improvements in students' diets. A set of handwritten menus dating from the early

1910s describes fare that, while potentially monotonous, at least appeared nutritious by the standards of the day:

Sat Nov 1st
>   Breakfast
>>   Oat Meal & milk
>>   Fried potatoes
>>   syrup
>>   bread & coffee
>   Dinner
>>   Boiled meat & gravy
>>   potatoes
>>   cabbage
>>   bread & water
>   Supper
>>   Roast Meat & gravy
>>   potatoes
>>   beans
>>   prunes
>>   bread & water

Mon Nov 3d
>   Breakfast
>>   Oat meal & milk
>>   Fried potatoes
>>   Syrup
>>   bread & coffee
>   Dinner
>>   Boiled meat
>>   dumplings & gravy
>>   potatoes
>>   beans
>>   light rolls
>>   water

Supper
    Meat & gravy
    potatoes
    parsnips
    apple sauce
    corn bread & tea
    butter

These menus show a heavy reliance on meat and staple foods, such as oatmeal, potatoes, beans, bread, and cornbread, containing complex carbohydrates. Fresh fruit is conspicuous by its absence, but the vitamin C in the cabbage at least would have prevented scurvy. Coffee at breakfast and milk only for breakfast oatmeal would not now be considered appropriate or adequate for children, but milk three times daily was uncommon before the universal adoption of pasteurization and on-site refrigeration. Otherwise, the menus indicate reasonably nutritious, if bland food.[7]

The menus say nothing about the quality of preparation, but a student of the era had pleasant memories of the food. Sara Buffalo attended Rapid City through grade seven and probably first enrolled before 1910, before leaving school to get married in 1917. Buffalo remembered Rapid City as "a real good school," where "we [ate] good food." After "yes" and "no," food names were some of the first English words children learned: "They didn't know much about what the words were and what they were talking about and if they were saying anything to us we didn't know. And finally one of us girls said she said in Indian, I know how to say the word gravy now she said cause we used to eat gravy. If you say gravy they'll pass you so that's how we learned you know." The children's hunger overrode the school's prohibitions against speaking Indian languages.[8]

A set of menus from 1929 shows considerable improvement in variety and the use of dairy products. These typed menus are particularly valuable evidence, for they contain handwritten corrections to show what was actually served on a given day. Furthermore, they are more complete than the earlier menus, covering entire weeks, with accurate dates:

Menu for week of March 10 to March 16, 1929.

Sunday

Breakfast: Corn flakes, bacon gravy, cocoa.

Dinner: Swiss steak, mashed potatoes, gravy, cabbage and pineapple salad, Fig and tapioca pudding, bread, milk.

Supper: Beans [replacing chili con carne], bread, peach sauce, cake.

Monday

Breakfast: Oatmeal, syrup, bread, milk, cocoa.

Dinner: Boiled beef, onions, dumplings, bread, cornbread.

Supper: Cream of potato soup, hash, hard bread [hardtack?], prune sauce, coffee cake.

Tuesday

Breakfast: Cracked wheat, gravy, bread, coffee [replacing cocoa], milk, coffee cake.

Dinner: Roast beef, browned potatoes, carrots.

Supper: Tomato soup, hard bread, apple sauce, bread.

Wednesday

Breakfast: Corn meal mush, syrup [replacing gravy], bread, cocoa, milk.

Dinner: Beef stew, carrots, [pickled beets deleted], bread, brown betty.

Supper: [Cream of tomato soup deleted], [hard bread deleted], Hash [replacing fried potatoes], apple sauce, ginger bread.

Thursday

Breakfast: Oatmeal, [syrup deleted], gravy, bread, coffee [replacing cocoa], milk.

Dinner: Meat pie, mashed potatoes, creamed cabbage, rice
           and raisin pudding, bread, corn bread.
Supper: Bean soup, hard bread, scalloped tomatoes, prunes.
Friday
Breakfast: Bran flakes, prune sauce, boiled eggs, butter,
           cocoa, milk.
Dinner: Creamed salmon, mashed potatoes, creamed corn,
           cabbage salad, bread, apples.
Supper: Meat loaf [replacing hot wieners], potato salad,
           bread, apple sauce, hot cross buns, butter.
Saturday
Breakfast: Corn flakes [replacing bran flakes], pork gravy,
           bread, [apple butter deleted], coffee [replacing
           cocoa], milk.
Dinner: Meat loaf, gravy, boiled potatoes, bread, apples.
Supper: Baked beans, bread, pineapple tapioca, cake.

Menus of this sort received considerable criticism in *The Problem of Indian Administration*, a weighty survey of Indian affairs compiled in 1928 by the Institute for Government Research, under the direction of Lewis Meriam. While the Meriam Report, as the survey came to be known, did not specifically mention Rapid City, it criticized boarding school diets that relied excessively on starch, meats, stews, and gravies.[9]

Starches, now known as complex carbohydrates, were better for the children than the authors of the Meriam Report realized. The report also criticized the schools for serving too few milk fats, such as butter and cream. A more valid criticism concerned the lack of fresh fruits and vegetables in boarding school diets. When boarding schools did not skip fresh fruits and vegetables altogether, they served them only seasonally and in small amounts. The Rapid City menus do not contradict these observations. The vegetables served, mainly onions, carrots, and cabbage, were all foods easily grown locally or in school gardens and readily stored in bulk in root cellars through the winter. Despite Rapid City's excellent rail connections, which made the city the center of Black Hills commerce, the school did not buy the fresh peaches, melons, or vegetables grown in Colorado and available through Denver, much less the produce of California's Imperial Valley. Nor was the food that made it to the students' tables always of good quality. In 1928, Elizabeth Tyon, Elsie Broken Rope, and Libbie Never Misses A Shot ran away from the Rapid City Indian School in part because of worms found in their applesauce and rice.[10]

Yet in comparison with the Canadian Indian students of St. Peter Claver's Indian School, whose experiences Basil Johnston describes in his memoir, *Indian School Days*, Rapid City students ate well. Johnston worked in the school henhouse, collecting eggs that the school sold in a nearby town or served only to staff, not to students. The school raised cattle for slaughter, which never showed up on student plates either. The Rapid City Indian School, not as hard-pressed for cash as St. Peter Claver's, at least let students eat what they worked to raise on the school farm. Johnston and his friends subsisted on porridge, known by the students as mush, and bread, lard, barley or pea soup, and an afternoon snack or collation of raw vegetables, supplemented by Boston baked beans on Tuesdays, Thursdays, and Sundays. Rapid City students ate institutional food of a sort not unfamiliar fifty years later and much improved over that served by the school in 1905.[11]

The 1929 menus reflect an only partially successful attempt the previous year by Superintendent Mote to bring more variety to the meals. In a memo to matron Theresa C. Kaufman, dated February 20, 1928, Mote observed that he "was in the dining room yesterday (Sunday) and noticed that the pupils were served roast beef instead of steak as was called for on the menu. I, myself, changed the menu when it went through this office calling for steak Sunday noon for the expressed purpose of giving some variety to the pupils' food. They get so much roast beef and boiled beef that I am sure they would welcome beefsteak fried occasionally. Please let me know why it was not possible to follow the menu." The reply, hand-written on the memo, indicated that the menu did not get out in time for changes to be made in kitchen routine that day. Mote noted that when additional bread had been requested, none had been available; moreover, most bread plates had been empty at the start of the meal. Informed that the allowance had been cut from seventy-five to sixty-five loaves per meal because of wastage, Mote ordered the allowance increased by an unspecified amount, telling Kaufman to give the children as much bread as they could eat. Wastage, he believed, should be controlled through increased super-vision in the dining room, not a reduction in food allowances.[12]

Although the bread incident indicates a tendency on the part of low-level staff to underfeed children rather than risk wastage, school officials took steps to insure that students would not suffer from outright hunger. In the 1920s, the school gave mid-morning and mid-afternoon milk lunches of a cup of milk and a cracker to underweight students. The office of the school superintendent or principal posted a list of the boys and girls required to take milk lunches and ordered teachers to add to the lists the names of any students who seemed to need the extra food. As many as sixty-eight boys and girls might be on the lists. If milk ran short, employees went without, not the students. When milk production at the school dairy fell off in September 1928, Superintendent Mote ordered the sale of milk to employees discontinued.[13]

Milk was one of the few foods Rapid City succeeded in pro-ducing in quantities sufficient for student consumption. As Carl Stevens, supervisor of Indian schools, noted in an inspection of the school in 1924, little of the school land was suitable for agriculture. The school owned 1,390 acres of land, but Stevens found that only 300 acres were intensively farmed and that the rest was too rough to be cultivated. Sharon Mote, inspecting the school in 1928 after his transfer to Flandreau Indian School, noted that only the irrigated part of the farm was productive. Clearly, a population of over 300 students could not be supported on 300 acres of South

Dakota land, particularly since not all of the land could be cropped
yearly, with some remaining fallow every year.[14]

In fact, little raised on the school farm went directly to the
students. Rapid City cultivated 175 acres of crops in 1924. That year,
despite hail damage, the school harvested 275 bushels of oats from
25 acres, 600 bushels of corn and 120 tons of silage from 40 acres, 90
tons of alfalfa from 30 acres, and 60 tons of prairie hay from 40 acres
of land. Potatoes represented the only crop raised for the direct
consumption of students: 270 bushels were harvested from 18 acres
of land. The rest of the crops raised on the farm went to support the
school herds, principally the dairy herd. In 1925, the school maintained a herd of 31 Holstein cows, which produced over a quart of
milk per day per child. This statistic compared favorably with the
pint per day average noted in the Meriam Report, which the
authors considered clearly inadequate. Not all of the milk reached
Rapid City students, however, for some of the milk had to be given
to the calves in the herd. Stevens thought too much milk went to
them and suggested that the male calves, of no use to the school,
be slaughtered. He also frowned on the practice of making butter,
believing it "preferable to give the children all the whole milk they
will consume first, before any of it is used for butter making." Still,
the children received milk at two meals each day.[15]

In addition to the dairy herd, the culls from which were either
sold or slaughtered for meat, Rapid City also raised hogs and kept
a small flock of chickens. In 1923, the school slaughtered eighteen
hogs, with a net weight of 3,900 pounds, not enough for the school
to be self-sufficient in pork. The small usable acreage of the school
farm limited pork production, for when crops were poor the school
had to buy grain to feed the hogs, a practice considered uneco-
nomical. Nor was self-sufficiency in egg products practical, in
Supervisor Stevens's opinion: while the school kept a flock of White
Plymouth Rock chickens, raised from chicks purchased in 1923,
Stevens opined that he was "always a little dubious about chickens
being a paying proposition, unless you have good buildings and a

man that gives them the best of care." Managing the school's food production meant using scarce resources of personnel and land. Only the dairy, producing a perishable product for immediate daily consumption, met the school's criterion of economy. Cost was an important consideration in the lean years of the 1920s, when the school's budget might be reduced 6 percent from one year to the next, as it was in 1925–26, with no corresponding decreases in enrollment.[16]

No matter how severe the pressures to cut costs, administrators remained aware of the critical practical and psychological roles played by food in the operation of the school and were wary of economizing unduly on the children's food. Carl Stevens spoke out strongly against lowering standards of care. "Our schools are providing much better food for the children during recent years, but we want to maintain the standard and if possible improve it, rather than lower it," he wrote in his 1925 inspection of the school. "We can not afford to do otherwise, else our efforts in behalf of better health, and our good reputation with the Indian parents and pupils will suffer." A good reputation was critical, for in an era when off-reservation boarding schools competed with not only reservation schools but mission and public schools for attendance, Rapid City's continued existence depended on the perception by Indian parents and children that the school adequately served their needs. The school could not afford to ignore the basic requirement that the students be well fed.[17]

In contrast to the improvement over time in school food, the Rapid City Indian School clothed children more adequately in the 1910s than in later years. In addition to the practical necessity of adequate clothing, especially in the cold South Dakota winters, clothing played a symbolic role in off-reservation boarding schools. In *The Phoenix Indian School*, Trennert puts the wearing of school uniforms in the context of the "de-Indianization" boarding school students endured. Along with haircuts, new students quickly received issues of dress clothing, school clothes, and work clothes. The wearing of uniforms was a part of the regimentation practiced at off-reservation boarding schools and denoted the students' progress from "savagery" to "civilization." As many parochial schools demonstrate today, uniforms also carry connotations of order and equality among students of varying economic backgrounds.[18]

Boys' dress uniforms resembled military uniforms. Before World War I brought tape puttees (wrapped leggings), riding pants, and the ubiquitous khaki to Indian schools, boys at the Rapid City Indian School wore long pants of dark wool and matching long-sleeved, high-collared tunics that buttoned at the throat. While data from Rapid City are lacking, photographs and descriptions of clothing from the Phoenix and Chilocco schools indicate that boys probably wore white shirts and plain belted slacks or dungarees to class and overalls to work assignments. Girls at the school wore dress uniforms of wool skirts and white blouses and gingham work dresses.[19]

In *They Called It Prairie Light*, Lomawaima notes the significance of girls' long woolen underwear, the ugly, baggy, outdated bloomers that school matrons forced girls to wear. Bloomers represented the school's attempts to control students' bodies and banish their sexuality. Variations on the "bloomer story," a bit of boarding school folklore where girls abandoned their bloomers outside the dormitory on the way to a dance only to have the bloomers recovered first by mischievous boys, highlight students' ingenuity in resistance to school control. Rapid City students had to find other ways to outwit the matrons in charge of the girls' dormitories, for bloomers were long gone by the 1920s. While Eva Enos, Arapaho, had to wear "them old fashioned bloomers" under her skirts while a student at St. Michael's Mission on the Wind River Reservation, Rapid City issued cotton panties. For Enos, freedom from the bloomers represented larger freedoms that became available as she transferred from St. Michael's to Rapid City.[20]

Despite the importance of uniform dress to the assimilation program of off-reservation boarding schools, clothing policy at the Rapid City Indian School exhibited a surprising flexibility. As Michael C. Coleman documents in *American Indian Children at School, 1850–1930*, boarding schools commonly took away children's "home clothing," which the students might never see again. Rapid City, deviating from the norm, let students keep their clothing. Corresponding with Mrs. Charles Snyder of Kadoka, South Dakota, in 1911, Superintendent House wrote that "pupils are allowed to wear their own clothing to school, if they so desire, excepting on Sundays [when] all pupils are required to dress in the school uniform. We have sufficient supply of everyday clothing, and you can suit yourself as to how much to furnish your children." Attending Rapid City in the 1920s, Eva Enos made sure she brought her own clothes to school her second year, after learning her first year that students could wear their own clothes outside school.[21]

Aside from the clothing students brought with them, the Rapid City Indian School sometimes allowed students with money on account at the school office to buy clothing in Rapid City. The school retained a large degree of control, however, for it did not always allow students cash and sometimes specified not only what students would buy, but where they would make their purchases. In 1911, for example, clerk F. A. Andersen gave a letter of credit to Silas Kills Plenty, a student of the school who had money to his credit, to take to clothiers Olson & Company of Rapid City. Andersen's letter, good only at Olson & Company, specified that Kills Plenty buy a suit. Andersen would be in town the following Saturday and promised to pay at that time. A postscript limited Kills Plenty's credit to $16, and the young man bought his suit for $15.[22]

In correspondence with parents, Superintendent House recognized good clothes for special occasions, such as Kills Plenty's suit, as the proper outlet for individuality. In 1917, parent Paul R.

Vincent wrote to House asking how he should outfit his son for school. House once again said that the school provided the children's everyday clothes, but advised Vincent that "most of the pupils provide themselves with a suit of clothes suitable for wearing to socials and other affairs of that kind." He did not acknowledge that school clothing was not suitable for better occasions, and sometimes not even for everyday wear. In 1920, Superintendent H. M. Tidwell of the Pine Ridge Reservation questioned House about this aspect of clothing policy. A young Pine Ridge woman, enrolled at Rapid City, had asked Tidwell for permission to spend her money on essential items of clothing. Was it true, Tidwell inquired, that girls enrolled at Rapid City had to buy their own outer garments, such as dresses, coats, stockings, and shoes?[23]

House denied the charge and replied that the school supplied children with all necessary clothing, as specified in BIA budget estimates. When children wrote home asking for money to buy clothes, he suggested that their real goal was to get spending money for other purposes. But pupils did spend some of their own money for clothing, House admitted: "Quite often pupils desire other clothing, such as shoes and suits for social affairs, etc., and where they have money to purchase these, I have rather encouraged it. Sometimes our stock of shoes, especially sizes that are required, is low and in these cases pupils sometimes purchase their own shoes." He recommended that if the girl had sufficient funds on account at the agency, Tidwell should give her $50 per year. If she had no money, House thought she could still get along quite well with the clothing the school issued.[24]

Students issued ill-fitting shoes when the right sizes were not available probably disagreed with House's assessment. Girls at BIA boarding schools particularly disliked the issue shoes. Lomawaima notes students' low regard for the heavy, high-topped government "bullhides," ugly, unfashionable shoes made of black leather, stitched together in prison workshops and issued to students at Indian boarding schools. Girls at the Chilocco Indian

School replaced them with their own shoes whenever possible. Rapid City girls liked the government-issue shoes no better. "Those shoes, oh I used to dread them things," Eva Enos said. "I don't know where they ever got them." When Enos went home, her grandmother always had tennis shoes or other comfortable shoes ready for her.[25]

In the 1920s, shortages extended from shoes to boys' uniforms, to the point that the Rapid City Indian School was reduced to begging funds from the students' home agencies to pay for school clothing. An early indication of trouble came in 1919, when Superintendent House turned down a request from Superintendent John B. Brown of the Phoenix Indian School for spare uniforms. Rapid City did not have enough uniforms for its own boys, and House faced the prospect, surely unpalatable for the superintendent of a BIA boarding school, of having boys clothed in two different styles of uniform.[26]

The release of World War I surplus brought some relief, at least to school superintendents. In 1925, Rapid City's Superintendent Mote asked the Sigmund Eisner Company of Red Bank, New Jersey, about the availability of uniform clothing. Government agencies shared stocks of surplus items, and the War Department gave the BIA uniforms from World War I. Mote secured woolen olive drab uniforms in adult sizes, suitable for the school's larger boys, but could find nothing similar for the small boys. Mote wanted to know if the Sigmund Eisner Company could supply something like the army uniforms, perhaps a Boy Scout uniform, for the small boys. He wrote to the company after failing to receive satisfactory bids from Sears, Roebuck and Company and the Lewis Company, another clothing supplier. Mote's request to the latter listed the items desired:

> 1 pr. All wool O.D. [olive drab] Riding Breeches, Size 30,
> 1 Army O.D. Wool Blouse,
> 1 O.D. Woll [sic] Overseas Cap,

1 pr. Army Russett Shoes, Munson last, Size 7,

1 pr. Spiral Wrap Leggings,

1 pr. Leather Puttees, Size 15,

1 Army Web Belt,

1 Leather Sam Brown Belt for officers,

1 U.S. Army O.D. Wool Shirt, Size 15.

If not simply matching new purchases to army surplus already on hand, then perhaps Mote was also Americanizing his boys by clothing them in the most patriotic dress of all: that of the American Expeditionary Force to France.[27]

At the same time, Superintendent Mote sent out letters to reservation superintendents, begging funds for boys' clothing. His letter to Superintendent W. E. Dunn of the Crow Creek Reservation in South Dakota detailed the children's plight: "The situation relative to proper clothing for our boys at Rapid City School is extremely unsatisfactory. Few of them have proper clothing of their own and the school finances will not warrant our making such purchases in any considerable quantity. Of course we have some uniforms but it seems that during the past few years even the uniforms and shoes have been curtailed to such an extent due to shortage of support funds that we now find ourselves in rather straitened circumstances when it comes to dressing up our boys properly." As a solution, Mote proposed that the reservation superintendents draw on the individual accounts of students who had lease, annuity, or other moneys in trust of the superintendents and send as much as $40 per boy to the school, though he would welcome even half that amount. For children without funds of their own on account at the agencies, Mote suggested that the superintendents ask the parents for however much money they could afford and that the funds be sent to the school and not to the boys themselves.[28]

Whatever funds reservation superintendents sent, whether from the students' accounts or their parents' pockets, had to be spent in supervised outings in Rapid City. Under the watchful eyes of school employees, the boys were to purchase a good suit, a hat, and shoes, to be locked up and kept from the boys except on special occasions. If the boys had money left, they were to buy a cheap suit and a second pair of shoes for daily wear at the school. Even when the school could not buy the students' clothing, it maintained control over what they would wear and when.[29]

The move to shift clothing costs to parents and the children's individual accounts brought into question the ability of Rapid City to fulfill its mission of educating children from impoverished families, who would receive no education at all if not from the federal government. Supervisor of Schools Stevens noted the problem in his inspection of the school in 1925. "It would seem . . . that we have reached the limit in reducing the clothing supply," he observed. "A great many children in schools like this buy a large part of their own clothing, and we can not ask much more in this respect. We naturally eliminate the most needy children, if we require them to purchase their own clothing."[30]

Curiously, the cost of girls' clothing became a matter of minor controversy not because such extreme shortages existed in girls' clothing as in boys', but because social pressures to dress well moved the costs of clothing, and therefore school attendance, out of the reach of some students. Standing Rock Reservation's Superintendent E. D. Mossman, sometimes given to lecturing his fellow superintendents, sent copies of a letter to the Haskell, Flandreau, Rapid City, Pierre, and Wahpeton boarding schools recounting the plight of a bright young woman of his jurisdiction whose relative poverty disadvantaged her at the boarding schools. The woman, then nineteen years of age, had recently returned from Flandreau, and Mossman hoped to see her placed at a more advanced school. The woman demurred, citing her lack of money. Unable to dress like other students, she did not want to go to a school where her poverty would cause her to be singled out by better-off students.[31]

Although the Mossman family did not need a domestic servant, Mossman's wife hired the young woman and provided her with a small wardrobe so she could go to school. Mossman complained that while getting students to dress neatly and fashionably was one of the goals of the off-reservation boarding schools, the amounts spent were clearly unreasonable. For what some students spent on clothing, their families could buy complete sets of home furnishings. Combining his thoughts on clothing with another of his criticisms of the off-reservation schools, his belief that such schools served whites and mixed-bloods to the exclusion of needier full-bloods, Mossman concluded he was "sending a few Indians in my various delegations this year and I hope they will not be frozen out by the well dressed whites attending your institutions."[32]

Superintendent Mote did not reply to Mossman's criticisms. He did, however, correspond with his colleagues at other boarding schools in 1929 about the possibility of requiring young women to make their own graduation dresses. The conclusion was that it was "a splendid project for the 9th grade clothing class" and that "[e]ach girl should choose her own material and design," with limitations on the amount that could be spent. While still allowing a degree of personal expression in clothing, this proposal put poor students on a more equal footing with those better off and furthered the vocational training goals of the school in the process.[33]

Health care for Indian students remained the most pressing need at the Rapid City Indian School. The school's years of operation, from 1898 to 1933, encompassed a critical period in Indian demographics. Threats to Indian survival did not end with the passing of the period of warfare on the Northern Plains or the gradual lessening of the severity of the smallpox epidemics that had devastated Indian populations from first contact with Europeans. Increased white settlement in the Northern Plains brought Indians into intimate contact with a variety of diseases, including measles, influenza, and, worst of all, tuberculosis. In *Parading*

*through History: The Making of the Crow Nation in America,
1805–1935,* Frederick E. Hoxie paints a grim portrait of Indian population loss. In 1880, the Crow tribe numbered 3,470 people. By
1920, the population had dropped by half, to 1,719. Only in 1920
did the ratio of births to deaths exceed unity, from a nadir of 0.71
in 1900. Traditional tree burials, still a part of reservation life before
World War I, were so common that one could not scan the horizon
from Crow Agency without seeing at least one bier or coffin
silhouetted against the sky.[34]

The BIA hoped that boarding schools would check the decline
of Indian population, as students learned white habits of hygiene
and methods of self-support. Instead, Indian boarding schools
acted as points of transmission for a variety of diseases. As parents
of young school-age children know, children share diseases in even
the most modern public schools of the late twentieth century.
Schools concentrate in a few buildings children from many different households; the sick mingle with the well, passing along
colds and worse from runny nose to hand to mouth and eyes. Once
sick, children bring their diseases home and infect other members
of their families.

In Indian boarding schools of the late nineteenth and early
twentieth centuries, conditions favored the transmission of diseases more serious than colds and mild flus, diseases for which the
limited medical knowledge of the time offered few treatments. As
Adams discusses in *Education for Extinction,* infection spread
readily when children shared towels, cups, books, and even the
mouthpieces of musical instruments, as was often the case in
Indian boarding schools. Physical and emotional stress brought on
by the rigors of boarding school life, with its dusk-to-dawn schedule and isolation from the family, lowered students' resistance to
disease just as they encountered an onslaught of pathogens. Vaccinations existed for only a few diseases, such as smallpox and
diphtheria, and antibiotics had yet to be developed. For most diseases, time and rest were the only available treatments. When an

epidemic of measles, for example, spread through a school, the staff could only nurse the sick and hope for their recovery. When time did not favor recovery, as when students wasted away from tuberculosis, schools often acceded to family wishes and sent the children home to die.[35]

The BIA quickly became aware of the dangers to student health lurking in Indian boarding schools. In 1901, Inspector William J. McConnell brought to commissioner of Indian affairs William A. Jones's attention both the magnitude of the crisis and some of the factors working against its resolution. At the Fort Totten Indian School in North Dakota, McConnell found that approximately ten percent of the children in attendance were infected with contagious diseases, several of them suffering from active tuberculosis. One of the tubercular students, Della R. Champagne, was so ill from pulmonary tuberculosis that she was confined to bed in the school's small sick room, which had a floor space of only 12 by 16 feet. Though doctors knew that tuberculosis was spread by sputum from infected patients and that droplets from every cough and sneeze of patients with active pulmonary tuberculosis carried the tuberculosis bacilli, the school regularly put Fort Totten students with other illnesses in the same room as the tubercular student, risking their infection and death. Many doctors in the Indian Service did not think tubercular students should be allowed in school. Yet as the physician in charge of the Fort Lapwai, Idaho, boarding school pointed out, if the school dismissed all the tubercular children, "there would, indeed, be a small attendance left." Limited expenditures for health care, and a reluctance to interfere with the operation of the schools, led administrators to continue practices that led inevitably to the deaths of Indian students.[36]

Many questions about mortality and the quality of care at Indian boarding schools could be answered if the schools had kept accurate records of illness and deaths. Unfortunately, they did not. Internal records of the Rapid City Indian School mention deaths at the school, but rarely in any detail. Typically, the school announced deaths in short memoranda from the superintendent to the matron and disciplinarian. "A short funeral service for Dorothy Crier who died here this morning will be held at Behren's undertaking parlors tomorrow morning at ten o'clock, Father O'Hara officiating," read one such memorandum from Superintendent Mote, dated October 13, 1927. "Her special friends at this school including employees and pupils and especially her classmates will be given an opportunity to attend."[37]

Official reports said little more. "Health of the school has been splendid," Superintendent Davis said in his annual report for 1901. "One pupil died during the year, making the first and only death that has ever occurred in the school. This does not mean that we have heretofore gotten the sick children home before dying. The contract physician, Dr. Joseph Van Buskirk, of Rapid City, has given his close personal attention to all matters pertaining to sickness and to the general health of the school. During the year the smallpox was raging all around us. The pupils and employees were vaccinated and the school quarantined." Davis did not name the student or state the cause of death. The collected annual reports published by the commissioner of Indian affairs almost never mentioned the names of individual Indians, and superintendents preferred to put the best light possible on health conditions in their jurisdictions.[38]

Rapid City's records say much more about procedures than about the fates of individual students. The physical that all new students had to pass before enrollment provided the school's first line of defense against infectious diseases. Since Rapid City drew many applicants, the school had no incentive to overlook students' ill health to maintain enrollment. Superintendents likewise tried to exclude students who fell sick while away on vacation. When the government physician at the Rosebud Agency diagnosed vacationing Rapid City student Nellie Hungry with swollen cervical (neck) glands, an early warning of tuberculosis, Rosebud day school inspector Julius Henke asked Superintendent House for instructions. Should students whom the physician suspected were physically unfit be returned to school at the end of summer vacation? House replied in the negative and emphasized that tubercular students should not be sent back to school.[39]

At the Rapid City Indian School, students received care from a full-time nurse, assisted by students, and a local physician employed part-time by the school. From 1915 until the conversion of the school to a sanatorium school for tubercular students in 1929, the school employed Rapid City physician Dr. Henry J. T. Ince, a graduate of New York's Bellevue Medical College. Ince was a "regular" doctor, as opposed to a homeopathic, "eclectic," or osteopathic doctor. For a salary of $720 per year, which rose to $1,000 in the mid-1920s, he visited the school either two or three times a week while the school was in session and made emergency calls when necessary. Ince's duties included examining all students at enrollment and vaccinating those who did not show evidence of a recent successful smallpox vaccination. He performed small surgeries, pulled teeth, tended to employees and their families as well as students, cared for any Indian adults who fell ill while visiting, and inspected sanitation and hygiene at the school.[40]

The Rapid City Indian School expected much of its physician, but paid very little. Superintendents House, Young, and Mote all found Ince's services to be unsatisfactory. House thought Ince qualified, but noted his lack of attention to work at the school and resented his "harsh and abrupt criticisms" of health conditions, criticisms that Ince did not follow with constructive suggestions or guidelines for improvement. House doubted that any doctor could be convinced to give the school and its students the attention they needed for only $720 a year when physicians made much better money in private practice in Rapid City. He wanted the work of school physician put up for bid, with the possibility that the school might pay more for satisfactory service than the $720 paid Ince. Succeeding House at Rapid City in 1922, Young revived the issue of contract physicians with commissioner of Indian affairs

E. B. Meritt. If Meritt's office would find a physician who could move to the school, Young wanted to shift money from other areas of the school's appropriation to hire a full-time physician at $1,200 per year. Young's proposal apparently came to naught, for Ince remained as part-time physician.[41]

Despite the problems securing physician services, the Rapid City Indian School weathered well one of the greatest health crises to face the school, the influenza pandemic of 1918–19. William H. McNeill, author of *Plagues and Peoples*, attributes the outbreak of particularly virulent strains of the influenza virus to the confluence in northern France of troops from America, Africa, and Europe at the end of World War I. Spreading quickly, the viruses infected nearly the world's entire population and killed an estimated 20 million people worldwide. Medical knowledge at the time was insufficient to treat the disease or even slow its spread.[42]

Influenza struck the Rapid City Indian School on September 22, 1918, when a student with influenza arrived with other pupils for the start of school. By October 5, there were fifteen cases of influenza. When two students from North Dakota arrived at the school sick, Superintendent House wired reservation superintendents and the railroad agents in charge of students' transportation to Rapid City and asked them to keep students away until the epidemic subsided. With 120 students already at the school, and another 30 already on the way, House canceled classes, closed the school, and assigned employees to the work of nursing the sick. Only after he had acted did House notify the office of the commissioner of Indian affairs. Aware of the magnitude of the crisis, assistant commissioner E. B. Meritt telegraphed approval of House's decisions.[43]

To minimize the risk of disease transmission among the 150 students at the school, House removed many of the students from the dormitories and dispersed them to buildings across the campus. Despite these measures, when special physician Dr. L. L. Culp arrived at the school on October 11, he found 120 students sick in bed, as well as Superintendent House and his daughter, Margaret. Ince was ill, but still at work, until Culp relieved him. Within days, the number of sick rose to 131 students and 16 employees. Pneumonia, the cause of death in most of the fatalities during the epidemic, complicated 16 cases. With so many people sick, and so few still able to care for them, only the extraordinary efforts of volunteer nurses from Rapid City kept the situation in hand. Over the course of the epidemic, 6 students died.[44]

Mortality at the Rapid City Indian School during the epidemic was comparable to mortality among both whites and Indians in the area. At a training camp for soldiers at the South Dakota School of Mines, in Rapid City, 7 died out of 130 cases. Among Indians camped near Rapid City, 200 fell ill and 11 died. There were an estimated 50 deaths among Rapid City residents, out of a population of roughly 5,800. Showing how bad the epidemic could be, influenza took a terrible toll among students at the Pierre Indian School in Pierre, South Dakota. "When you told me over the phone that it was simply awful and the worst that you had ever experienced I knew it was a calamity proper, but you had not seen same at its worst," Pierre's Superintendent C. J. Crandall told House. "Pierre has been hard hit, harder than you can realize but you alone can form some conception. We have lost 15 of our children. In two families, there have been two deaths making the blow double. Have lost as high as two and three a day. Last night was the first one for several days that there has not been a death call. I have had as high as 15 or more special nurses; now the nurses begin to succumb and take sick. Had the people in town realized the danger, I would not have been able to get a single nurse." Crandall's daughter, Dorliska, left her job in Pierre to nurse sick students before she, too, fell ill. Of 190 students at the Pierre Indian School when the influenza epidemic hit, 16 eventually died, and 5 students fled the school, nearly setting off a panic. "Pierre will not recover from this sad blow in 20 years," Crandall said.[45]

In the wake of the influenza epidemic, other diseases struck students at the Rapid City Indian School. On December 2, 1919, Superintendent House reported two cases of scarlet fever and one of smallpox. The boy with smallpox had been attending the public high school in Rapid City; since there were cases of smallpox in town, House assumed he had caught the disease there. Fearing epidemic, he imposed a partial quarantine at the school and isolated the sick students in separate rooms of Home 2, a house usually used as living quarters for some of the older girls. All students who did not have good smallpox vaccination scars received new vaccinations, although the work was held up for several days when Ince ran out of vaccination materials. Concerned about the lack of effective quarantine in Rapid City, where new cases of smallpox and scarlet fever were appearing, House urged reservation superintendents to keep Indians away from both the school and the city. A nationwide coal shortage caused by coal strikes complicated matters. With temperatures in Rapid City ranging from zero to ten to twenty below, the Indian School burned ten tons of coal a day, up from the usual winter consumption of five tons a day. By December 12, the school had run out of coal. House purchased wood for the school's boilers while he negotiated the release of several cars of coal from Wyoming coal companies. A break in the cold, the arrival of coal, and effective quarantine averted crisis. Thirteen Rapid City students contracted scarlet fever, and nine smallpox, but none died.[46]

The Rapid City Indian School did not face another potential outbreak of epidemic disease until 1933, when Pennington County health officer Dr. F. J. Austin quarantined the school following an outbreak of cerebro-spinal meningitis. The infrequency of epidemic disease did not, however, mean that health at the school could be considered good. Recognizing the magnitude of some of the health problems at the school, Superintendent Mote vigorously promoted "Health Week." In 1926, February 21–28 was devoted to preventa-

tive health care. The Reverend C. J. Semans opened the week with
a Sunday evening sermon on health. All students received physical
examinations, and the county health officer, county nurse, and city
nurse all inspected the school. Mote assigned the kitchen the task
of exterminating mice and ordered the bakery rid of roaches. In a
Tuesday evening assembly, students sang health songs, many
borrowed from the Chilocco Indian School, set to popular tunes of
the day. To "Yankee Doodle," students sang,

> The best six doctors anywhere, And no one can deny it
> Are sunshine, water, rest and air, And exercise and diet.
> These will gladly you attend, If only you are willing,
> Your mind they'll cheer, your ills they'll mend,
> And charge you not one shilling.

Students kept daily health records in which they awarded themselves points for their performance of twenty different tasks,
including eating vegetables, skipping tea and coffee, and having
regular bowel movements. Isabel Rouillard scored high all week,
even if she lost points when she could not be happy all day, as
required by the health record.[47]

But happy thoughts and vegetables were not enough to cure
tuberculosis or trachoma. Worried that a number of students were
on the verge of active tuberculosis, Mote made arrangements with
the Sac and Fox Sanitarium, a BIA tuberculosis sanitarium in
Toledo, Ohio, to take up to twenty students, hoping that rest and
care would check the progress of the disease. He also initiated a
campaign against trachoma that led to a broader investigation of
health conditions at the school. Trachoma, a chronic, contagious
eye infection, caused the formation of nodules on the inside of the
eyelid. Left untreated, the nodules irritated the cornea, causing
pain, sensitivity to light, and impairment of vision or even blind-
ness. The available treatment for trachoma, an operation called
tarsectomy, involved turning the eyelid inside out, scraping away

the nodules with a scalpel or toothbrush, and cauterizing or disinfecting the scraped section of the eyelid. A Rapid City eye specialist, Dr. J. M. Walsh, found that many Rapid City students had trachoma and recommended tarsectomies. Judging an outside specialist too expensive, the BIA assigned special physician Dr. C. E. Yates to the task. Yates found forty-six cases of trachoma and fifty-one cases of tonsillitis requiring operation, and the school sent out permission forms to the students' parents, asking their authorization for the procedures. Yates did not proceed with the operations, however, because of the persistence of measles and erysipelas at the school.[48]

Alarmed at the high rates of measles and erysipelas, the BIA authorized inspections of the Rapid City Indian School by district medical director Dr. Emil Krulish. Krulish visited the school in 1926, 1927, and 1928, detailing each time problems that the school did not have the money to correct. He repeatedly criticized hospital facilities at the school. The school enrolled 330 students, but had only 20 hospital beds. Krulish recommended 35 beds, the construction of isolation facilities, and the addition of an operating room. Medical care under the contract physician system was inadequate. Ince did all the work Krulish expected of someone receiving $1,000 per year, which was much less work than Ince's contract specified. Ince performed only superficial medical examinations of students, gave them little personal attention, saw only those patients confined to bed on his twice-weekly visits, missed many developing cases of tuberculosis, and sometimes responded to emergency calls hours late. "There has been considerable sickness among the pupils this school year," Krulish reported in 1927, "including 10 cases of erysipelas, and epidemics of chicken pox, measles, and German measles." Mote called Ince's attention to Krulish's criticisms, but the school's budget did not allow Mote to hire a full-time replacement. When Krulish returned in 1928, he found little changed. "As usual," he noted, "there has been considerable sickness among pupils." Poor health conditions had become the norm at the Rapid City Indian School.[49]

The Rapid City Indian School compiled a mixed record on issues of student care. School food, poorly prepared and of insufficient variety and quantity during the school's first decade, improved dramatically over time. By the 1920s, Rapid City students ate well, despite increasing pressures on the school's budget. Having made substantial improvements in the school diet, administrators did not wish to jeopardize their achievements. They made the decision fully aware that students and parents participated in the process of schooling. Their goodwill had to be retained.

The Rapid City Indian School did less well in clothing its students. Decisions to economize on clothing purchases in the 1910s and 1920s yielded increased freedom of expression for students who were not only permitted but in fact required to buy or make much of their own clothing. This freedom of expression perhaps allowed class differences to surface between those who could easily afford clothes and those for whom the added expenses constituted an unwanted burden. In becoming something more approximating a regular high school, where students could pursue social activities in clothes purchased for special occasions, Rapid City sacrificed something of its original mission, providing education to those who would in the school's absence receive no other, to cater to the increasing sophistication of Indian young people.

The school's greatest failing was its inability to provide adequate health care for students, a problem directly attributable to inadequate appropriations. Rapid City staff responded well to crises, as when Superintendent House closed the school during the 1918 influenza outbreak and assigned employees to nurse the students. But the contract physician system and inadequate expenditures on hospital facilities and preventative care worked against the long-term maintenance of student health. The school became a breeding ground for trachoma, measles, and other diseases and often did not catch incipient cases of tuberculosis. By the mid-1920s, the Rapid City Indian School was not a healthy environment for children.

Critical changes had occurred, however, in the mission of off-reservation boarding schools. When Inspector William J. McConnell criticized health conditions in Indian boarding schools in 1901, BIA administrators could justifiably be accused of squandering the lives of Indian children in their rush to implement a program of assimilative education. By the 1920s, boarding schools had become welfare providers of last resort for Indian families. The Rapid City Indian School remained overcrowded not because its superintendents wanted to put every last Indian child on the road to assimilation, but because Indian parents and reservation officials enrolled children who could not be fed, clothed, and housed anywhere else. Seen in that light, Rapid City's problems were less serious and were rooted outside the school, in insufficient congressional appropriations and all the causes of reservation poverty. For all its deficiencies, the school still offered the children of Jule Matt better care than they were likely to find on the streets of Ronan, Montana.

CHAPTER 3

CURRICULUM

Language was a critical issue at federal Indian boarding schools. First and foremost, the BIA wanted Indian children taught the English language. As Commissioner J. D. C. Atkins (1885–88) said, "the first step to be taken toward civilization, toward teaching the Indians the mischief and folly of continuing in their barbarous practices, is to teach them the English language." The content of American civilization and citizenship, he concluded, could not be transmitted through Indian languages, but only through English.[1]

The emphasis on learning English extended to a ban on teaching Indian children in their native tongues, a ban that Atkins applied to both government schools and mission schools operating on reservations. He questioned the practicality of teaching in the many languages and dialects extant in Indian country. Furthermore, he believed the use of Indian languages in instruction would prejudice Indian students against the English language and by extension against government schools. Most importantly, however, Atkins simply did not want Indian languages to survive. He thought English permitted a greater range of thought, facilitated communication among tribes as well as with the larger society, and made possible assimilation. Native languages were dead weight, he believed, to be lifted from Indian students as quickly as possible.

English was good enough for whites and blacks, so it was good enough for Indians, too.[2]

The belief that newcomers to American society should speak English was not confined to commissioners of Indian affairs. As Lawrence A. Cremin notes in *The Transformation of the School: Progressivism in American Education, 1876–1957*, language was a common concern of "old stock" Americans, descended from immigrants from western Europe and particularly Britain, as they encountered the "new immigrants" from southern and eastern Europe who dominated the immigrant stream from the 1880s until World War I. Urban areas in the East and Midwest favored by immigrants became home to a welter of languages, all incomprehensible to monolingual Americans who identified English with American democracy and civilization. Immigrants dressed, worshiped, and behaved in ways bewilderingly foreign, too. Only education could fit these newcomers for American society, but how could teachers cope with classrooms where students spoke a half-dozen different languages? Cremin points out that "the problem went far beyond language, for each language implied a unique heritage and unique attitudes toward teacher, parents, schoolmates—indeed, toward the school itself. Not only baths, but a vast variety of other activities that could not be found in any syllabus began to appear. Manners, cleanliness, dress, the simple business of getting along together in the schoolroom—these things had to be taught more insistently and self-consciously than ever." Students had to be fitted for the classroom before the process of education, and with it Americanization, could begin.[3]

Much of the content of boarding school education can be found in responses to the basic issues Cremin cites. BIA educators focused on English and instruction in the simplest behaviors to bridge the gap between teachers and Indian students. Pedagogy drew inspiration from industrial education or manual training. Manual training arose out of dissatisfactions with traditional education, with its emphasis on "book learning," and training for the professions. When only a small minority of public school students went beyond the eighth grade, why force on students grindingly dull routines of textbook-based lessons that taught them to abhor work? Students' faculties of learning, and a proper love of labor and respect for work, could be cultivated more effectively through training in crafts that taught students to use their hands as well as their heads. Regardless of the value of the crafts, the belief went, manual training bred necessary traits of character. Yet for Indian students, manual training also promised the speedy acquisition of work skills that would facilitate their assimilation and allow the BIA to wash its hands of them.[4]

Manual training also found a place in educators' prescriptions for immigrants. There were differences, however, between the needs of immigrants, as perceived by old stock Americans, and those of Indians. Immigrants, some schooled in socialist thought and most Roman Catholic, Greek or Russian Orthodox, or Jewish, posed a political and social challenge to the society old stock Americans jealously guarded. Such Americans approached immigrants in the burgeoning urban areas of the East and Midwest with a certain amount of fear. Indians, in contrast, may have been obstacles to settlement in the West, but represented to whites a dying race. This conviction raised expectations of the boarding schools, especially in the area of manual training, where the curriculum and its goals were particularly poorly defined. How could Indian students be prepared for immediate entry into the work force, for economic assimilation? Could manual training, as a pedagogical technique, be made into vocational education that would give Indian students the skills to survive when, as the BIA anticipated, allotment eliminated reservations?

At church-run mission schools and government boarding schools alike, educators tried to reconcile schooling for survival, as they defined it, with a basic education in academic skills through the half-and-half schedule. Students spent half a day in the classroom learning academic subjects and half a day in the sewing room, shop, or field learning vocational skills that the BIA hoped would prepare them for life beyond the school. Atkins's contempt for Indians' "barbarous practices" reflected a wider belief among whites that Indian ways of life, the skills students learned at home, were inappropriate or worse in a civilized society. The BIA therefore tried to teach Indian students entirely new sets of skills. Burdened with such sweeping expectations, and limited by available funding, the Rapid City Indian School never entirely reconciled schooling for economic assimilation with its mission of educating Indian students in academic skills. Experience showed the half-and-half to be not a solution to the problems of Indian education, but rather a persistent obstacle to their resolution.

Large, off-reservation boarding schools like the Rapid City Indian School bore more resemblance to urban schools of the late nineteenth and early twentieth centuries than to rural schools of the same period. In 1910, schools in rural areas enrolled two out of every three American children of all races. Many rural schools were one-room schools, the "little red schoolhouse" of American tradition. In 1917, there were 195,000 one-room schools in the country. A decade later, there were 153,000, enrolling roughly 4,000,000 children. One-room schools existed in disproportionate numbers in the newly formed school districts of sparsely populated western states. In Nebraska and Montana, more than 40 percent of teachers taught in one-teacher schools. In North Dakota, more than 50 percent taught in one-teacher schools. In South Dakota, fully 80 percent of teachers taught in such schools.[5]

In *How Teachers Taught: Constancy and Change in American Classrooms, 1880–1990*, Larry Cuban describes teaching in one-room schools. Students of all ages and educational levels sat in the same room, with the young children in front and the older, taller students in back. A single teacher, who sometimes lacked even a high school education, taught all subjects to all grade levels. The necessity of teaching many different lessons in the same day fragmented the teacher's time and attention. The teacher faced a hectic day. Students received little individual attention, none of it prolonged. Instruction centered on textbooks: the teacher assigned readings and ordered recitations, with questions designed to elicit specific facts that students were to have learned from the textbooks. The teacher relied on drill and rote memorization, enforced extraordinary control over children's movements, such as requiring them to sit perfectly still and not look anywhere but at their desks or the front of the room, and used corporal punishment. Nevertheless, many students of such schools recalled their experiences fondly.[6]

When Albert H. Kneale and his wife, Edith, arrived at the No. 10 Day School on Wounded Knee Creek on the Pine Ridge Reservation in 1899, they found a one-room schoolhouse, conforming in plan and operation to the rural schools of the day. One of thirty-two day schools on the Pine Ridge Reservation, No. 10 consisted of a teacher's residence, two outhouses, a crude stable for the teacher's horses, and a small schoolhouse. The school had a small entryway, windows on three sides, and a blackboard, map of the United States, and clock on the fourth side. A wood stove supplied heat. Rows of desks faced the front of the room, where the teacher sat at a table in front of the blackboard. Students from seven to seventeen years of age attended. Working on the half-and-half schedule, the Kneales succeeded in teaching very little, for the students knew little English and the Kneales less Lakota (although they tried to learn). The students of No. 10 had little opportunity or incentive to learn English, for the Kneales were the only English speakers in the vicinity, save for a returned student of the Carlisle Indian School. The former Carlisle student, a Porcupine resident visiting relatives at Wounded Knee Creek, used her English to teach the Kneales Lakota.[7]

From its opening in 1898, the Rapid City Indian School bore little resemblance to Pine Ridge No. 10 Day School. Unlike the often isolated day schools, the Indian School was two miles west of the Rapid City depot of the Chicago and Northwestern Railway, within walking distance of town. The original school building was a two-story, brick structure containing boys' and girls' dormitories, a dining room, a kitchen, play rooms, a chapel, and two school rooms. The school employed two teachers, one instructing young students and one the older students. The school had an enrollment of eighty students. Superintendent Collins suspended the half-and-half schedule for 1898, owing to the lack of preparation of some of the students, and kept the children in academic instruction for two-hour periods in both the morning and afternoon and an additional one-hour period in the evening. With its partial age grading, the school occupied a place somewhere between rural and urban schools. Rapid City's teachers did not have to teach students of all ages and levels of schooling at the same time, but they taught a wider range than teachers in large urban districts of the time, who commonly taught only a single grade.[8]

In 1901, the Rapid City Indian School received congressional authorization for an increase in enrollment to 150, with accompanying increases in expenditures. Even with only 100 students at the school, Superintendent Davis was less than satisfied with academic instruction at his two-classroom institution. Teachers Manie B. Cone and Rilla A. Pettis shouldered the entire burden of classroom teaching, and Davis noted that academic instruction was only "as satisfactory as two teachers could render it." In 1903, the BIA funded an extensive program of renovation and expansion, which included the construction of a girls' dormitory, a new school building, and the conversion of the old main building into a boys' dormitory. The improvements and additions raised the school's capacity to 250 students, but only doubled the number of classrooms. In 1906, with 253 students enrolled, teachers Anna Cranford, Ellen B. Riley, Maude A. Chamberlain, and Henrietta Fremont taught academic subjects, and Cranford did double duty as temporary principal. As late as 1916, Rapid City still employed only four teachers of academic subjects.[9]

Understaffing in the academic department seriously impaired teaching at the school. When Supervisor Peyton Carter inspected the school in 1921, he found 285 to 290 students instructed by five teachers. The three teachers in charge of the older students each taught two classes, totaling from 65 to 45 students, and had as much work on their hands as they could handle. Clara M. Peters, in charge of 40 third graders, had a room so small that she could teach only half the children at a time, with the result that the children attended school only every other day. Maude E. Hopkins taught 20 children in the second grade and 60 in the first, and these children, too, were in class only half the time. A new school building then under construction promised to alleviate the problems of insufficient classroom space, but the school still needed another teacher, so students in the important primary grades could be in school every day. Perhaps because Carter so emphasized the need for another teacher, calling it "the crying need at present," the school did hire a sixth teacher for 1922 and subsequent years.[10]

The BIA exercised a measure of control over the content of teaching at Rapid City and other government schools. Commissioner Thomas J. Morgan made the adoption of a uniform course of study part of his original blueprint for Indian schooling. The work of systematization received fresh impetus in 1898, with the appointment of Estelle Reel to the post of superintendent of Indian schools. Reel had considerable experience in public education in Wyoming, as a teacher, as a county school superintendent in Laramie County, and as the elected state superintendent of public instruction. Reel was also a figure of considerable power in Republican politics in Wyoming, and her role in carrying Wyoming for William McKinley in 1898 earned her appointment as superintendent of Indian schools.[11]

Reel began her work with a thorough survey of federal Indian schools, traveling 65,900 miles in three years to inspect the far-flung network. In 1901, having seen the work of Indian schooling firsthand, she distributed a course of study to be followed in all

Indian schools. In the accompanying message to Indian agents, school superintendents, and teachers, Reel offered a curious blend of progressive teaching ideologies and her own, limited vision of practical education for Indian students. She believed that a child learned English "through doing the work that must be accomplished in any well-regulated home," work that also taught "habits of industry, cleanliness, and system. He learns to read by telling of his daily interests and work with the chalk on the blackboard. In dealing with barrels of fruit, bushels of wheat, yards of gingham, and quarts of milk . . . he becomes familiar with numbers in such a practical way that he knows how to use them in daily life as well as on the blackboard in the schoolroom." The development of curiosity and the ability to apply knowledge, coupled with knowledge of everyday subjects, was more important to Reel than the memorization of "definitions and useless dates."[12]

In *A Final Promise: The Campaign to Assimilate the Indians, 1880–1920*, Frederick E. Hoxie argues convincingly that by the beginning of the twentieth century, the BIA had abandoned an earlier commitment to educate Indians for full participation in American society. Instead, the BIA hoped to fit Indians into the lower rungs of a social and economic hierarchy built on the principal of white supremacy. There is much to support his argument in Estelle Reel's "Course of Study." For Indians, who were "just starting on the road to civilization," she proposed only the most modest of objectives: the goal of the course was "to give the Indian child a knowledge of the English language, and to equip him with the ability to become self-supporting as speedily as possible." The government had no plans for Indian children, apparently, beyond ridding itself of them.[13]

Reel's low expectations were grounded in a profound misapprehension of Indian intellectual abilities. The Indian children she imagined were not only blank slates, but very small slates, at that. In First Year Arithmetic, the teacher first tried to find out if incoming children could count not to ten, but to one. Reel suggested unspecified special exercises directed toward training the senses and developing judgment, faculties she believed Indians lacked. Teachers were not to introduce addition until the second year and multiplication and division in the fifth. For the sixth and final year, Reel proposed problems no more complicated than adding up the sides of a field to determine its perimeter and the amount of fencing required or calculating the square yards of carpet needed to cover a 6 by 12 foot floor. The "Course of Study" made no mention of long division, calculation of volumes, or multiplication of numbers greater than twelve. If Reel thought this was the education that best suited Indians for life, she plainly saw little potential in Indian students and envisioned for them only the most restricted lives.[14]

Any reading of Reel and her "Course of Study" must be open to the nuances of her prejudices, however, for she was a complex individual. Her refusal to recognize Indian intelligence coexisted with a willingness to work with the children's Indian pasts. Teachers were to begin history instruction by teaching the children their tribal histories and by having students relate the stories told to them by their parents. "The parents have lived through pages of history," Reel told teachers. "Oral and written reproduction of all such historical stories should form an important part of the work." At a time when her superiors in the BIA still emphasized farming as the ideal occupation for Indians, seeking to create a class of Indian yeoman farmers, Reel wanted Indian students taught to see the cultural continuities between buffalo economies and cattle ranching.[15]

Reel's "Course of Study" also attempted to make fundamental changes in the ways teachers taught. Cuban identifies two distinct, competing traditions in American education: teacher-centered instruction, where teachers control the content, methods, and pace of instruction; and student-centered instruction, in which students "exercise a substantial degree of responsibility for what is taught, how it is learned, and for movement within the classroom." Observable measures of mode of instruction include the amount of talk by teachers or students, the relative uses of textbooks as opposed to more varied instructional materials, and the opportunities for group work by the students.[16]

Reel emphatically opposed the textbook-dominated routine of recitation and drill characteristic of teacher-centered instruction. Instead, she urged teachers to cultivate children's faculties by drawing lessons from observations of their school environments, using objects as teaching aids (such as teaching fractions with actual quart and pint measures), and by encouraging children's interests in adult activities. Reel's approach was in the Swiss tradition of "object teaching" popularized in America by Edward Sheldon and bore strong resemblances to the "New Education" of Francis Parker. At the Cook County Normal School, later to become Chicago State University, Parker ran a "Practice School" where children explored the links between academic subjects, learned basic skills through integrated content, expressed themselves through the arts, and received instruction in manual tasks such as cooking, sewing, and gardening. Educator John Dewey sent his children Fred and Evelyn to Parker's Practice School before enrolling them in his newly formed Laboratory School at the University of Chicago in 1896. Cuban characterizes the Laboratory School's curriculum as one centered on "the work that people did rather than upon separate subjects, upon reading and writing through learned activities rather than through isolated tasks, and upon group work guided rather than directed by teachers." In Reel's "Course of Study" one sees the intersection of the best progressive, student-centered teaching methods of the day with the racial hierarchies of Anglo-Saxonism.[17]

Student-centered teaching required considerable time and effort on the part of teachers, however, as well as willingness to experiment with the bases of order and authority in the classroom. The costs were obvious, the benefits less so. Reel's "Course of Study" enjoyed no more lasting success, and probably less, than Dewey's progressivism. In the nation's schools as a whole, teaching from 1900 into the 1930s remained teacher-centered. Teachers taught from the front of the room, taught entire classes as single groups, and spent most of the day "lecturing to, explaining to, and questioning students while they listened, answered, read, and wrote." BIA schools, dependent on teachers trained outside the BIA in traditional methodologies, were in no position to swim against the tide of educational conservatism. When Estelle Reel retired in 1910, student-centered teaching lost its strongest proponent within the BIA.[18]

Perhaps in response to the waning enthusiasm for Reel's "Course of Study," Superintendent House put the Rapid City Indian School on South Dakota's state course of study in 1910. Under this plan, which the school followed until the BIA issued a new course of study for the 1916–17 school year, instruction was decidedly teacher-centered. In Elizabeth Bishop's first-grade class of twenty-nine students, for example, the children learned to read from the *New Education Reader*. The children read the lesson, and Bishop wrote a list of difficult words on the blackboard as well as the text of the lesson. The children then spelled the words, first as a class and then individually. The children read the text silently then aloud from the blackboard, and Bishop questioned them about forming plurals. The lesson lasted a half hour and could have been taken from any urban public school.[19]

Student-oriented teaching of the simplest form survived in Olive Turner's second grade class, where thirty-five students learned numbers from coins. In describing the method on an evaluation form, Principal Frank L. Hoyt wrote that "[p]upils were taught the different denominations of coins (objectively)." Since there could be nothing subjective about learning United States coinage, it can be surmised that he was referring to Sheldon's method of "object teaching," where students learned academic subjects through handling relevant objects. Hoyt reinforced traditional methods of measuring student progress by suggesting that Turner require more of the pupils to recite.[20]

If student-centered teaching received short shrift under Superintendent House, so too did Reel's dismissal of Indian students' intellectual abilities. House placed no arbitrary limits on the achievements of Rapid City students. The school offered only eight grades; but by following the state course of study, the school prepared students for entry into South Dakota high schools. Graduates of the Rapid City Indian School passed examinations given by the county superintendent and received diplomas admitting them to any South Dakota high school. Those who entered high school usually stayed at the Indian school, which provided room and board, and commuted to the public high school in Rapid City. Since the students and their parents were not residents of Pennington County or Rapid City, students had to pay tuition, which for the 1916–17 school year was $36 for the entire year. Eight Indian school graduates attended Rapid City High School that year, and one, Robert Emery, was both captain of the football team and president of the senior class, elected by a vote of 34 to 4. Other Indian school graduates attended the Rapid City Business College to take courses in stenography, accounting, and other business skills.[21]

Pursuing education beyond the Rapid City Indian School demanded both courage and personal sacrifice. Lakota student Nancy Schmidt, one of the five students in the first class to graduate under the state course of study in 1911, went on to graduate from Rapid City High School in 1916. In 1917, she gained admission to the State Normal School (teachers' college) at Aberdeen, South Dakota. Schmidt applied for money from her share of Rosebud Reservation tribal funds to pay her expenses; though the application went out from the Rosebud office in May, the September date for the beginning of school came and went with no reply from the BIA in Washington, D.C. House intervened with Normal School president Willis E. Johnson to keep Schmidt's place open, while prodding the Rosebud superintendent to come up with Schmidt's tuition. The money finally came in mid-October, over a month after the start of classes. Schmidt arrived in Aberdeen late and alone, with no place to stay. The dean, Miss Moore, picked her up at the train station, took her to lunch, and helped her find a room. After meeting Johnson, Schmidt ate dinner at the house of old Indian Service friends of House's. "It's a good thing they are here," she wrote House, "or I'd be tempted to take the next train home."[22]

Being far from home in an unfamiliar environment proved difficult for Schmidt. "To-day has been a trying day everything is so new and so many strange faces, they all look alike to me," she wrote House. "I feel worse than I did when I entered high school, for there there were other Indian students. Tho' Esther and Ethel [her new roommates] have been so good to me, I feel absolutely lost." Schmidt stuck it out for the whole year then returned to Rosebud and worked as a clerk and teacher. She also worked at the courthouse in White River, South Dakota, before marrying fellow Rapid City Indian School graduate Arthur T. Arrow. After her marriage and the birth of a child, she worked at the school as an assistant matron.[23]

Schmidt's example did not blaze new trails for graduates of the Rapid City Indian School, however, for the BIA choked off opportunities for advanced study by mandating the adoption of a new, restricted course of study during the 1916–17 school year. Commissioner Cato Sells claimed that the effort of the BIA in implementing the new course of study was "directed toward training Indian boys and girls for efficient and useful lives under the conditions which they must meet after leaving school." Under Sells, the BIA evaluated academic subjects and determined the emphasis they received by their "relative value and importance as a means of solving the problems of the farmer, mechanic, and housewife." The BIA sent a clear message. It had limited expectations for Indian men, and it defined Indian women only in terms of the home.[24]

Reflecting Sells's biases against academically oriented education for Indians, the course of study divided the program into two divisions: a Prevocational Course, corresponding to grades four through six, and a Vocational Course, corresponding to the seventh through tenth grades. Although the new course of study went further than the state course, which only went through eighth grade, it was less demanding academically, and Superintendent House did not believe it prepared students for high school. He continued his efforts to prepare students for high school until 1920, when poor attendance and failing grades from students already in high school led him to discontinue support for Indian students at the public high school altogether. Thereafter, higher education for graduates of the Rapid City Indian School meant going on to other BIA schools, most notably the Haskell Institute in Lawrence, Kansas.[25]

The course of study adopted in 1916 did not soften the impact of the half-and-half schedule, which remained a serious obstacle to effective teaching. After visiting Rapid City classrooms in 1925, Supervisor of Schools Stevens harshly criticized the half-and-half plan, declaring it almost impossible to do the work required in only a three-hour period. Students and teachers at Rapid City had half a day to cover material that took a full day in public schools. As Indian schools added health education to the curriculum, Stevens found "teachers almost in despair as to where they will find the time for this additional work." Any added time for instruction had to come out of the students' free time, which was almost negligible. The schedule seriously retarded learning. Mary Stewart, a teacher with an M.A. from Indiana University in history and international relations, requested a transfer from the Rapid City Indian School to the Haskell Institute after only a semester of teaching. She had discovered Rapid City students were simply not well enough prepared. Stewart was appalled at having "to talk to eighth grade pupils as though they were fifth graders—yet realize, even then, that they had missed what one meant to say."[26]

Researchers for the Institute for Government Research had the final word on the half-and-half schedule. The Meriam Report called for the outright elimination of the half-and-half schedule for the first six grades. To provide Indian children with educational opportunities at least approximating those enjoyed by white children, Indian children needed full-time schooling, with time for play and recreation, through age fourteen. But like many of the Meriam Report's recommendations, the elimination of the half-and-half could not be accomplished without time, money, and considerable support from the highest levels of the BIA. The Rapid City Indian School remained on the half-and-half.[27]

The half-and-half had its roots in both schooling ideology and the economics of running a BIA boarding school. Pratt began the practice of assigning work to his first "students," Indian prisoners from the Red River War held at Fort Marion, Florida, as a way of mitigating the impact of their imprisonment. He dismissed white guards and assigned the prisoners to guard details, making them responsible for their own conduct, and assigned them tasks such as cleaning their areas, maintaining their uniforms, and cooking. The work kept the prisoners occupied, while teaching them some of the skills Pratt thought necessary for Indian assimilation into white culture.[28]

When Pratt sent volunteers among the former prisoners to the Hampton Institute, they encountered a more fully developed ideology of work and manual training. In *Indians at Hampton Institute*, Donal F. Lindsey explores the roots of the practices of school head General Samuel Armstrong in his personal beliefs. Armstrong had fought as a volunteer for the Union in the Civil War, yet spoke well of slavery as a civilizing force for African Americans. Under slavery, he concluded, African Americans had learned the English language, Christianity, habits of labor, and work skills. To bring Indians to a comparable state of civilization, Armstrong wanted Indians deprived of government support on the reservations and thus forced to learn civilization from the ground up, by the sweat of their brows. African Americans, Armstrong believed, knew how to work, but slavery had not taught them to see the dignity in their work. Indians knew nothing at all of work and had to learn work, and thereby civilization, through the use of their hands at the simplest tasks of manual labor.[29]

In BIA boarding schools, the doctrines of Pratt and Armstrong dovetailed with institutional needs. What better way to teach work and industry to Indian students, and save money to boot, than to have them do the labor necessary for the upkeep and operation of BIA boarding schools? When working in the school kitchen, sewing room, or farm, Indian students could learn valuable skills, while enabling the institutions to function with a minimum of expenditure. As Robert A. Trennert, Jr., shows in "Educating Indian Girls at Nonreservation Boarding Schools, 1878–1920," pedagogy rationalized the economically expedient step of using student labor in the boarding schools.[30]

Not surprisingly, the programs of student labor that emerged at BIA boarding schools also expressed the gender distinctions common in the cultural backgrounds of BIA officials. In *They Called It Prairie Light*, K. Tsianina Lomawaima offers an interpretation of gender biases in close accord with Trennert's work. Both writers demonstrate the gender distinctions in the work details and vocational programs forced on Indian students, based on ideas of gender roles that, while common for the time among whites, were particularly burdensome for young Indian women. Young Indian men learned skills that would help them to farm their allotments or to work as day laborers. Women learned the skills of domestic servitude, whether as home-bound helpmates for Indian husbands or as domestic labor for white households. Trennert suggests that the division of labor at BIA boarding schools, with the large quantities of sewing, cooking, mending, and cleaning to be done, put an undue burden on female students, who found themselves doing much of the labor needed to keep the schools operating.[31]

Early visitors to the Rapid City Indian School noted the students' contribution to the operation of the institution as well as the gender distinctions in the work assigned. In 1900, a reporter from the *Rapid City Daily Journal* watched approvingly as a half-dozen girls mended clothes under the direction of a seamstress. Besides making their own beds and mending clothes, girls learned to "cook, wash, iron, scrub, and do all kinds of housework." Boys also made beds, learned carpentry, and worked on the school farm, caring for cattle and horses, sawing and splitting wood, and doing other farm tasks. Boys learned to smoke cigarettes, too, and "smoked like little engines," disregarding the ban on the practice. All told, the students did much of the work at the school, with school employees supervising but contributing relatively little of the actual labor.[32]

By 1916, the Rapid City Indian School grouped seven areas of instruction in its Industrial Department and made varying claims for the utility of each to the school and to the students. The catalog description of the school's dairying program stated that "[m]ilking, separating cream, care of stock, feeding, give opportunity for practical training in a branch of work of great importance on the reservations." Poultry was "a prominent industry," though the catalog did not claim that it would become prominent on reservations, too. Learning how to repair the school's buildings and wagons in the carpentry program gave boys training that was "generally useful." Likewise, shoe and harness making would "prove useful in later life." Laundry, however, was important primarily for the school, which needed clean clothes and uniforms for the students, though the catalog claimed that girls would be "taught to be painstaking in every particular of the work of washing and ironing." Both large and small girls would learn sewing, too, but their work was to make uniforms and workdresses and keep the school's linens mended. Domestic science, where girls would learn "all the branches of housekeeping," followed the BIA's course of study, and the catalog noted proudly that "the equipment and work done is regarded as the equal of any school in the service."[33]

But the catalog was misleading, for it listed courses that the Rapid City Indian School did not offer and had no intention of adding to its curriculum. The catalog listed a ten-week course in farm blacksmithing, for example, designed to teach boys enough blacksmithing to enable them to repair farm equipment. No such course in blacksmithing existed, perhaps because the school lacked a blacksmith shop. The four-year engineering course was to have taught boys both steam and gas engines, but the school had only steam engines. Rather than providing an accurate listing of the courses actually taught at the school, the catalog apparently offered boilerplate descriptions of courses taken from Commissioner Cato Sells's 1916–17 course of study.[34]

Rapid City's vocational curriculum emerged out of a process of negotiation between Cato Sells, who wanted strict compliance with his new course of study, and Superintendent House, who tried to reconcile Sells's demands with the limitations of the school plant, work force, and budget. Perhaps fearing that superintendents would stray from or simply ignore his directive, Sells ordered copies of the course of study given to every school employee at every BIA school, from principals and teachers to cooks and laundresses. He further commanded that the work of implementing the course of study be overseen by a force of supervising superintendents, who were to report to him personally on the progress of other superintendents within their jurisdictions. Sells named House supervising superintendent for the Crow Creek, Lower Brule, Pine Ridge, and Rosebud Reservations.[35]

Putting enforcement for much of South Dakota in House's hands proved to be a mistake on Sells's part, for House was not particularly enthusiastic about the course of study. Supervisor of Schools Peairs reported to Sells that House had left implementation of the course of study at Rapid City almost entirely to principal Frank L. Hoyt and that many of Rapid City's employees appeared to have given little thought to meeting the course's requirements. Sells responded by asking House to describe the process by which Rapid City's staff had prepared new courses and to provide detailed plans for the implementation of the course of study at the school. He wanted to know precisely how House would schedule teachers, students, and subjects to move students through to graduation.[36]

House had a ready-made excuse for his inattention: as supervising superintendent, he had been helping instructors at other schools with the course of study. He defended Hoyt's work in planning the vocational curriculum at Rapid City and pointed to the problems of adjusting instruction and application in light of the school's need for productive student labor. Sells wanted classroom instruction followed by hands-on application, as students applied knowledge to concrete tasks. House started from the labor needs of the school and tried to find ways students and the school could get credit for tasks students were already performing around the campus. To return to the example of engineering, the school had steam heat and ran its laundry with steam power. In operating the systems, House decided, students could learn about boilers, steam engines, and steam pumps. The school also had electric lighting, and in repairing and improving the wiring, students could apply their lessons in electric wiring. The school's sewer system and plumbing provided foundations for classes in those branches of knowledge.[37]

When Sells complained that House had scheduled students in a way that failed to lead to their orderly progression through the course of study, House argued that the school's need for student labor made full compliance impossible. Students were supposed to receive application after instruction; they should go to work applying the skills just imparted in the classroom. House wanted authority to assign students to work details outside their areas of instruction. "I wish to ask if a boy who has had his lesson in plant production, dairying or stock raising, as the case may be, may be permitted to report at [the] dormitory building to assist in care of rooms after having received his instruction," he wrote. "Or in case such details cannot be made, how is the necessary cleaning of rooms and building to be performed?"[38]

A disjointed curriculum thus emerged, where students were exposed to skills in the classroom then went about the work of maintaining the school with little reference made to the classroom work. Carpenter George M. Rasque's course in farm carpentry clearly displayed the conflicts between learning and productive labor. Over a one-week period, Rasque instructed boys on making plans for a house and a barn. Application consisted of unrelated repair work and simple labor. Among other tasks, the boys under Rasque's direction repaired windows at the school house and power house, fixed dining room chairs, repaired picture frames for employee Benjamin Black Fox, and moved furniture from the lumber shed and stacked lumber in its place. The closest the class came to any actual construction was putting up forms for the foundation of a new paint shop. The other fourteen tasks completed for the week involved routine maintenance around the school.[39]

Instruction for girls seemed little better and, in addition, was bound by the conventions of gender. The "Vocational Record Card for Prevocational and Junior Vocational Sewing" listed a number of tasks the Bureau of Indian Affairs expected young Indian women to learn as part of their education at the Rapid City Indian School. Under problems to be completed in the first year, the card listed such tasks as cleaning and oiling a sewing machine, cleaning and pressing a wool skirt, and making a dress. Second-year tasks included making a tub dress, renovating a hat, and making the dreaded bloomers. After each task the card listed the maximum possible credits (the possible credits for a whole year totaling 100) and left a space where the instructor could enter the credits actually earned.[40]

Agnes Hawkins, a Lakota student from the Pine Ridge Reservation, entered the second-year sewing course on January 28, 1924, and finished on April 7 of the same year. Of the eleven tasks to be completed, the instructor assigned only two, renovating a hat and making a plain petticoat. Hawkins received perfect scores of 15 and 20, respectively. The instructor assigned the additional problem of making boys' trousers, for which Hawkins received a score of 40, with an overall score of 75 for the course. Hawkins's instruction in sewing was primarily devoted to supplying the school, but at least she was able to practice her skills. Of the eleven problems listed for the Kitchen Gardening course, the instructor awarded credit only for planning a garden, giving Hawkins a 5 out of 5. Hawkins received no credit for planting, cultivating, harvesting, or other essential tasks. Why? In 1924, the school offered the course from January 2 to January 12, and the students "[o]nly had theory, weather was too cold for planting seed." In a display of creative arithmetic, the instructor changed Hawkins's 5 points for planning a garden to an 80 for the course.[41]

Agnes Hawkins's experiences were not unusual. Girls in seamstress Margaret A. Coverston's class spent the week of May 8, 1916, measuring and shrinking gingham and calico for the work dresses to be worn by other students. In the sewing room, four students made corset covers, gingham dresses, and princess aprons while six others made and hemstitched handkerchiefs. The seventeen students in the mending room did the "usual mending for [the] week," including hemming towels for the school's system of Pullman towels (continuous hand towels rolled through a dispenser). Students in A. Foster's nursing class learned the importance of taking pulse in diagnosing disease by copying from their text. The application was "mainly to get notes in note-book." Not surprisingly, there was "somewhat of a lack of interest in the work on the part of the instructor and of course it would be felt in the class."[42]

Eva Enos was happy to get away from such dull routine in her work at Rapid City. After working in the dining hall and kitchen, Enos was assigned to the cottage of one of the school nurses, where she kept house and cared for the nurse's children. "That was a good job," Enos recalled. "I got away from the building, that big building." In addition to sparing students the drudgery and close supervision of the regular work details, working as domestics kept them away from the most hazardous assignments. At Rapid City, the laundry was particularly dangerous. The laundry had little relevance to the curriculum, for it was an institutional laundry, powered by steam, as would be found in a professional laundry or hospital or other large institution. Student labor in the laundry offered little of pedagogical value, and a steam laundry was no place for children. Lizzie Blackman, age fifteen, suffered severe burns to the back of her hand when she accidentally placed it on the hot rolls of the mangle, a machine that ironed laundry by passing it under pressure between heated rolls. Blackman's hand recovered, and she went home to the Cheyenne River Reservation. Sadie Plenty Holes, Lakota, lost the fingers of one of her hands in another accident involving the mangle. Her hand touched one of the rolls, and the heat burned her hand so badly that the fingers had to be amputated. Her parents, in Rapid City for the Stock Meeting (a livestock exhibition), visited her at the school. When Superintendent House would not give them permission to take their daughter home, they employed a ruse to spirit her back to Pine Ridge. Alma Provost, an Indian employee of the Rapid City Indian School, suffered similar injuries. The mangle started while Provost was changing the covers of the rolls, and the pressure and heat crushed and burned her left hand so badly that all the fingers had to be amputated.[43]

The dangers to children in the laundry detail and other such work went beyond accidents. The Meriam Report noted that "the labor of children as carried on in Indian boarding schools would, it is believed, constitute a violation of child labor laws in most states." Because of the scarcity of older students, children ten to twelve years of age worked four hours daily "in more or less heavy industrial work—dairying, kitchen work, laundry, shop. The work is bad for children of this age, especially children not physically well-nourished; most of it is in no sense educational, since the operations are large-scale and bear little relation to either home or industrial life outside; and it is admittedly unsatisfactory even from the point of view of getting the work done." The half-and-half lingered on at Rapid City and elsewhere for no other reason than that congressional appropriations made it impossible to pay adults to do the work students performed under the guise of education.[44]

The Meriam Report added that "very little of the work provided in Indian boarding schools is directly vocational in the sense that it is aimed at a specific vocation which the youngster is to pursue, or based upon a study of known industrial opportunities." But, as Lomawaima notes, for one line of work, the vocational education of Indian boarding schools prepared students quite well: staying on to work in an Indian school, where graduates could continue the labor they had learned as students. In 1909, Superintendent House asked that the BIA modify his spending authorizations to permit the temporary employment of recent graduates as laborers. Instead of employing white laborers for forty days at $2.50 per day, House wanted to employ Indian labor at $1.25 per day, plus room and board at the school, with students. BIA chief clerk C. F. Hawke even argued that labor at the school should be done for free by the students. However, the BIA grudgingly authorized House to spend up to $300 per annum to employ recent graduates as temporary labor.[45]

The Rapid City Indian School generally employed graduates as assistants to other, usually white employees. Indeed, BIA policy mandated that assistant positions be reserved for Indians. When House wanted to employ Jay Allen, a white, in an assistant position, he had to secure special permission from the BIA, which it granted only on the condition that Allen "be relieved as soon as the services of a competent Indian are procured, it being the wish of the Office that worthy Indians always be given the preference for appointment to minor positions of this character." In 1912, nine of Rapid City's thirty-one employees were Indian. Six—Thomas Standing Elk, Benjamin Prairie Hen, Earl Heddrick, Lizzie

Williams, Lizzie Allen, and Maggie Good Voice—filled assistant positions at $300 per year. The assistants were all in their early twenties and were under the discipline and regulations of the school in much the same way as students. House generally considered any graduate of a reservation or nonreservation boarding school competent to fill an assistant position and required that applicants be "of good character." The young men had to be willing to abstain from liquor, and the young women "willing to abide by the general rules prescribed for girls of the school." The school's supervision of personal lives extended to young Indian employees, as well as students.[46]

Though assistant positions turned over rapidly, as assistants left for better work or marriage, some Rapid City graduates moved from assistant positions to higher-paying jobs at the school. Margaret Clifford, who attended Holy Rosary Mission at Pine Ridge and the Rapid City Indian School, became laundress at Rapid City in 1915 at an annual salary of $540. Jessie Bissonette, a 1914 Rapid City graduate employed as her assistant, replaced her in 1916, when Clifford resigned because of poor health. As laundress, Bissonette supervised girls who had been her fellow students only a few years before. Nevertheless, she received high marks from Superintendent House, who noted that she did "remarkably well in directing and caring for the work of her department." Rapid City graduate Mary Primeau (née Janis), Bissonette's assistant, became laundress when Bissonette resigned and held the position until the school closed in 1933. In addition to her work as laundress, Primeau coached the girls' basketball team.[47]

Other Rapid City graduates found opportunities elsewhere in the Indian Service. Samuel Eagle Shield, a 1913 graduate, found employment in 1916 at the land office on the Standing Rock reservation, after passing a noncompetitive Civil Service examination for the position. Lakota Benjamin Black Fox, a 1914 Rapid City graduate who later took courses at the South Dakota School of Mines in Rapid City, started as a student assistant engineer at the school. In that position, Black Fox worked as a repairman and fired the school's boilers, for an annual salary of $300. In 1915, he went to work at the Rosebud Boarding School as assistant engineer at $600. Quarters for married couples were not available at the Rosebud school, so Black Fox transferred to the Crow Agency in Montana, where his pay rose to $720. From 1917 to 1919, he worked at the Genoa Indian School in Genoa, Nebraska, until housing problems led him to transfer again, this time back to Rapid City, with his salary still $720. Black Fox stayed at Rapid City as assistant engineer until the school closed in 1933.[48]

Few Rapid City students traveled as far as Jesse H. Rouillard. Rouillard entered the Indian Service as a truck driver at Rapid City in 1922 and became an industrial teacher at the school in 1924. In 1926, he followed former Rapid City superintendent S. A. M. Young to the Charles H. Burke School at Fort Wingate, New Mexico, where he served as disciplinarian for Navajo boys. Rouillard reacted to the Southwest as any newcomer might: the scenery, though fantastic, soon tired him; language and culture separated him from his Navajo charges; and distance from his beloved Black Hills and Rapid City left him homesick. Also, the Burke school was new, neither fully equipped nor fully staffed, and Rouillard did the work of the dining room matron in addition to his regular duties and played organ in the chapel as well. He soon fell passionately in love with a young teacher from Washington, D.C., to the detriment of his work as disciplinarian. When Young offered Rouillard a transfer to Colorado River at a reduction in pay, he instead resigned and soon married. When Mote inquired about hiring Rouillard back in 1928, he was working as a truck driver in Gallup, New Mexico, and playing in a local band. Returning to the Rapid City Indian School, Rouillard worked as a bus and truck driver until the school closed in 1933.[49]

In 1916, Special Officer J. L. McBrien, assigned to the Interior Department's Bureau of Education, asked Superintendent House to consider alternatives to the off-reservation boarding school. If a reservation school were as well equipped as on off-reservation school and included in its work force agricultural extension agents as provided for rural counties in the Smith-Lever Act of 1914, could it offer instruction as good as that provided at the Rapid City Indian School? House did not think so. The Rapid City Indian School benefited from its proximity to the Rapid City public high school, the South Dakota School of Mines, and the Business College. In House's opinion, the educational environment of Rapid City and the opportunities open to Indian students at other institutions were decided advantages in favor of the off-reservation boarding school.[50]

Within four years, however, the Rapid City Indian School quit sending Indian students to the public high school and the Business College. The advantages cited by House ceased to exist. In the program that remained students spent half the day in class, learning from a watered-down academic curriculum, and half the day at vocational instruction that taught farming and housekeeping skills the students could have learned at home, aided by extension agents. Institutional needs for unpaid student labor compromised even the limited goals of transmitting "home" knowledge. Agnes Hawkins spent her time in sewing class making boys' trousers not for the pedagogical benefit of the work, but because the school needed boys' trousers to clothe its male students and could not afford to buy the clothing. Because students spent much of their time doing such "productive" labor, they learned far less than they might have in their academic subjects.

Despite the deficiencies of the curriculum, Lakota Sara Buffalo thought she got a fine education. "It's a real good school. Of course, I didn't go to no other school just there, but it was a good school. I learned more. I wasn't the girl that didn't know how to talk English after I came out of there." In addition to her English, Buffalo learned domestic science, how to cook and sew. She worked in the laundry, too, washing and ironing for the whole school. As Northern

Arapaho Winnie St. Clair remembered, Rapid City did not educate students to go elsewhere. It schooled them to stay in place, "to take care of your home and raise your family."[51]

Thomas Jefferson Morgan would have considered such education a partial success, at best. Buffalo and St. Clair learned English and the domestic skills the majority society expected of women. The homes they made, however, were on reservations, which continued to exist despite allotment. Rapid City taught students skills, but failed to force their assimilation into the majority society. There, perhaps, lay the reason for Buffalo's satisfaction with the school. In its partial success, the Rapid City Indian School better met Indian needs of the time than it would have had it fulfilled a loftier set of goals. When Indian education was designed to "kill the Indian, and save the man," a mediocre school was better than one that worked entirely as planned.

The original school building at the Rapid City Indian School. Later converted to a boys' dormitory, this building burned in 1923. Photo courtesy of South Dakota State Historical Society—State Archives.

The school campus. The old school building is at the center. The building in the left foreground is a girls' dormitory. Leaves appear to have been added to the trees with an artist's brush. Photo courtesy of South Dakota State Historical Society— State Archives.

The Rapid City Indian School football team, 1916, from the 1916–17 school catalog. Photo courtesy of National Archives—Central Plains Region, Kansas City, Missouri.

Interior of a small girls' dormitory, showing four rows of beds. From the 1928 school catalog. Photo courtesy of National Archives—Central Plains Region, Kansas City, Missouri.

One of the three-bed rooms for the older girls, showing beds, a dresser, and electric lights. From the 1928 school catalog. Photo courtesy of National Archives—Central Plains Region, Kansas City, Missouri.

The sitting room in the girls' dormitory, from the 1916–17 school catalog. Photo courtesy of National Archives—Central Plains Region, Kansas City, Missouri.

Meal time. There are seven or eight children of various ages at each table, boys on one side, girls on the other. From the 1928 school catalog. Photo courtesy of National Archives—Central Plains Region, Kansas City, Missouri.

The 1923 graduating class. Top row—Cecelia LeDeRoute, Sophia White Coyote, Corena DeMarsche, Victoria Little Bull, Zella M. Guthrie (teacher), Mabel Runs Against, Virginia Conroy, Millie Big Crow, Elizabeth Little Bull. Middle row—Lucille Carpenter, Pamela Powell, Mary Powell, Elvira Philbrick, Edith Ledo, Jennie Cashen (Florence Kimmel not pictured). Bottom row—Dawson Morrisette, William Yellow Robe, Paul White Turtle, Silas White Shield, Joseph Lyman, LeRoy Cummings, Raymond DeSheuquette, Harry Jacobs. From the 1923 school catalog. Photo courtesy of National Archives—Central Plains Region, Kansas City, Missouri.

The girls' basketball teams at the 1929 tournament at the Rapid City Indian School. The Bismarck Indian School team is front and center in the white sweat shirts, with the Rapid City team above them in the top two rows. The teams on the left and right are the Pine Ridge and Pierre Indian School teams, but it is not clear which is which. Photo courtesy of National Archives—Central Plains Region, Kansas City, Missouri.

The 133rd Motor Transport Company of the South Dakota National Guard, on summer maneuvers, June 18, 1929. The 133rd Motor Transport Company was composed of Rapid City Indian School students and staff. The company's trucks are not in the photo. Photo courtesy of National Archives—Central Plains Region, Kansas City, Missouri.

CHAPTER 4

CYCLES OF DAYS AND YEARS

On June 25, 1904, Indians from reservations in South Dakota and Montana began arriving at Rapid City for the "Council of Nations," a political and social gathering of northern tribes meeting under the guise of celebrating the Fourth of July. A single party of 650 Cheyennes arrived at Rapid City four days later. By July 1, 2,000 people had camped at South Park outside town, with their 400 tents arrayed in a great circle. Rapid City merchants did a brisk business in groceries, clothing, and firecrackers and brought in nine barrels of bread from Deadwood when local bakers failed to keep up with demand.[1]

The Fourth of July yielded a fine day for Indians and townspeople alike, heralded at dawn in the patriotic fashion by explosions of giant powder.[2] The Grand Parade began at 9:00 in the morning, with students of the Rapid City Indian School leading the way. Visiting Indians, many of them the students' families, followed in traditional ceremonial clothing. South Dakota's Congressman E. W. Martin addressed the city at Court House Square at 10:00. Yellow Owl, a Lakota from the Cheyenne River Reservation representing the Indians assembled, spoke at 11:00. Indian School cadets gave a demonstration of marching and drill at 11:30, passing in review before Congressman Martin and Mayor F. N. Emrick.[3]

Afternoon festivities began with a foot race down Main Street at 1:30, which Indian school student William Bordeux won for a prize of five dollars. After a pony race, a baseball game, and a polo game, citizens presented gifts donated by business houses and others to the Indian visitors in a Gift Ceremonial. Indian school students warmed up the crowd for the evening fireworks with gymnastics demonstrations. The day ended with ballroom dancing at the Armory Hall, sponsored by Company M of the South Dakota National Guard.[4]

Although Indians and whites alike participated in the Fourth of July, they did not always agree on the celebration's meanings. For white inhabitants of Rapid City, the day celebrated nationhood and the achievements of their state and municipality. For Yellow Owl, it provided an opportunity to voice the concerns of the gathered tribes and remind whites of their treaty obligations and to call on them to share the wealth flowing out of the Black Hills. And as the *Rapid City Daily Journal* reminded its readers, July 5 was truly the Indians' day. Once gathered together to pay homage to the United States on its day of independence, Indians held dances of their own, feasts and giveaways, and sham battles between Indians and cavalry, Indians and cowboys, and Lakotas and Crows.[5]

The Fourth of July had many meanings, for it was also a time for Indian families to renew ties between the generations. Among the other events of midsummer, the Rapid City Indian School held its closing exercises on June 25. Indian parents traveled to Rapid City not only to gather in council and celebrate, but also to pick up their children for summer vacation. Out of these yearly rituals came a rich tapestry of events, some occasions for joy, others for loss and sadness. Intricate daily and seasonal schedules governed the lives of students. Some, like the demanding daily routine, were core elements of the boarding school program, meant to restructure the habits and perspectives of Indian students. Others, like the football and basketball seasons, became social institutions promoted vigorously by the staff and remembered fondly by students. Even as they marked the passage of time, the cycles of days and years became enduring elements of life at the school.

The school year began on a variety of schedules, not all of them set by the school superintendents. Fall harvests worked to the detriment of prompt enrollment at the beginning of September. On September 28, 1909, J. J. Duncan, day school inspector on the Pine Ridge Reservation, noted that many Pine Ridge students were still not in school. The work fund available to employ Indian laborers on the reservation proved small, in comparison to the great demand for potato pickers off the reservation, and families so employed had not been able to bring their children to school on time. Aware of the economic needs of Indian families, authorities at Pine Ridge had not pressed them to bring their children immediately to school.[6]

Fall harvests also brought fall fairs, many of which took place in September. Sponsored by reservation officials, the fairs instructed Indians in agriculture at a time of year when pleasant weather favored travel and Indian farmers could take time away from their fields. The gatherings also provided opportunities for Indian families to meet and socialize. In 1917, C. C. Covey, superintendent of the Rosebud Agency, South Dakota, opened reservation schools the first week of September and expected students to be in school within a day of the opening date. Covey warned agency employees not to let students of off-reservation schools remain on the reservation until after the Rosebud Fair. J. J. Duncan, in 1917 the principal and day school inspector at the Cheyenne River Agency, South Dakota, complained that the people of the Cherry Creek district, in the southwest corner of the reservation, went "to every fair in the country nearly, and many do not pretend to go to school for about a month after school opens."[7]

Superintendent House thought it would be better not to open schools until after the reservation fairs and then to make an effort to get students to school promptly. C. J. Crandall, superintendent of the Pierre Indian School, also believed it preferable to open school late in September or on October 1, on account of the fairs. The BIA did not agree, though, so school continued to open the first week of September. Superintendent Young's moving pictures and student social during the first week were an attempt to get students in on time. Superintendent Mote moved the festivities to the second week of school.[8]

Whenever school opened, traveling there could be a frightening experience for young people. Arapaho Eva Enos was scared the first time she took the train from the Wind River Reservation in Wyoming to Rapid City. The Wind River students boarded the train at Lander, Wyoming, early in the morning, traveled all day, and stopped at Chadron, Nebraska, for the night. There were no adults to guide the party, only older students who had made the trip before. "[W]e had to go over to a rooming house," Enos remembered. "[T]hat was kinda scary cause we didn't know whether . . . where you was headin' or what." The Wind River students stayed overnight in Chadron and took the train into Rapid City the next morning. On her return trip at the end of the year, Enos knew what to expect and lost her fear.[9]

For reasons of economy, Rapid City superintendents preferred to have students travel unescorted, with an older student guiding each group. Superintendent Mote bitterly disputed travel vouchers submitted by Martha Pereau, a seamstress from the reservation boarding school at Fort Peck, Montana, who escorted a group of Fort Peck students to Rapid City in 1927. Pereau's claim on Mote's transportation funds left him livid, because it threatened his control of an account already depleted. Mustering his arguments against payment of Pereau's vouchers, Mote saw no reason why an escort was needed to bring a party of "five or six full grown girls" from Fort Peck to Rapid City. As he pointed out to Fort Peck superintendent Charles Eggers, Pereau's superior, two other Fort

Peck girls had traveled from beyond Fort Peck to Rapid City by themselves with no incidents. Mote considered Helen Iron Bear, one of the older girls in the party escorted by Pereau, to be entirely capable of leading the group herself. Had not Assistant Commissioner E. B. Meritt intervened in the dispute to support Eggers and Pereau, Mote would have refused Pereau's vouchers. Meritt did not issue a general ruling requiring the use of escorts, but he thought the length and complexity of the route from Fort Peck (to get to Rapid City, the students had to go through Fargo, North Dakota, where they spent a night in a hotel) justified Eggers's insistence on an escort for the students.[10]

The following year, Mote decided to avoid the roundabout and expensive train trip by sending the Rapid City Indian School's own automobile bus to Fort Peck to pick up students. By 1930, Rapid City was making extensive use of the bus. On a single trip to the Pine Ridge Reservation on August 25, 1930, the bus driver collected fourteen students and would have picked up more, had students not already left for Rapid City by wagon. As reservation roads improved and cars became more common, parents sometimes drove their children to school. To the dismay of Superintendent Young, parents who brought their own children expected to be reimbursed for their expenses. Young, guarding his transportation funds, preferred to buy train tickets for students who could not afford the expense of travel to the school and paid the parents nothing.[11]

Arrival at an off-reservation boarding school thrust children into a busy, bewildering world that ran by its own rules and rhythms. In *American Indian Children at School*, Coleman describes the jarring dislocations Indian children faced when they entered boarding schools for the first time. School staff took children's "home clothes" away from them, scrubbed them down, cut their hair, supposedly to prevent lice, and clothed them in uncomfortable, ill-fitting school uniforms, sometimes against the children's physical resistance. The

loss of culturally significant clothing and long hair could be profoundly unsettling. The total effect completely transformed the
children's exterior selves.[12]

The transitions were perhaps less abrupt at the Rapid City
Indian School. For most students, this was not their first school. In
1917, only 24 of 342 pupils listed on the rolls enrolled at Rapid City
with no prior schooling. In 1927, 18 of 341 had no prior schooling.
Some students entered Rapid City with six or more years of school
to their credit. Even for students from mission or reservation
boarding schools, though, the transfer to a big off-reservation
school like Rapid City brought changes. Eva Enos had never left
the Wind River Reservation before going to Rapid City. At St.
Michael's Mission in Ethete, Wyoming, she had lived in a cottage
with fifteen other Arapaho students. On arrival at Rapid City, she
moved into a dormitory housing as many as sixty students, from
different tribes. Enos and the other Wind River students were
"kinda scared, you don't know what's going to happen to you."[13]

The tyranny of the bell represented another constant of boarding
school life. Boarding schools ran on busy daily schedules, punctuated by ringing bells or steam whistles from school power houses.
Coleman suggests that for boarding school students, the bell
"probably became for them what the alarm clock is for many
twentieth-century Euro-Americans—a sound which, no matter
where heard or when, startles the whole system." In 1914, the
school ran on the following Monday–Saturday schedule, approved
by Second Assistant Commissioner C. F. Hawke after Superintendent House included instructional periods for work details and a
play and exercise time for small children:

A.M.	
5:30	Rising Bell.
6:30	Mess Call and Breakfast.
7:20	First Work Call. (Two blasts of the Whistle.)
7:30	Second Work Call. (One blast of the Whistle.)

7:30–8:00	Instruction of Work Detail.
8:25	First School Call.
8:30	School Call. (Bell.)
11:30	Recall from work and school.
	(Blast from Whistle.)
11:50	Mess Call and Dinner.
P.M.	
12:50	First Work Call (Two blasts of the whistle.)
1:00	Second Work Call (One blast of the whistle.)
1:00–1:30	Instruction of Work Detail.
1:15	School Call. (Bell.)
4:00	Recall from school.
4:00 to 4:30	Group athletics for small children.
5:30	Recall from work. (Blast of whistle.)
5:55	Mess Call and Supper.
7:00	Evening Hour (Winter.)
7:30	" " (Spring and Fall.)
8:30	Taps (Winter)
9:00	" (Spring and Fall.)

Children typically worked a half day at tasks that the BIA defined as vocational training but were in fact routine work necessary to keep the school running and attended academic classes the other half day. Sunday brought relief from the whistle, but not the bell. Students still rose to a 6:00 A.M. bell, with Sunday school or Mass in the morning, and all-campus, nondenominational chapel services (in which Catholic priests participated) and Young Men's Christian Association (YMCA) or Young Women's Christian Association (YWCA) meetings in the afternoon and evening.[14]

No new student could hope to understand Rapid City's complex schedule without considerable practice and coaching. When Enos and the other Wind River students arrived at Rapid City, "we was green, we didn't know nothing about you know that kind of boarding school." Enos learned the routine of the school from older and more experienced students. It was not enough that students respond to the bells and whistles and be in their places on time. Students had to learn to stand in lines, to form up in companies, and, above all, to march. Sara Buffalo, Lakota, said that Rapid City "was a military school and we had to drill and practice our marching. We march even to the dining room. There was four companies of girls, A, B, C, D. And we all had to march."[15]

The daily routine at the Rapid City Indian School resembled that of basic training in the military, a resemblance that intensified during and after World War I. Unlike basic training, however, the routine lasted all year. Students rose early to the cacophonous sound of a bell, getting out of bed well before dawn in the long darkness of Dakota winters. In the hour between rising and breakfast, students made their beds, washed up, dressed, and brought their beds, lockers, and clothing to military standards of perfection. Students with early morning duties, such as milking cows or working in the mess hall, rose earlier and had less time to prepare before going to work. Mess call was an occasion for inspection as the children formed up outside in companies, before marching to breakfast. After breakfast, students had a few minutes to return to their dormitories before going on work details or going to class. The day was already long by the time students formed up for dinner (lunch). Students switched activities in the afternoon: those who worked in the morning went to school in the afternoon, and those who studied in the morning went on afternoon work details. World War I brought increased instruction in military drill and marching for boys, in addition to their burden of classes and work details. Only after a late supper did students have time to themselves, when they could catch up on shining shoes, repairing clothes, and all the other details the military refers to as "personal maintenance." Students found time for themselves in the late hours before taps, or in minutes stolen here and there during work details, or in between duties.[16]

Under the unrelenting regimen, days blended into weeks and weeks into months, with the passage of time marked by the changing seasons of the South Dakota year and the occasional holiday. The 1916–17 school catalog listed only a short Midyear Vacation from December 25 to January 1 and Closing Week exercises June 17–20 that included religious services, athletic and literary programs, and closing ceremonies. The school did hold socials for students, although something of their character can be inferred from Superintendent House's prohibition against dancing. He was willing to reconsider his ban, though, when he failed to find a suitable substitute for the entertainment of the students. In 1917, Rapid City's Principal George E. Peters wrote Charles F. Peirce of the Flandreau Indian School (Flandreau, South Dakota) to ask if Peirce permitted dancing. If so, Peters wanted to know how often he allowed dancing, how Flandreau conducted dances, and what effects dancing had on pupils. It almost goes without saying that the dances Peters had in mind were not Indian dances, which the school never permitted, but formal affairs like those conducted at white high schools.[17]

The 1916–17 catalog did not list the event, but students did celebrate Thanksgiving Day with a program put on at the school for residents of Rapid City and an evening banquet for the students of roast turkeys with cranberry sauce and pumpkin pie. A description of a Thanksgiving program presented in 1928 evokes the tenor of such ceremonies at the Rapid City Indian School. The program began with the assembled students singing "America." Performances included student Agnes Clifford's recital of "The First Thanksgiving," Marjorie Ann Whipple's reading of "Turkey Time," a piano solo by Norma Silverthorne, and the singing of "America the Beautiful" by the assembled students. The program gave students an opportunity to exhibit and receive praise for their achievements, but only in a context that glorified the history of the Anglo-American conquerors. Lest anyone miss the messages contained in the celebration, the written program concluded with a quote from nineteenth-century English clergyman and novelist Charles Kingsley: "Thank God every morning when you get up, that you have something to do that day which must be done whether you like it or not. Being forced to work, and forced to do your best, will breed in you a hundred virtues which the idle never knew." If forced labor bred virtues, the students of the Rapid City Indian School at their long work details were candidates for sainthood.[18]

In the 1920s, the Rapid City Indian School began to resemble city high schools of the era in many of its extracurricular activities. Movies alternated with student socials on a weekly basis. When ordering films, Superintendent Mote wanted comedies, but not slapstick. He would consider feature films, too, if they were not too expensive and suitable for children. Films had to be "wholesome and uplifting in their nature but at the same time entertaining and instructive, if possible." The students liked outdoor pictures, and Mote put in special requests with agencies in Minneapolis and Denver for outdoor movies and westerns. Some of the films Mote ordered included such forgettable titles as *Great Main* [not *Train*] *Robbery*, *Harvester*, *Freckles*, *Alex the Great*, and *When the Law Rides*. In the winter months, the school offered basketball as an alternative to the movies, depending on its success in securing games with other teams.[19]

The socials enjoyed broad participation. Young students had their socials from 6:30 to 7:30 Saturday evenings, and older students from 7:45 to 9:30. Various student organizations took charge of the socials, with boys' and girls' organizations alternating. In October 1927, the Sons of Pahasapa, a student fraternal organization, sponsored the first social, the YWCA sponsored the second, and Company A of the Boy's Battalion the third. In November, Company A of the Girl's Battalion took the first social, and Company B of the Boy's Battalion the second. The school held a Halloween party, variously described as a social or a masquerade carnival. Committees composed of white and Indian staff and Indian students oversaw booths, stunts and prizes, refreshments, and decorating. The prizes included two first prizes for the "boy and girl wearing the most beautiful and original costume." Second prizes were to go to the boy and girl wearing the most comical costumes. Perhaps to make sure that nothing got out of hand, the committee in charge of stunts and prizes consisted of principal Carl Wilcox, disciplinarian Chauncey Yellow Robe, and matron Theresa Kaufman, the three highest-ranking employees in direct daily contact with students.[20]

The Student Activities Association had responsibility for all student activities, including the school store, athletics, and the band and orchestra. The association was composed of the previous year's honor students, one boy and one girl elected from each of the three highest grades, and the student officers (students who held positions in the military organization of the student companies and battalions). A faculty advisory committee that included the superintendent, principal, disciplinarian, matron, and the athletic coaches oversaw the association's work. A pay social, a pay movie, and receipts from the school store funded it. From November 17 to December 15, 1925, the association earned $69.41 from the social, $16.35 from the movie, and $169.46 from the store. The store listed inventories of basic school supplies, including 133 pencils and 140 erasers, and an astonishing variety of snack food, including 91 Ding Dongs, 77 Fat Emmas, 7 1/6 dozen oranges, and 180 ice cream cones. Eva Enos remembered the store fondly, for purchases there tided her over between care packages from home. While care packages might come once a month, or even less frequently, "at that little store we could buy a lot of things for maybe fifty cents."[21]

The school always offered entertainment featuring students to the white citizens of Rapid City. The Fourth of July gymnastics demonstrations were perhaps the most innocuous. On December 12, 1914, a large advertisement in the *Rapid City Daily Journal* promoted an appearance by the Indian School Minstrels, billed as "20 Full Blood Sioux Indians." The three-part entertainment, held on a Saturday night at the Elks Theater, consisted of hit songs and music, a "Darky Imitation of a Grand Opera," and a performance of the skit "Breach of Promise." Seats were fifty and thirty-five cents. Perhaps Indian performers brought a new twist to the traditional minstrel fare of actors in blackface mocking stereotypes of African Americans. Certainly it was safer in Rapid City for Indians to lampoon African Americans than whites. This was not an isolated incident, as shown by the 1913 closing exercises of the Osage Boarding School, which included a Sambo character in the skit "The Jolly Waiters."[22]

The Rapid City Indian School exercised the dramatic talents of its students in other performances that played on white stereotypes and misrepresentations of Indian cultures. In the 1910s, the school put on "The Pioneer's Papoose, A Light Opera in Two Acts." Set in the eastern woodlands, "The Pioneer's Papoose" tells the story of two fictional tribes, the Tomahawks and the Arrowheads. In act 1, the Arrowheads threaten war against the Tomahawks unless Prince White Face (played by Roy Azure), son of Chief Tomahawk (Jesse Rouillard), marries the ugly Lillamush (Alma Morigeau), daughter of Chief Arrowhead. The Pioneer, a Western Pathfinder (Harry Albert McGaa), enters the scene with a grievance against the Arrowheads, and war begins, ending act 1. In act 2, Layemout, Medicine Man of the Tomahawks (Richard Friday), gives a "glowing account of the battle." Lillamush returns as a prisoner of war, whereupon Chief Tomahawk and the Pioneer make a discovery. The synopsis does not give away the ending, although one can guess from the title and the Pioneer's enmity with the Arrowheads that either Prince White Face or the ugly Lillamush is the Pioneer's lost child. The opera ends with a victory dance. Choruses of Indian "Maids" and "Braves" provided counterpoints to the stories of the principal characters.[23]

In 1925, the Girls' and Boys' Glee Clubs presented "The Indian Princess," a musical version of John Smith's traditional Pocahontas story, billed as "true history." Roy Azure, moving up to better parts, played John Smith. With the exception of Chief Powhatan (Dallas DeCory) and his two Scouts (Charles White Wolf and

Stephen Red Ear Horse), most of the characters with speaking parts are white men. Smith rates fully five "Friends," played by James Stirk, Henry LaRance, Joe Laderoute, Michael Tree Top, and Isaac High Elk. Choruses of Indian "Braves," "Squaws," and "Sailors" round out the cast, with the Girls' Glee Club providing the "Indian Girls from neighboring village" and Pocahontas's friends.[24]

For profound defamation of Indian cultures and histories, the operetta "Lelawala, The Maid of Niagara" ranked first. The operetta is based on the "Legend of Niagara," an astonishing invention in which the Great Spirit orders the sacrifice of a virgin to ease a famine. Necia, the daughter of the Chief of the Oniahgahras, volunteers to be the sacrifice. On the appointed day, she drifts over Niagara Falls in a white canoe decked with flowers, appeasing the Great Spirit and ending the famine. The operetta is set in a later time of crisis, when the fictional Oniahgahras face annihilation in war at the hands of the powerful Delawares. The tribe appeals to the Spirit of the Waters, who again demands a virgin sacrifice. Once more, the daughter of a chief volunteers to die in the "Thunder Waters." Lelawala, played in 1929 by Effie Whipple, is to be the dutiful (and beautiful) victim, but plot complications enter in the form of a rejected suitor, Shungela (Isaac Long), and a number of white characters. Shungela kidnaps Lelawala, only to be captured in turn by the Oniahgahras, at which point the John Smith–Pocahontas motif pops up as Lelawala intervenes to spare Shungela's life. Lelawala, once more with her tribe, is about to enter the sacrificial canoe when word arrives that Shungela's tribe has defeated the Delawares and slain their chief. Wrapping up the dreadful story, the Medicine-man (William Lends His Horse) receives word from the Great Spirit that a sacrifice is no longer necessary, and the sacrificial canoe becomes part of a new wedding ceremony.[25]

The effects on Indian students of these white fantasies of Indian life can only be imagined. As Robert F. Berkhofer, Jr., discusses in *The White Man's Indian: Images of the American Indian from Columbus to the Present*, the western became an established part of American literary tradition after the Civil War. Plains Indians, particularly Lakotas, became the quintessential American Indians. In South Dakota, however, white-Indian warfare on the Plains was local history, and recent, too. All three plays are set in the distant past of white-Indian conflict in the Eastern Woodlands, the safe and well-known haunts of James Fenimore Cooper's *Leatherstocking Tales*, rather than the Plains warfare that was the heritage of Indians and whites alike in South Dakota.[26]

Oratory also enlivened the long winter and spring months at the Rapid City Indian School. Though not as offensive as "Lelawala," the subject matter for the declamatory contests was no more oriented to the students' own lives. Instead, students read pieces that would not have been out of place at the city high school. For the 1926–27 school year, Principal Wilcox organized preliminary declamatory contests between the sixth and seventh grades to be held Wednesday evening, April 15, and a contest between the eighth and ninth grades to be held Thursday evening, April 16. He invited school employees and all others interested to the Saturday evening finals, held in the school auditorium. The orchestra opened the evening with selected marches. Viola Hornbeck was the first of the twelve contestants, reading "The Trouble with Rastus." Other pieces included "An Old Sweetheart of Mine," read by Lillian Swain; "The Red Man Eloquent," read by Godfrey Broken Rope; and the final piece, "The Necessity of War, March, 1775," read by Mortimer Hernandez. The contest ended with more music from the orchestra and the classes performing their class songs and yells, before the judges rendered their decision. Hernandez took first. Albert McGaa came in second with his reading of "The Union Soldier," and Alvina Fallis third with "Jane—from Sixteen." Hernandez and McGaa won first and second, respectively, in a declamatory contest at the Pierre Indian School, a one-two punch for Rapid City students with patriotic speeches.[27]

As important as public speaking was to the school, though, it could not match the appeal of athletics. In *Education for Extinction,* Adams shows the importance of football at the Carlisle Indian School. For Carlisle's Superintendent Richard Pratt, football was a powerful advertisement for the school, and the possibilities of Indian achievement, in an era when upper-middle-class whites celebrated sport as the epitome of civilized virtues. Football was also an acculturating force, where Indian players learned "the value of precision, teamwork, order, discipline, obedience, efficiency, and how all these interconnected in the business of 'winning.'" The BIA forced Pratt out by 1904, but football lived on at Carlisle. Under the legendary coach Glen "Pop" Warner, Carlisle fielded an outstanding team that made its reputation roughing up such early football powers as the University of Pennsylvania, the University of Chicago, Harvard, and the University of Minnesota. The 1907 team had a 10–1 record, and the 1911–13 teams were nearly as successful. The Carlisle football team's national tours, and the later successes of the Haskell Institute team and the incomparable Jim Thorpe, indelibly linked Indian schools to football in the minds of American sports fans.[28]

The Rapid City Indian School did its best to uphold the reputation of Indian athletics, but it was never the powerhouse that Carlisle and Haskell were in their heydays. Rapid City athletes were younger, rarely out of their teenage years, and the school did not have the national recruiting base of Carlisle and Haskell. Early football games against the Rapid City High School in 1902 ended in 17–2 and 26–0 victories for the high school. The Indian School apparently spent 1903–4 rebuilding, venturing out only to beat the South Dakota School of Mines, located in Rapid City, at baseball, 9–5; and to lose to Lead High School, Lead, South Dakota, 23–9 at basketball. The 1904–5 season went poorly. School of Mines beat the Indian School 54–0 in a football game that ended at halftime because of darkness and obvious disparities in the levels of play. The basketball team also did not fare well, losing 16–13 and 16–6 to the Rapid City Athletic Club, before winning a game with Sturgis 28–20. A return trip to Lead brought another loss, 28–18.[29]

As the results suggest, the Rapid City Indian School's early efforts were haphazard, with few games scheduled. While the students enjoyed the games, particularly the away games, the boys (girls had yet to get their own teams in the first decade of the 1900s) were not well trained and had yet to reconcile their vices with athletics. John Whipple, a lead player of the football team and apparently every other team, described a 1905 trip to Spearfish, South Dakota, for the *Rapid City Daily Journal*, which ran the interview on the front page. The boys had played basketball in Spearfish; nonetheless, Whipple showed much more interest in the rodeo. A natural raconteur, he entertained readers with the story of a steer that escaped the rodeo and ran loose in the streets of Spearfish, where it met up with and ran down its owner (no one was hurt). The boys finished the trip to Spearfish with a track meet, where the Spearfish boys beat the Indian School team so badly that the Indian boys were ashamed of themselves, and even the victors wished the Indians had won a few more events. Whipple blamed the loss on the boys themselves: they smoked too many cigarettes, and hardly any could run more than 100 yards. When asked to explain, Superintendent House said that the boys did not smoke openly or in the presence of employees and had often been lectured on the subject.[30]

Although athletics matured somewhat under House's direction, he did not promote them as Pratt promoted football at Carlisle. In the 1916–17 school catalog, House claimed that the Rapid City Indian School's athletic field was "unequaled in this section of the state." The gymnasium, 48 feet by 96 feet, had floor space "ample for basketball games and other indoor sports." He pointed to frequent opportunities to play other schools and club teams in football, basketball, baseball, and track and field. But athletics received "due attention," a phrase that suggests a certain restraint, and House made no claims for the benefits of sports, beyond developing the *individuality* of the players. Sports made the school interesting and attractive, and House lumped them together with amusements in the catalog. He showed no interest in sports as an acculturating activity, as promoted by Pratt and later "Pop" Warner at Carlisle.[31]

Sports at the Indian School flourished only after the arrival of Superintendent Mote in 1925. Transferred to Rapid City from the Haskell Institute, Mote brought with him that institution's passion for football, only to find that superintendents House and Young had done little to cultivate the students' pigskin talents. Due to lack of uniforms and other equipment, for which the school had no funds in 1925, Mote could not even get up a good scrimmage. Remembering a box full of old football uniforms in storage at Haskell, he wrote his friend R. E. Hanley, Haskell's director of athletics, to get the uniforms shipped to Rapid City before Hanley threw them out. A determined Mote knew his team could not hope to challenge Haskell in their first year, but promised Hanley a "Waterloo in South Dakota some day."[32]

Superintendent Mote tried to secure membership for the Rapid City Indian School in the South Dakota High School Athletic Association. That organization's Board of Control rebuffed his application, with R. E. Rawlins, the secretary-treasurer, explaining that association rules limited membership to the public high schools of the state and the high school of the University of South Dakota, excluding the Indian School. Mote nonetheless scheduled full seasons for Rapid City Indian School basketball teams against a variety of opponents. In 1925–26, the boys' team played Holy Rosary Mission (Pine Ridge), Belle Fourche High School, Scenic High School, Nisland High School, Pine Ridge Boarding School, Pierre Indian School, and the local Methodists. The "midgets" team played the Nemo Bantams and the Rapid City Junior High team. The girls' team played the Whitewood, Scenic, Nisland, Nemo, and Deadwood high school teams. Only the "midgets" had a winning season. In 1927–28, Indian School teams played the Sturgis, Nisland, New Underwood, Midland, Belle Fourche, Piedmont, Newell,

Pringle, and Philip High School teams, as well as the St. Francis Mission (Rosebud), Holy Rosary Mission, and Pine Ridge Boarding School. Many of the matches included both boys' and girls' teams. With the exception of Pierre Indian School, another off-reservation boarding school, Rapid City played teams in western South Dakota, avoiding long trips.[33]

Mote had less success with the football team. Winters were long in South Dakota, and fall and football seasons brief. Nearby high schools were unwilling to schedule games with the big Indian School boys, whom Mote described as husky but inexperienced, some never having played a game before. The Murdo, South Dakota, high school and the Sundance, Wyoming, high school both begged off, explaining that their weekends were already full. The soldiers at nearby Fort Meade (outside Sturgis) were willing to play, though, as were the young men of the Spearfish Normal School football team. Dan O. Root, director of physical education at Spearfish Normal School, guaranteed the entire travel expenses of the Rapid City team if they would play in Spearfish, an arrangement that was not unusual. He also offered half the gate receipts, which he thought would be considerable, since football was popular in Spearfish and Indians were "always a great attraction athletically." Indian football was popular in Rapid City, too, even if the local teams would not play the older Indian School boys. For the school's first homecoming game, part of a celebration Mote elected to call "Indian Day," the school met the Pierre Indian School downtown on the Rapid City High School's field. A flyer boldly advertised "FOOTBALL!" as the Pierre Indians met the Rapid City Indians, admission fifty cents.[34]

Basketball remained the most successful sport, probably because as an indoor sport it could be played through the long, harsh South Dakota winters. At the end of October 1928, the Rapid City Indian School had only two confirmed home football games scheduled for the season, but at least ten basketball games, most of which were double headers, featuring both boys' and girls' teams. The girls' team was particularly strong. The previous season, it had beaten all the local high school teams so soundly, often holding them to single digit scores, that Mote tried unsuccessfully to set up an exhibition game with a college team that had overwhelmed the Flandreau Indian School girls' basketball team. To help finance such fine performances, the school sold season tickets, good for both football and basketball. Those who held two tickets could bring their entire families at no extra charge. Mote sent one of the $1.50 tickets to each school employee, with an accompanying memo all but ordering the recipient to accept the ticket and pay up. Through its faculty members, the Student Activities Association sold tickets in town, too, mainly to local businesses. Such pillars of the Rapid City business community as the Pennington County Bank, First National Bank, the Rapid City Motor Company, and Henry Behrens, the undertaker, all bought tickets.[35]

In addition to its revenues from season tickets, the school store, and the pay movies and socials, the Student Activity Association used gate receipts to pay for uniforms, referees, and game expenses. The association apparently received fixed sums of money from host schools to pay the expenses of away games, collected gate receipts on home games, and paid fixed sums to visiting teams to cover their costs. Rapid City received twenty-five dollars per trip for basketball games at Pine Ridge Boarding School and Holy Rosary Mission, while St. Francis Mission at Rosebud paid thirty-five dollars, and Sundance High School in Wyoming forty dollars. The Rapid City Indian School used employees' cars to transport the teams, minimizing expenses. Employees who owned cars might find themselves asked to "volunteer" when Mote was short of transportation.[36]

In January 1928, Superintendent Mote floated a proposal among the other Indian schools in South Dakota and northern Nebraska for a Northern Indian School Association. He modeled the Indian School Association after the South Dakota State High School Athletic Association, which had refused to grant membership to Indian schools. The proposal went out to the Pierre, Flandreau,

Rosebud, and Pine Ridge Indian Schools and the St. Francis and Holy Rosary Missions in South Dakota, the Genoa Indian School in Nebraska, and the Wahpeton Indian School in North Dakota. The proposal evoked mixed reactions, however, with several superintendents declining on grounds of cost or distance, and the idea ultimately died.[37]

Within a month, however, District Supervisor James H. McGregor proposed an annual contest with athletic, public speaking, and group singing events for the mission and government Indian schools of South Dakota, with the option of forming a permanent association if the annual events went well. McGregor, whose invitation could not well be refused, arranged for the contest to be held at Pierre, the state capital, where South Dakota's Governor W. H. Bulow would be on hand to present the trophies. C. R. Whitlock, superintendent of the Pierre Indian School, hosted the two-day event. Though McGregor originally intended the meet to encompass only his district, he allowed C. B. Dickinson, superintendent of the Bismarck Indian School, North Dakota, to enter a Bismarck delegation and was willing to enter Wahpeton, Pipestone, and Genoa in subsequent years. Rapid City entered a strong contingent, with Albert McGaa trying his luck in the Boys' Orations with "I Am an American." The strongest contenders with the Rapid City contingent, though, were Alvina Fallis in the Girls' Dramatic category and Alberta Horne in Girls' Humorous, with near perfect scores in a preliminary contest for their readings of "The Soldier's Reprieve" and "The Football Fan," respectively.[38]

With McGregor's backing, Superintendent Mote organized what he initially billed as a Tri-State Indian School Basketball tournament, to be held March 15–16, 1929. The states represented slipped to two, though, when the Pipestone Indian School in Minnesota declined to participate on account of bad winter weather. The snows were so deep that the 25-mile road between Pipestone and Flandreau had been closed for two weeks, and Pipestone had disbanded its teams for the season. Fort Yates and Bismarck in North

Dakota managed to send teams to Rapid City; the Bismarck Indian School students traveled 600 miles round trip to spend one day at the tournament. The South Dakota School of Mines in Rapid City made all arrangements for the tournament, including officiating, and allowed its $100,000 gymnasium to be used for the finals.[39]

Bad weather held down attendance and revenues, but the tournament emerged as a success for the Indian School. The Rapid City team of Cecelia Janis, Julia Black Fox, Alice DeMarshe, Mildred McGaa, Eloise LaPlante, Agnes Marin, Margaret Two Bulls, Nellie Craven, Agnes Clifford, and Mabel Newman defeated the favored Bismarck team, 23–16, buoyed by the cheering crowd. The Flandreau boys' team, confident from wins in the eastern part of South Dakota, fell to the Rapid City team of Edward Quick Bear, Raymond Picotte, Jacob Two Bulls, David Spotted Horse, William Lends His Horse, Max One Feather, Bert Afraid of Hawk, Dominic Day Eagle, and Ambrose Day Eagle by the score of 25–14. The Holy Rosary Mission boys' team picked up the Class B cup (for smaller boys) after defeating Pine Ridge, and the trophy for most sportsmanlike conduct went to the Bismarck girls.[40]

Spring brought better weather and a successful trip to the Pierre Declamatory Contest, Track Meet, and Music Contest. Principal Kirk K. Newport held a general school assembly in the auditorium on the evening of May 10, 1929, to celebrate the successes of Rapid City students. Roy McLeod reported on the trip to Pierre, Alberta Horne on the declamatory contest, Albert McGaa on the track meet, and Agnes Clifford on the music contest. McLeod and Sam LaPointe presented the Class A (older students) cup, with Agnes Clifford receiving it on behalf of the Class A girls. Rose Swimmer presented the Class B (younger students) cup, with James Gayton receiving. Mote offered concluding remarks.

The Pierre meet was the last big event of a Rapid City year, for classes ended with the arrival of summer and many students went home. Superintendent Davis began the tradition of offering year-end entertainments in 1904. He promised the students a public entertainment if they did well in their studies; when they met his expectations, he arranged a demonstration of student gymnastics and singing in the Armory Hall in Rapid City. Under Superintendent House, the year-end program became a regular affair and much more elaborate. In 1905, House reserved the first performance, held at the school, for Indian parents. Over time, the year-end program became a commencement ceremony and less a public entertainment, though superintendents continued to invite prominent citizens of Rapid City as well as the students' families. Marching drills, piano solos and duets, and the march "Salute to Washington," played by the band, marked the graduation of James LaPointe, Paul Presho, William Schmidt, James H. Tatiyopa, and Nancy Schmidt, class of 1911, the Rapid City Indian School's first graduating class. By 1916, the graduating class had grown to sixteen. Jennie L. Brown was salutatorian, Millie Runs Over Them valedictorian, and the ceremony began and ended with music from the school orchestra.[41]

Commencement ceremonies meant extra work, as students worked double details to clean up the buildings and the school grounds. They also meant transitions, and not just for the graduating class. Students whose three-year terms of enlistment had run out were free to go home, with the school paying their transportation, whether they had stayed long enough to graduate or not. Other students left, too, for Indian parents succeeded in keeping summer vacations for most students. In 1905, commissioner of Indian affairs Francis E. Leupp, believing students lost too much of their learning and boarding school habits over summer vacations, ordered vacations eliminated for students of off-reservation boarding schools. Parents of students at the Indian School did not learn of the change in policy until they arrived at Rapid City for the school's closing exercises and the annual Fourth of July celebration. On finding out that they could not take their children home with them, parents were understandably upset and said that they would not send their children to Rapid City in the future.[42]

So strong were the parents' feelings that Superintendent House took the matter to local civic and business leaders. These "prominent men of the city" sent telegrams of protest to South Dakota's congressional delegation, who prevailed on the BIA to allow the children thirty days' vacation. After talking with parents, Mayor Emrick concluded that, unless Leupp's order was rescinded or further modified, attendance at the Rapid City Indian School would suffer. The *Rapid City Daily Journal*, reminding its readers that "Indians have the same feelings as white people" in regard to their children, urged that the matter of vacations be pursued and that the children be given full summer vacations. Good business sense demanded that the needs of Indian families be respected.[43]

Superintendent House arranged a compromise whereby the BIA authorized him to release pupils for the summer on the conditions that their parents promise to return them in the fall and that the government bear none of the expense of the students' transportation. Summer vacations for students were not unknown at off-reservation boarding schools, yet they were not the norm. House had to secure permission from the BIA in 1909 and 1910 to continue the practice.[44]

By 1910, House had settled on a system where students or their families left a deposit sufficient to cover return transportation before releasing the children for the summer. That way, there were no delays while parents collected money for transportation back to the school. The deposit requirement only applied to students brought to the school at government expense. As House explained to His Roan Horse, a Lakota parent from the Cheyenne River Reservation, parents who brought their children to the school themselves and received no reimbursement from the government could take their children back without paying the deposit.[45]

The deposit system was not unique to Rapid City. Chilocco Indian School also required parents to deposit money sufficient to cover students' transportation expenses. In *They Called It Prairie Light*, Lomawaima writes that "[m]ost families were able and eager to pay for transportation, and their children spent summers at home." Deposits did not keep many Rapid City students at school over the summer, either. In 1915, only 20 students out of 300, some of them orphans, stayed on during the summer. At schools serving other communities, the deposit requirement, which had become BIA policy, was burdensome. In "A Bitter Lesson," Child puts the cost of round-trip travel from the Flandreau Indian School, South Dakota, to Chippewa reservations in Minnesota or Wisconsin at over $30 per child in the 1920s. Many Chippewa families could not afford the expense.[46]

Yet even when families could pay the deposits, as was the case for most Rapid City students, bringing their children home could mean great sacrifices. Fares for Rapid City students in 1925 ranged from $1.52 one way to Scenic, South Dakota, near the Pine Ridge Reservation to $15.71 one way to Lander, Wyoming, for students from the Wind River Reservation. Children twelve years of age and younger traveled at half fare. The costs to families with more than one child at Rapid City would have been considerable, particularly for families from reservations more distant than Pine Ridge and Rosebud. Flandreau Indian School's Superintendent Charles F. Peirce complained to Pine Ridge's Superintendent Brennan that parents were destituting themselves to pay their children's fares. Peirce knew of instances when parents mortgaged and sold property, even the family cow, to pay children's fares. Bringing their children home sometimes left families so poor that the children, once home, had nothing to eat. Peirce used the problem of transportation costs to argue that reservation superintendents should restrict home visits. Another solution, one that the superintendents apparently never explored, would have been for the BIA to pay at least part of the students' transportation expenses.[47]

Not surprisingly, some students remained at the school over the summer, sometimes as many as thirty-five. In addition to those who could not afford to go home, other students chose to stay at the school over the summer and work for pay, as did some Chilocco students. Another class of students had no choice in the matter: in 1912, House began keeping runaways at school over the summer, a practice his successors largely continued.[48]

The superintendents of the Rapid City Indian School and the reservations also collaborated in denying vacations to students whose home conditions the superintendents deemed unhealthy. In one case, Rosebud officials persuaded Agnes Yellow Cloud to permit the enrollment of her daughter Edith at the Rapid City Indian School. Though Edith was sixteen, she was in the third grade and therefore ineligible for enrollment at Rapid City. Superintendent House nonetheless enrolled Edith because Rosebud's Supervisor in Charge C. L. Davis considered the mother to be of "rather unsavory reputation" and feared the daughter "would be ruined if she remains at home." A condition of Edith's enrollment was that she stay at the school over the summer. When Agnes Yellow Cloud asked for her daughter's return at the beginning of the summer, House refused on the advice of Rosebud's Superintendent Covey. Edith worked as a cook at the employees' club and got along fine with employees and the other older girls who were spending the summer at the school. House considered it better that she stay at the school and earn money than return home. In another case, a girl from the Fort Peck Agency, Montana, had attempted suicide and would give Fort Peck's Superintendent Mossman no other reason than that her father had been "mean" to her. Not knowing what had gone on between the girl and her father, but concerned for her welfare, Mossman and House agreed that the girl should stay at Rapid City over the summer.[49]

While the attempted suicide of a student was unusual, House's response was not. The purpose of Rapid City and other boarding schools was, after all, to separate children from their parents so that cultural ties could be severed through education and indoctrination. The schools' interests lay in preparing Indian children for assimilation, not in preserving Indian families, and so the schools were not reluctant to retain children, whatever the cost to their families. Child documents the frustration and grief Chippewa families endured when boarding schools kept their children, often without explaining the reasons to the parents. If the reservation superintendent agreed with the school superintendent's decision to keep a child, families had little recourse. And while reservation and school superintendents might squabble over enrollments in their respective schools, giving families greater leeway to choose which schools children would attend, divisions of authority were less apparent in custody decisions. When the decision was not which school a child would attend, but whether the child would stay at school or return to the family, the superintendents confronting Indian families shared not only race and culture, but also a belief in their authority to interfere in Indian lives.[50]

Whatever their reasons for staying at Rapid City over the summer, students at the school shared a routine. Though there were no classes, much of the work of the school continued. There were clothes to be made and mended, meals to be cooked, and fields to be planted and cultivated. Some students, like Edith Yellow Cloud, worked for wages. Summer work in the fields was harder than the school-year duties, but the schedule was far simpler, consisting only of meals and two work periods, and students had evenings to themselves. The days were long, the nights short, and brief, violent thunderstorms interrupted the heat of a South Dakota summer. In August or September, other students began arriving at the Rapid City Indian School, and a new year began.[51]

The rhythms of the Rapid City Indian School defined much of the life of its students. Their days began early, with the clamor of a ringing bell, and electric bells and a steam whistle drove them through a complex schedule that demanded much work, frequent marching, and regular formations and allowed little free time. The superintendents fine-tuned the schedule over the years, with the military routine remaining a constant of life at the school.

The longer rhythms of the year remained constant, too. The superintendents preferred that school begin the first week of September. Nevertheless, the agricultural rhythms of the harvest and the cultural rhythms of reservation fairs dictated later beginnings. The Rapid City Indian School always held Christmas celebrations, but BIA policy did not allow children to go home for a midwinter break, even if the school superintendents had wanted such a break. School ended late, at the end of June through the 1910s and the end of May thereafter. Parents' demands that their children have summer vacations forced a partial accommodation by the superintendents. Most but not all Rapid City students had summer vacations. All had the opportunity to go home at government expense at the end of their three-year terms of enlistment at the school.

In the intermediate rhythms of weekly entertainment, of movies and socials, basketball games, and declamatory contests, the Rapid City Indian School showed the most development over time. These excursions from the demanding daily routine, though present in the 1900s, developed fully only in the 1920s. They set Rapid City apart from mission or reservation boarding schools. Eva Enos, who started school at St. Michael's Mission on the Wind River Reservation in Wyoming, found Rapid City to be freer than the mission. The Indian School had town days, when students with money could go into Rapid City to shop. Enos bought makeup. And Rapid City had dances, where students waltzed and tried the Charleston, as well as foot races, basketball, and "all kinds of sports." Enos really liked the school, once she got used to it, even given the rigors of the daily schedule.[52]

CHAPTER 5

DISCIPLINE, PUNISHMENT, AND VIOLENCE

For hundreds of young Indian students, the Rapid City Indian School represented a place of transitions: from childhood to the beginnings of adulthood, from the cultures of their upbringing to the threshold of the often hostile majority culture. They made these transitions in an environment that proved to be far from ideal. As Adams shows in *Education for Extinction*, it was an article of faith among white educators and BIA officials that Indian youth could and should be prepared for assimilation through education. The transformation could best be effected by physically distancing the children from their roots in family and tribe. Superintendent House phrased the role of the nonreservation boarding school in deceptively mild terms, finding it "better fitted owing to location and environment for creating interest in education." White educators seized the opportunity not only to act *in loco parentis*, but to usurp the role of Indian parents in the upbringing of their children.[1]

This policy created, unintentionally, an environment where children outnumbered adults by overwhelming margins. In 1916, the BIA authorized a payroll of thirty-two employees at the Rapid City Indian School, and two positions went unfilled. Several employees, such as the clerk and assistant clerk, worked in the superintendent's office and had no contact with students. The school employed four teachers and a principal, who carried the entire burden of academic instruction. Other employees, such as the nurse, farmer, carpenter, and cook, were responsible for teaching students their respective trades and supervised students on work details. Only seven employees—the disciplinarian, matron, and five assistant matrons—assumed the primary responsibilities of child-rearing. These seven employees, assisted when possible by other staff, served as surrogate parents for 250 to 300 children.[2]

These extreme child-adult ratios provided a key dynamic at the school, shaping the conduct of everyday life and the structures and moods of staff-student relationships. The numbers restricted the possibilities for nurturance and individual guidance. Combined with the assimilationist agendas of BIA educators, the skewed child-adult ratios produced a rigid, unforgiving environment. Life at the school took on an impersonal, regimented character, with expanded definitions of deviance and correspondingly harsh punishments that stood in stark contrast to the gentler child-rearing practices of the students' families. At the Rapid City Indian School, the important transitional periods in students' lives became complicated by the hazards of institutional life in an assimilationist setting.

The most visible evidence of the regimented nature of life at an off-reservation boarding school could be seen in the BIA's imposition of a system of military conduct and discipline for students. In *American Indian Children at School*, Coleman describes the shocked reactions of students newly arrived at off-reservation schools as school employees took away their home clothing, scrubbed them with harsh soaps, and sheared the students' much-loved, and often culturally significant, long hair. Ill-fitting uniform clothes and heavy, uncomfortable shoes followed. So did introduction into a regimented world where school authorities and student officers enforced a bewildering system of rules and regulations, punctuated by ringing bells and the measured tread of marching feet. As on an army post, boarding school students lined up in rows and columns for inspections and parades and marched in neat formation wherever they went on campus. The Indian School followed the common pattern. "We march even to the dining room," Sara Buffalo remembered.[3]

The use of military discipline in the BIA's off-reservation boarding schools had deep roots. U.S. Army Captain Richard Henry Pratt, the leading exponent of off-reservation boarding schools for Indian youth, made the imposition of military standards of dress, movement, and conduct the centerpiece of his work with Indian prisoners from the Red River War housed at Fort Marion, Florida. Nothing so quickly erased the image of the "savage" in the white mind as a haircut, a uniform, and the abilities to stand at attention and march in step. As Lindsey discusses in *Indians at Hampton Institute*, Armstrong employed a similar system of military organization and discipline. The results profoundly impressed and reassured whites, whether the objects of the makeover were Indians or African-American freedmen.[4]

Beyond its immediate visual impact, military drill and discipline had meanings that white educators valued. White stereotypes of Indians invariably included elements of "wildness," of disorder and a lack of discipline or self-restraint. Products of a Protestant culture that placed paramount value on self-restraint and demanded order and discipline, white educators saw powerful meaning in military drill as the antithesis of the supposed Indian character. Where proponents of allotment under the Dawes Act saw the solution to the "Indian problem" in the virtues of private property and the values its possession would presumably teach, educators saw in military drill and discipline necessary lessons of cleanliness, promptness, attention to detail, obedience, order, and self-discipline.[5]

Studies of Indian education have focused on these pedagogical aspects of the military program. But military drill was more than a moral exercise or even symbolic evidence of civilization. Drill had its roots in the practical necessities of the battlefields of the seventeenth and eighteenth centuries, where success in battle depended on the ability of a relative handful of officers to control the movements of hundreds or thousands of soldiers. While Coleman emphasizes the pedagogical aspects of military discipline, he also notes the advantages of drill in maintaining physical control of students. Drill made it possible to enforce order on an environment where chaos might otherwise have ruled. Adams shares Coleman's interpretation of drill's ultimate purpose and recognizes the role of drill in coping with "the sheer organizational problems created by having to house, feed, teach, and, most significantly, control several hundred 'uncivilized' youths."[6]

The records of the Rapid City Indian School suggest that its civilian superintendents, living with the day-to-day consequences of the BIA's decision to concentrate Indian children in boarding schools, appreciated the utilitarian aspects of military drill and discipline, irrespective of their supposed pedagogical value. The emphasis the school placed on orderly movement, on marching and straight lines, can be seen in the responses to children's uncontrolled activities. As a group of domestic science students learned, the bounds of permissible behavior were narrow, to the point that normal childhood activities became expressions of deviance. The students spent much of their day's instruction in the Domestic Science cottage sewing, an activity that demanded concentration and allowed little movement. When let out of the enforced quiet of the cottage by teacher Agnes Greiner, the young women unwound like so many tightly coiled springs. They raced around the campus, shouting to each other and playing ball, releasing their tensions as any children might. The students made the most of their recess, enjoying the last seconds of freedom until they were once more in the cottage.[7]

Unfortunately, their exuberance drew the attention of Superintendent Mote. "I think that the D.S. girls set a very poor example just now of returning to work after recess," he reprimanded Greiner. "While all the rest of the school is marching orderly to the school building, the D.S. girls are running around the lines, yelling, throwing a ball, etc., to the confusion of the marchers." If the young women needed a recess, and Mote was not sure that they did, they could at least go to and from their recess in an orderly manner. He instructed Greiner not to permit play when it interfered with the orderly handling of large groups of students. Greiner would not deny her students their recess, but promised changes in their behavior. She preserved play at the cost of spontaneity and release. To Mote, the maintenance of order was paramount. For administrative convenience, the military regimen of marching and straight lines had to prevail over the students' natural modes of childhood behavior.[8]

But the discipline of bells, marching, and straight, orderly lines encompassed more than a system of restraints. It offered as well a set of demands, of *dos* as well as *don'ts*, requiring prompt and thorough obedience from the students. As Trennert writes in *The Phoenix Indian School*, an Indian school campus ran on a schedule, where every activity had a proper time and place. The demanding routine sometimes evoked a passive, quiet resistance from Rapid City students. Getting the children moved around the campus and to their classes and assigned duties on time presented a challenge for the staff, too few in number to supervise the students in all their movements. The matrons and disciplinarian were responsible for their charges; but quite often students determined their degree of compliance with the complex routine of the school. Sometimes the students made their lives easier by skipping inconvenient parts of the routine. Science teacher Kirk K. Newport complained that children, especially girls, returned to school too early after recess and noon, apparently showing up in the halls and classrooms before the teachers were ready for them. The students' schedule required them to return to the dormitories after recess and noon and stay there until the first whistle blew. They then had five minutes to get to their classes. While Newport thought five minutes ample time to get anywhere on campus, some of the girls apparently thought otherwise and simply left out the scheduled return to the dormitories.[9]

More often, boys violated the school's strict routines, sometimes with the connivance of school employees. Superintendent Mote cautioned employees Benjamin Black Fox, Jesse Rouillard, and Fred Basler about their evening basketball games. Mote counted at least six boys in the game, at an hour when the students were supposed to be at religious instruction. If employees were to continue to have access to the gym after hours, they would have to keep the students out. To see that the boys did not sneak back in after the employees left, Mote wanted the employees to keep closer track of the keys. They were to fetch the keys themselves and not just send a boy to pick them up.[10]

Mote similarly corrected assistant farmer Emerson Hill. Boys congregated in the farm shop near the horse barn, gathering around the stove to parch corn and pass the time. Mote wanted the shop kept as a work space, locked when not in use, and the boys kept out except when there on work with Hill, another employee, or a "responsible boy" in charge. Maintaining the intricate routine of the school required the active cooperation of all of the staff, aided by collaborating students.[11]

While employment data on Hill are not included in the school files, his name suggests that he was Indian and he occupied one of the assistant positions usually reserved for Indians, often themselves graduates of federal boarding schools. Black Fox and Rouillard were Indian, suggesting the possibility that some of the problems Mote perceived grew from a camaraderie between Indian employees and students and the boys' need for companionship and the company of older men as mentors and role models. For the boys playing basketball off-hours, separated from their families for months at a time and living in an environment where the scarcity of adults made adult nurturance a rare and valuable experience, friendship with Indian employees may have filled an acute need. If so, such relationships formed in the face of official opposition from Superintendent Mote, who again saw a need for strict order in the school.[12]

Other aspects of student conduct are more easily interpreted. To satisfy adolescent hunger, a need not entirely met by school diets, boys went through a window in the horse barn to get corn to parch. Students broke the padlock on the commissary under the dining room, taking food. Boys driving the school trucks on delivery runs from Rapid City to the school helped themselves to groceries out of their loads. Boys pulled the padlocked door of the farm shop open far enough to allow entry and exit, giving them a place to congregate away from the eyes of school employees. A house behind the small boys' dormitory became a place for unsupervised and messy play, incurring Superintendent Mote's wrath. Boys hung around the bakery, where a detail of girls worked, when the superintendent thought they should be elsewhere.[13]

Indeed, boys often surfaced where superintendents thought they ought not to be and sometimes authored much mischief. By 1911, Superintendent House concluded that boys should not be detailed to assist the night watchman. On a Saturday night, while two boys supposedly watched, other students broke into the bakery and did considerable damage. School boundaries were surprisingly porous: in 1915, Rienzie Dillon, Alexander Larvie, and Joseph Chipps, all students at the school, had the misfortune to be involved in an accident while playing at an old brick yard a mile from the school. Finding a tramway once used for hauling bricks and sand, the three pulled the wheels of a tramway truck up a hill, then released them down the track. The wheels struck a cow grazing by the track, breaking its hind legs. The cow had to be killed, and its owner and Superintendent House dunned the boys' parents for damages.[14]

As automobiles became more common in Rapid City, opportunities for dangerous play multiplied. In 1923, Superintendent Young found that boys from the school jumped onto the running boards of cars that passed school grounds. Boys also played chicken, running in front of cars at the last possible moment. Young ordered disciplinarian Yellow Robe and small boys' matron Ema D. Walters to put an immediate stop to both activities. In 1928, students Earl McLeod and George Williams allegedly took an unauthorized joy ride into town in an automobile belonging to employee Audrey Carr. Superintendent Mote made the boys pay for the "use and abuse" of the car.[15]

Taken together, the misdeeds of Rapid City boys suggest a certain laxity in the school's supervision of its students, which probably stemmed from its student-staff ratios. A boarding school's myriad rules could only be enforced, after all, when staff were both present and willing to exert themselves to secure students' compliance. On the Indian School's sprawling campus, with students often scattered among numerous work and training details, staff were plainly insufficient to supervise the activities of all students. Gender differences complicated student behavior and staff responses, too, particularly when female employees of the school confronted the large boys. Teacher Frances Masden, for example, wrote directly to Superintendent Mote about the problems she encountered getting the older boys to choir practice on time. Head matron Kaufman always had the choir girls lined up and ready at the appointed time and substituted other girls to make up the required number when special duties kept the regular choir girls from attending practice. The small boys usually arrived at practice in a body, on time. But the large boys arrived late when they went to choir practice at all, coming in by ones and twos at times that suited them, not Masden. The teacher sent the list of choir boys to disciplinarian Yellow Robe several times and reported the boys who failed to attend practice, but he did not respond.[16]

Clearer intimations of conflict come from the correspondence of Mrs. Russell. "In spite of all the talking Mr. Otopoby and I have done there in the dining room to some of the large boys, we still have trouble with them," she said to Mote. A group of young men persisted in defying her, damaging or destroying cutlery and speaking in language Russell did not think appropriate at the table. Talking to the young men did not do any good. "If I were a man," she added, "I'd throw some of them out of the dining room."[17]

The evidence does not suggest a conflict between female staff and male students as much as it does an unwillingness on the part of male staff to support their female co-workers. Masden's quarrel was with Yellow Robe. And if gender-linked physical or social constraints kept Russell from exercising her full authority in the dining room, no such constraints limited Otopoby. Why, then, did Russell find it necessary to complain to Mote about the behavior of the large boys in the dining room? And why did Masden have to go over Yellow Robe's head about the behavior of boys under his care? The possibilities range from a lack of respect for female staff by male co-workers to a conscious use of conflicts with the large boys as a means of embarrassing and undermining female staff. The result further diluted authority at the school: Masden's students felt free to skip or be late for choir practice, and Russell could not enforce decorum in the dining room.

However, divisions between female and male staff did not make female staff powerless in their interactions with male students. Power relationships at the school still favored staff over Indian students, regardless of gender. Teachers sometimes subjected students to humiliating verbal abuse that denigrated their tribal heritages. Lakota student Charley DeSheuquette described one such incident. After entering the classroom of teacher Daisy Haines for an afternoon class, DeSheuquette stood at the window and watched the girls march past. Haines ordered DeSheuquette to his seat, and he complied. As the girls filed into the classroom, Haines informed DeSheuquette that he would stand at the window at the end of class and remain there all evening as punishment.[18]

DeSheuquette retorted: "You cannot make me stand there." Haines responded by humiliating him in front of the class. In disciplinarian Yellow Robe's boyhood, Haines told her students, the old way of courting was for a boy to sit down away from camp and look at a girl. The boy and girl looked at each other. Then the boy wrapped himself in a blanket and walked up to the girl and wrapped the blanket around her and stole her away. In that way a boy and a girl would become married. Haines told the class, "Charley DeSheuquette will do the same thing some time."[19]

In the boarding school context, where the inculcation of Christian values stood second in importance only to literacy in English, Haines had labeled DeSheuquette a future adulterer. Angered, he replied, "Think twice before you speak." During the ensuing interchange, Haines said that the superintendent of the Lower Brule Reservation had sent the DeSheuquettes to school only because they were too lazy to be put to hard labor on the rock pile. When DeSheuquette lost his temper and called the superintendent "nothing but a damn liar," Haines started looking about the room for a weapon to use on him. Had she a hammer, she told him, she would use it on his head. Only the arrival of Lakota student Ada Shuck with the news that Principal Peters wanted DeSheuquette in his office spared DeSheuquette further humiliation and possible injury in Haines's classroom.[20]

While verbal abuse was potentially as damaging to the students as physical abuse, physical violence against students was more likely to draw the attention of both parents and school superintendents. In 1910, Mitchell Desersa was incensed to learn that the matron E. O. Stilwell had struck his daughter, Delphine. Corporal punishment, Desersa said, "I positively will not stand and especially when it is in striking my daughter on the head when she is already afflicted with poor hearing." Desersa, a Rosebud resident, promised to go to Rapid City if necessary, for this was the second time Stilwell had struck his daughter.[21]

Theresa C. Kaufman, Stilwell's replacement as matron, drew no complaints. But Philomine Bierly complained to Superintendent Young in 1924 about a spanking her son Narcisse received at the hands of Ema D. Walters, assistant matron under Kaufman. Walters spanked Narcisse Bierly for wetting his bed, an action his mother thought inappropriate. Her son's problem was medical and in no way warranted disciplinary action. Young agreed. The superintendent had the doctor look at the boy and told Walters to use some punishment other than spanking, if the boy deserved any punishment at all.[22]

The superintendents of the Rapid City Indian School continued to be concerned about containing violence against students. Superintendent House reprimanded cook Maggie F. Porter for striking and otherwise punishing students at work in the kitchen. Augusta Thompson's father made particular complaint to House of Porter's mistreatment of his daughter. While House was aware that work in the kitchen was demanding and that "conditions [were] such as to make [Porter] and the pupils nervous," he could not tolerate a cook striking students. If any girls on Porter's detail failed to obey instructions, she was to send them to the matron, who would decide what, if any, punishments were necessary. Taking disciplinary functions from the hands of other employees was "necessary to protect both [Porter] and the school."[23]

Similar but more serious conflicts led to the resignation of Earl G. Kelsey, carpenter. A former first lieutenant in the army, Kelsey "carried his army tactics in too pronounced a degree into his school work." He taught the boys military drill as well as carpentry, and students disliked his overbearing ways. His abuse of students during drill and on the carpentry detail earned Kelsey the enmity of students and staff alike. In 1923, Superintendent Young took him to task for violently disciplining Albert Tall Bull, Jacob Brown Otter, and Edward Schmidt. In each case, Kelsey had torn the students' clothing, and he had struck Tall Bull in the back with his fist. Warning Kelsey that such actions would destroy his influence with the boys, Young reminded him that discipline should be left to disciplinarian Yellow Robe. Young demanded an explanation in writing, to be placed in Kelsey's file. Kelsey denied the accusations and blamed Yellow Robe for carrying students' stories to Young. The following year, Superintendent Young once again told Kelsey not to shake or strike boys, but to leave corporal punishment to Yellow Robe. This time, Kelsey's offense was against a physically disabled boy, Henry Kennedy. Within a month, Kelsey had departed. He chose to resign when Young threatened to initiate disciplinary action with the office of the commissioner of Indian affairs.[24]

Yet if Kelsey's military background served him poorly at the Rapid City Indian School, military models of discipline similarly failed the superintendents when students absented themselves from school. Much as soldiers deserted their units at army posts in the West, Indian students ran away from boarding schools. Students began running away from Rapid City within months of the school's opening. The first pupils arrived on September 21, 1898. After the New Year, six boys from the first class to attend the school ran away. Of those six, the school farmer recaptured two, after tracking the boys to a ranch near the mouth of the Belle Fourche River. Reservation officials on the Pine Ridge Reservation detained two more. The last two made it safely to their homes at Pine Ridge, only to be returned to the school by their parents. In 1920, out of an enrollment of approximately 300, 38 boys and 12 girls ran away from the school, some of them as many as three to five times in a year. Because of the nearness of the school to the Pine Ridge and Rosebud Reservations, nearly all of the runaways hailed from those two reservations.[25]

In keeping with the military model, Rapid City, like other Indian boarding schools, applied to running away the term "desertion." In the process of enrollment, students signed for three- to five-year terms of enlistment with the government school. In the eyes of school officials, leaving before one's term of enlistment was up was a gross breach of contract and honor, a disgrace of the worst sort because it betrayed one's duty and a written commitment. The army that subjugated the western Indians, the pre–World War I regular army, did not ordinarily allow men under twenty-one years of age to sign away their rights and freedoms through enlistment. Yet the Rapid City Indian School demanded the same stern commitment of children and punished infractions with a severity that often rivaled that of the old army.[26]

Some of the methods of punishment might have been taken from army practice. A student who attended Rapid City in the early 1900s saw seven runaway boys brought back to the school in chains. The boys, about ten years old, were chained together so that if one stumbled or got out of step they all fell down. School employees shaved the boys' heads. They then forced the boys to march back and forth across the campus until they had marched as many miles as they had run away. When they were not marching, the boys were locked in a jail cell. The girls cried at the sight of the boys marching. Employees forced an older boy who ran away to wear a ball and chain and split firewood all day. Such punishments might have come from an army post of the late nineteenth century. That the school applied them to *children* reinforces the point that these were the children of subject nations, some of them former enemies, that the government hoped to destroy. Little wonder, then, that the school treated runaways harshly and meted out punishments consistent with a disciplinary model that equated running away with desertion.[27]

Recent studies of Indian boarding schools have suggested a more accurate and interpretively useful meaning of running away: it was an act of resistance. In "A Bitter Lesson," Child casts running away as an expression of students' overwhelming frustration with school life. Students ran away because of poor food, mistreatment by teachers, overwork, the restrictions of school life, and homesickness. Adams adds fears of deculturation by Indian students and cognitive dissonance caused by the process of acculturation.[28]

Certainly such interpretations go far toward explaining student motivations, an issue school officials rarely explored. Superintendent Mote understood something of the problems of homesickness and the difficulties of adjusting to the school regimen. Rapid City's other superintendents apparently gave little thought to the matter. Perhaps they did not care to look too closely at the dilemmas boarding school life placed before their students. In part because school officials treated running away as desertion, it became an act fraught with hazard, a decision that placed students at odds not only with school officials but sometimes with their families as well. Running away was never without costs, whether to students or their families.[29]

Running away was physically dangerous, for even students from the Pine Ridge Reservation were too far from home to venture safely onto the prairie by themselves. South Dakota winters were particularly dangerous for runaways. Blizzards lasting three days or more, combining blinding snow, disorienting wind, and subzero temperatures, often descended with little warning, killing people caught on the treeless prairie far from shelter. Even without taking wind chill into account, winter temperatures might drop to 40 degrees below zero. Winter winds cut right through the open weave of issue wool clothing and quickly froze unprotected skin.

Winter took a brutal toll in late December 1909, when four boys ran away from the Rapid City Indian School in cold weather. Nine days later, two of the boys, Paul Loves War and Henry Bull, turned up near Wounded Knee on the Pine Ridge Reservation, suffering from frostbite. Though treated by physician and amateur ethnologist Dr. James Walker, both boys lost their lower legs, amputated below the knee. Pine Ridge had no facilities for the care of amputees, and the parents of Loves War, at least, wanted their son sent back to the school. A school employee brought the boys back to Rapid City by train. Aware that the boys' parents could not pay for artificial limbs, Superintendent House had them fitted at the school's expense. The maimed students remained at the school to finish their terms of enrollment.[30]

Another tragedy occurred less than a year later, when six boys ran away from school on October 15, 1910. On this warm, clear, Saturday evening, the six hoped to reach Scenic, South Dakota, where an Indian celebration would begin on Monday. The boys walked along the railroad tracks and then decided to stop and rest. James Means and Mark Sherman, both from the Pine Ridge Reservation, would not sleep along the embankment because of the thistles growing there. Instead, the two went to sleep with their heads resting on the rails. One of the other boys heard a train whistle, but Sherman thought it was a cow bell. Not long after, an eastbound train from Rapid City struck the two, killing Sherman instantly and fatally injuring Means.[31]

Child has noted that Indian families worried about the safety of their children if they should run away from school. Parents particularly worried that their children might run away in winter and sometimes urged school officials to keep a close eye on potential runaways. Similar concerns motivated the parents of Rapid City students, but they were more likely to argue that their children should be sent home or allowed to stay home if they had already run away. On October 3, 1921, Todd Smith went to J. A. Buntin, superintendent of the Rosebud Reservation, to tell him that his son Clarence, who had run away from the Rapid City Indian School, had arrived home. Clarence had run away twice, and Smith thought he might simply run away again if sent back. He worried that his son's repeated desertions might prove a detriment to the school and was particularly concerned that Clarence might run away later in the year and be caught in a storm. Buntin described Smith as "a man who favors educating his children and endeavors to keep them in school; neither does he wish to encourage the boy in disobedience in the way of running off." But Smith wanted to keep his son home, and neither Buntin nor House objected.[32]

Such willingness to accommodate parental fears was not exceptional. In 1930, Rosebud's Superintendent W. O. Roberts wrote Superintendent Young on behalf of the parents of George and Peter Wilcox. The two boys were "very much discontented" at the off-reservation boarding school, and the parents requested that the boys return home, lest they run away in cold weather and perish. If returned home, the boys would be sent to a reservation day school. Roberts favored the boys' return and offered to trade three other boys for the two Wilcox boys. Young declined the trade, but sent the Wilcox boys home.[33]

Another parent, George R. Brown, kept his boy Joe out of school after the boy ran away, but for disciplinary reasons. Brown was starting a trip to Rosebud and then to the Sand Hills to round up horses and planned to keep Joe with him, "as he needs a little strating [sic] out and correcting." Two other boys, Jim Wilson and George Jensen, had made their escape with Joe Brown, and George Brown told Superintendent House the two would get the best of care with his wife until they could be returned to the school. Brown wanted advice on how to put a scare into the three runaways. The three had made their escape from Rapid City by train, huddled on the steps of a sleeping car. All three admitted that they were asleep when the train crossed the Cheyenne River on the way to Kadoka, South Dakota. Brown did not like children taking such risks and wanted to be sure they did not do so again.[34]

School officials, too, worried that children might be hurt catching rides on trains and certainly disliked the mobility a stolen ride gave a runaway. Superintendent Mote ordered a poster showing the dangers of boys' stealing rides on a train put up where the boys could see it and told school employees to "try in every way to prevent our boys in taking chances which might result in crippling them for life." He also wrote E. E. Benjamin, general agent for the Chicago and North Western Railway in Deadwood, South Dakota, to complain about train crews allowing students to steal rides. Three runaways captured north of Pierre, South Dakota, claimed the crew of a passenger train knew they were riding for free, but made no effort to put them off. Benjamin forwarded Mote's complaint to the railway's Superintendent S. S. Long in Chadron, Nebraska, who responded with a bulletin to train and engine men. To prevent injury, and to keep boys from running away, Long ordered personnel to keep runaway students off the trains. "Please make an effort to keep these boys from stealing rides on our trains," he wrote, "but in doing so use the usual good judgement that is expected and do not put them off the trains except at suitable places where they can find protection from the weather."[35]

The increasing car and truck traffic on roads did not reassure adults, either. When asked by Superintendent Mote why he had not returned two runaways to the Rapid City Indian School, Rosebud's Superintendent E. E. McKean explained that he had found it necessary to place the two children in the St. Francis and Rosebud boarding schools. The two runaways, a boy and a girl, "declared several times in my office that they would run away again from Rapid City if they were forced to return. Their parents were very much worried regarding these children, fearing that they would run away and be frozen in the winter or injured by some truck or automobile, and in order to avoid such a possibility and also in order to maintain the cordial feeling on the part of the Indians of this jurisdiction toward your school and schools in general I consented to follow the wishes of the old people in these two instances." While reservation and off-reservation boarding schools sometimes competed for pupils, McKean noted that the reservation schools were already far over capacity. Yet he bowed to parental concerns and the wishes of the community and enrolled the two children.[36]

The world outside school and reservation held more hazards than bad weather or accidents. Runaway students, caught up in the heady feeling of freedom, sometimes engaged in activities older, wiser heads could have warned them against. In 1928, Sheriff George Waln of Wheatland, Wyoming, held two runaway boys on felony charges, after they were allegedly caught breaking seals on railroad box cars in Guernsey, Wyoming. After notifying the boys' parents and the superintendents of the Flathead and Rosebud Reservations, where the boys lived, Superintendent Mote washed his hands of the matter. The parents and the reservation superintendents had to decide how to respond to the allegations. If the judge trying the case thought the offenses were serious enough to warrant sending the boys to a reform school, Mote did not want them back.[37]

Mote's reaction was extreme, but illustrates one response of Indian school superintendents to runaways. Their responsibility for the safety of students and the perceived need to maintain discipline in the school inclined superintendents to seek the return and punishment of runaways. Yet, at some point, runaways became liabilities. They distracted school personnel and consumed time and energies that might better be spent educating the children who stayed in school. Considerations of children's welfare might enter into decisions, too, as when superintendents allowed chronic runaways to be enrolled in other schools rather than run the risk that the children might be injured or killed running away.

Superintendent House usually placed discipline and punishment first. He demonstrated some flexibility in his emphasis on discipline, for he sometimes allowed runaway children to be enrolled in reservation day or boarding schools if their reliable attendance could be secured. Students' health also factored into his decisions. In May 1912, House let Garnet Goings, a witness to the deaths of Sherman and Means, remain at his home on the Pine Ridge Reservation. In poor health, Goings had been improving under a regimen that allowed him "quite a good deal of liberty." Efforts to restrict his freedom would impair his health, so House allowed him to remain at home.[38]

Adolph Cuny, who ran away with Goings, had no such health problems, and House granted him no leniency. Cuny, Felix Pretty Bird, Joseph New Holy, and Willie Mexican ran away several times during the 1911–12 school year, and House went to extraordinary lengths to keep them in school. In January, he began keeping the boys locked in the school jail when they were not in classes or working. In late February, Cuny's mother informed Pine Ridge day school supervisor J. J. Duncan that House told her son he would stay in jail until June. "I don't think it is write [sic] to treat a poor boy that way," she objected, and she asked Duncan to take up the

matter with Pine Ridge's Superintendent Brennan. House apparently relented, for in late May, Cuny, Pretty Bird, and New Holy
again ran away. House excused Mexican from school because of the
death of his sister and was incensed to learn that the sister had
actually died the previous fall. Determined to make an example of
the four boys, House asked Brennan to send them back to spend
summer vacation at the school. House had work enough on the
school farm to keep the four boys busy and thought a summer away
from home might convince them to change their ways. By late June,
with none of the boys captured, House had had second thoughts
and was willing to wait until fall to round them up. Brennan persisted, however, and by the time his police and employees caught
the four in mid-July, the search had consumed so much time and
effort that House had little choice but to take the boys back.[39]

Despite the problems experienced capturing Cuny and his
friends, their forced labor over the summer set a precedent for the
treatment of runaways at the Rapid City Indian School. Superintendent House came to rely on denial of vacation as punishment
for running away to such an extent that he produced a form letter
for the benefit of parents. It explained that for disciplinary reasons
no deserters would be allowed to go home before July 1, and repeat
offenders might be kept for longer periods. Stressing the dangers
of desertion to students and to the school, the letter demanded that
parents work to keep their children in school. If parents wanted
exceptions made, they should go through their reservation superintendent, for House would not consider any special case except on
the reservation superintendent's recommendation. The letter
addressed only the parents of runaway boys and made no mention
of girls.[40]

Denial of vacation time was only partially effective, for students
continued to run away. In 1920, Francis C. Goings, chief of police
at Pine Ridge, reported to House that his son, William Goings, had
returned home with some reluctance; the elder Goings said that
his son had returned when he "could not stand it any longer on

the out side." William dreaded the thought of returning to school, knowing that he would have to spend part of his vacation there. Goings told his son that he should have thought of that before he ran away.[41]

House came to understand that knowledge of the punishments for running away did not necessarily check students, particularly when they were as close to home as those from Pine Ridge and Rosebud. By 1920, he was expressing some doubt about his methods. Keeping runaways for all or part of their summer vacations had succeeded as a deterrent for a year or two, but it no longer worked. He still held runaways into the summer, although he considered allowing them to return home if their parents would reimburse the school for its costs in catching their children. But because this action would penalize parents, and not the children, House appeared reluctant to institute such a measure.[42]

House's successor at the school, S. A. M. Young, became far less willing to compel attendance when students were not only prone to running away but troublesome to school officials in other ways. When Peter Quilt ran away from school, Young hoped he would not return and did not buy him a train ticket back to Rapid City. Quilt paid his own transportation back to the school, but gave Young and his staff "a great deal of trouble" before once more running away. Young saw no point in returning Quilt to the school only to expel him and wanted both the young man and his relatives and neighbors on the Lower Brule Reservation told why he did not want him back.[43]

In at least one case, though, that of a runaway girl, Young did have the student returned to be expelled. When students were of mature age, particularly if they were approaching or already beyond eighteen, Young was more likely simply to let them go. In one incident, after reviewing the cases of three older students caught running away, he ordered them released from custody, with the suggestion that if they wished to return to school they could come back the way they left. In no other area of administration,

Young confessed to H. B. Peairs, chief supervisor of education, did he feel less sure of himself. When Young constantly received applications from pupils begging to get into Rapid City, why did he "spend considerable sums of Government money to have apparently worthless pupils return?"[44]

Peairs replied with guidelines drawn from his experiences at the Haskell Institute in Lawrence, Kansas. At Haskell, Peairs said, runaways were rarely punished for first offenses. Instead, school officials talked to runaways and made them explain their motivations. Repentant runaways got a second chance. Those who ran away again posed a more serious problem. With so many students seeking admission to government schools, Peairs saw little point in chasing students eighteen or older, unless discipline required that they be punished before being expelled. He pointed out that parents often sent children to off-reservation boarding schools to give them more discipline than could be provided at home. In such cases, parents should bear the cost of returning runaways. The knowledge that other students waited to take the runaways' place offered the most effective deterrent to runaways.[45]

Commissioner of Indian affairs Charles H. Burke held a somewhat different view of the matter. He took Young to task for allowing Stephen Sun Goes Slow, Fred Piche, Leo Brown Otter, and Louis Primeau to stay home at Standing Rock after running away from the Rapid City Indian School in January 1923. If the boys were detrimental to the school, Young should have reported the matter to Burke, in compliance with paragraphs 107–9 of the BIA's School Rules. Young, who had no idea that letting the four stay home was a violation of BIA regulations, protested that he had not reported the students to Burke's office prior to their desertion because he had hoped to reform them. Once they ran away, it was in keeping with the customs of the Indian Service to let them be. Burke, however, wanted the four in reform school and let the matter rest only after Young pointed out that three of the students were over eighteen and therefore not eligible for admission to the South

Dakota State Reform School. The official decision was that the young men could provide for themselves.[46]

By outlook and training, the superintendents of the Rapid City Indian School were for the most part ill prepared to understand why Indian children ran away from an institution designed, built, and operated for the benefit of Indians, as defined by the BIA. Committed to a belief in the value of assimilative education and offered little guidance by the BIA, the superintendents often resorted to the most inappropriate punishments when faced with a problem they did not understand. Rapid City superintendents tried to control violence growing out of classroom or drill field conflicts between staff and students, but allowed violence to flourish in their responses to runaways.

In keeping with the equation of running away with desertion, superintendents continued to rely, consciously or otherwise, on models of punishment taken from the military. The use of shackles and the ball and chain recalled punishments employed in the nineteenth century in army posts in the West, when post commanders enjoyed an autonomy born of isolation, not unlike that later experienced by the superintendents of off-reservation boarding schools. The guardhouse, or makeshift jail, was another institution of the old army that found its way into the boarding schools. House maintained one until 1912, primarily for the incarceration of runaways like Cuny, New Holy, Pretty Bird, and Mexican. Explaining his decision to close the jail, House remarked that "it seemed that as soon as it was empty some others would desert and consequently it meant from one to half a dozen in jail a good part of the time." Finding incarceration ineffective, he had the space converted into a play room, though he sometimes regretted his decision as desertions rose. Mote revived the practice of keeping a jail, only to discontinue it in 1927, several months before the BIA ordered the abolition of jails and cages in boarding schools.[47]

A quicker and more direct instrument of violence existed in the strap, used to beat children who deserted or in other ways violated school rules. School staff may not have been able to supervise students closely enough to keep them out of trouble, but they could certainly beat those they caught in the act. Yet even in an era when the majority society condoned corporal punishment for children, the line between acceptable punishment and outright abuse was thin and easily crossed. In 1919, R. W. Hunt, a white resident of Scenic, South Dakota, reported to Superintendent House a conversation he had with Sewell Avery, a school employee. Hunt met Avery at the train depot, looking for runaways. When Hunt asked him what would happen to the runaways if they were caught, Avery bragged about whipping two runaway boys several weeks previously. He claimed to have held the boys bent over a chair while another man beat them with the unfinished side of a razor strop, blistering their buttocks and genitals. Angered by this story of abuse, Scenic residents very nearly did the same to Avery at the train depot. When Hunt reported the incident to House, House checked with disciplinarian Yellow Robe, who denied that any beatings so severe had occurred. But the "judicious use of a strap" remained a standard punishment for runaways not just through House's tenure at the school, but through Superintendent Young's as well.[48]

Superintendent Mote, who had worked at the Haskell Institute prior to his posting to Rapid City, resorted to the strap when students ignored his attempts to sympathize and reason with them in the Haskell style. One Sunday in September 1926, not long after the start of school, Lakota students Rose Romero and Eunice Plenty Holes ran away from Rapid City. The school alerted local officials, and the sheriff took the two girls off a northbound train at Sturgis on Sunday afternoon. It is unclear why the girls went in that direction, away from their homes on the Pine Ridge Reservation; but they were not pleased to be taken back to Rapid City and used language with a deputy sheriff and school employee that Mote thought "quite indecent and disgraceful." After a Monday morning spent in classes, Romero and Plenty Holes went to Mote's

office and told him they did not like the school and wanted to quit.
Mote

> tried to sympathize with them and made them feel that this
> was the place for them to be and that they would soon over-
> come their lonesomeness and of course told them I would
> not approve of their stopping school just after enrolling. They
> left the office supposedly to return to school but instead
> walked right out the front gate and before we could overtake
> them they had hid some place and we were unable to get
> them until Tuesday morning when we brought them back
> from Piedmont. A very good strapping was administered to
> each and Rose Romero was locked in her room and deprived
> of her street clothing while Eunice Plenty Holes, a ninth
> grade pupil, was discharged from the institution in the cus-
> tody of her mother.

One wonders what Mote considered a "very good strapping" and
whether the girls and their families saw anything good about the
beatings. Mote hoped Romero would reconcile herself to the school
after spending a day or two locked up. If not, he would send her
home, too.[49]

Despite the beatings Romero, Plenty Holes, and others endured
at the Rapid City Indian School, Indian families and communities
were divided in their responses to runaways. In their efforts to
recapture runaways, school authorities could count on the cooperation of other BIA employees on the reservations and at other
schools. Yet as many runaways found out, people other than white
employees of the BIA had an interest in seeing them returned to
boarding school. Indian employees of the school and Indian police
on the reservations worked to return runaways to the school.
Whether or not students succeeded in escaping the Indian School
often depended on the extent to which their parents supported
their efforts.

Students running away from Rapid City used a variety of means of transportation. Some, like Paul Loves War and Henry Bull, set out across country on foot. Others, like Jim Wilson and George Jensen, caught rides on trains. Elizabeth Tyon and Elsie Broken Rope of Pine Ridge, together with Rosebud student Libbie Never Misses a Shot, walked from Rapid City to Hermosa and then caught a ride with a white man to Hot Springs. Another white man took them to Pine Ridge, where they went to the home of Oliver Tyon. But whatever their mode of travel, runaways followed predictable paths. Rarely did they try to settle into white communities. As one might expect, students usually tried to return to their own families. Others, like Mark Sherman and James Means, ran away to attend Indian fairs and ceremonies in nearby towns, where they could expect to find refuge and hospitality in Indian camps.[50]

In either case, school officials anticipated the routes and destinations of the runaways and used the telephone and telegraph to alert county, railroad, or reservation officials along the runaways' anticipated routes home. When school officials thought students might have succeeded in reaching their homes, as in the cases of Loves War and Bull, they contacted the reservation superintendents. The superintendents then contacted the district farmers and reservation police, who checked on the students' families to see if they had knowledge of the runaways. In this way, Pine Ridge employees found Loves War and Bull with Loves War's family. When superintendents knew parents personally, they sometimes contacted the parents directly. In 1910, Superintendent House wrote Willard Standing Bear to inform him that his son Richard had run away and asked him to return both Richard and another son, Stephen. If possible, House wanted the matter settled without involving agency officials at Pine Ridge. If Standing Bear refused to return the children, though, House threatened to report them as runaways, to be collected by Indian police. Sometimes threats were unnecessary. When Tyon, Broken Rope, and Never Misses a Shot reached Oliver Tyon's home, the elder Tyon turned the girls in to Pine Ridge's Superintendent E. W. Jermark.[51]

Families sometimes resisted turning over their runaway children, even to the point of violence. Cecelia Old Coyote left the Rapid City Indian School with the help of her father, who drove Cecelia and another girl home to the Crow Reservation in Montana in his automobile. Superintendent Mote went to the reservation with a school employee, intent on getting Cecelia back. The Crow Agency's Superintendent C. H. Asbury sent the reservation special officer, a reservation farmer, and the school inspector with the party as reinforcements. The family, though, "put up such a strenuous fight that it seemed the only way to get the girl was to have a knock-down and drag-out procedure and perhaps have to lock her mother up and it was the feeling of our officers that they did not care to take such drastic action; consequently the girl was left at home." Pearl Eastman's family took a less direct but no less effective approach: when Mote arrived at their home at Lodge Grass in his car, with two other runaways on board, the mother told him that Pearl was eleven miles out in the country and would not return for several days. With two runaways on his hands, Mote had no choice but to leave without Pearl.[52]

It was in fact common for families to help runaways or to encourage children to run away, when Rapid City superintendents refused to excuse children from school. Superintendent House complained that when he denied parents permission to remove a child from school, "it would appear that they write to him directly or at least he knows what is going on, and if the case is not decided to his satisfaction he deserts the school." Apparently Rapid City staff did not regularly censor students' mail. Sometimes letters fell into the wrong hands, however, as when disciplinarian Yellow Robe confiscated a letter F. F. Jewett of the Cheyenne River reservation wrote to his brother Cleophus, urging him to run away and offering advice. "[M]y Dad said you are to [sic] old to go to school anyhow and he is willing to help you out and my Dad said if you want running away why he said you ought to go toward South where the Ogala [sic] Indians are." Yellow Robe forwarded the letter to the superintendent at Cheyenne River, who ordered F. F. Jewett brought in to the agency for unspecified punishment. When BIA officials held such power over Indian lives, encouraging a child to run away from boarding school was an act of resistance both powerful and hazardous.[53]

Not all runaways had the support of their families, however. When Caine Afraid of Hawk ran away from the Rapid City Indian School, his father, Richard Afraid of Hawk, visited the school to ask for Superintendent House's help in finding his boy. Caine had run away from the family as well. When running away evoked such mixed responses from students' families, little wonder that Charles Dog with Horns remembered running away as being futile. "A lot of them run away. But they get them back, the school. When they get home, policeman [sic], they chase them around and catch them, take them back." The reservation police were, of course, Indian men who knew their communities and the families involved. Reservation gossip worked against runaways, too. After Jacob Douglas, Joe Primeaux, and Eugene Blue Lips ran away from Rapid City in 1917, several students still in school received letters from home saying that the three boys had reached their homes on the Standing Rock Reservation and were hiding out. Police searched carefully, but could not find the three. Then Primeau turned up on the adjacent Cheyenne River Reservation. After questioning, he told where Douglas and Blue Lips could be found. Such gossip and betrayals suggest a less than united response to runaways in reservation communities.[54]

To supplement the Indian police on the reservations, the Rapid City Indian School created its own force of Indian volunteers to capture and return runaway students. In 1917, Superintendent House wrote a letter for George Eagle Bear, of the Cheyenne River Reservation, authorizing him to arrest and detain runaway students and giving him "full police authority in all matters pertaining to deserters or runaway pupils." Three years later, Ralph Old Horse of Kyle, South Dakota, wrote House, asking for a job catching runaway boys. Old Horse had been in the business of catching runaways before and wanted his old job back. House did not offer him a job, but promised to pay him for his trouble and expenses, should he capture any runaway boys in his area of the Pine Ridge Reservation.[55]

Superintendent Mote made a similar arrangement with Mark Spotted Horse, also from Kyle. Mote appointed Spotted Horse his deputy policeman and authorized him "to apprehend any Indian boys or girls belonging to the Rapid City Indian School who seemed to be absent without leave." He instructed Spotted Horse to call the school long distance to arrange for a school employee to come get any runaways captured. Spotted Horse was not to make his own transportation arrangements or bring back runaways on his own without Mote's authorization. Mote would allow exceptions, though, when it was necessary to transport students quickly to prevent them from escaping again. He wrote to Spotted Horse that the appointment "carries no compensation except that when you apprehend any of our pupils, you will be reimbursed for your expenses and allowed a reasonable amount for your compensation in each particular case." In essence, Mote hired a bounty hunter.[56]

In addition to Indian police on the reservations and the superintendents' own special deputies, school superintendents commanded a work force that included Indian employees. As disciplinarian, Chauncey Yellow Robe was supposed to prevent the escape of students and was responsible for punishing the male runaways who were returned to the school. In a typical communication, Principal Wilcox wrote Yellow Robe a note demanding to know where three missing boys were and told him that they "should be hunted up and immediately punished." Leon Holy, one of the boys who ran away with Paul Loves War, went back to school with another runaway, James Buffalo, under the supervision of Thomas Standing Elk, an assistant farmer at the school. Concentrated in low-paying assistant positions, Indian men working for the school often had no fixed responsibilities and were easily detailed to various odd jobs. Who better to send to a reservation to pick up a runaway student?[57]

The Meriam Report recommended that off-reservation boarding schools give attention "to boys and girls as individuals rather than in the mass." A prerequisite of any effort to individualize students was that the schools practice "less of the marching and regimentation that look showy to outside visitors but hide real dangers." The marching and regimentation, though, were not merely for show. Long after Richard Henry Pratt's dismissal from the Indian Service in 1904, marching and drill persisted in off-reservation boarding schools, outlasting school superintendents, commissioners of Indian affairs, and more than one change in educational policy. Marching and drill were core elements of a program designed to maintain staff control in an institutional setting, where primary responsibilities for the care of three hundred students might fall on a mere seven adults.[58]

The "real dangers" of military discipline alluded to in the Meriam Report lay in the disrupted lives of students who did not flourish under the system, who were part of the human cost of the BIA's usurpation of the rights and roles of Indian parents. Perhaps the most eloquent testimonies to the hazards of growing up at the Rapid City Indian School were the maimed bodies of Paul Loves War and Henry Bull. The two boys "have been very patient and are favorites with the nurses and others," Superintendent House reported after the boys' return to the school. House had knee-pads made so they could get about on their hands and knees and later arranged for the two to be fitted with artificial limbs. For Loves War and Bull, the school's combination of harsh discipline and inadequate supervision had lifelong consequences.[59]

CHAPTER 6

EMPLOYEES

The superintendents of the Rapid City Indian School were the most publicly visible members of its staff. They represented the school to Rapid City residents, businesses, and civic organizations, spoke to reservation officials, corresponded with parents, and traveled to reservations to meet prospective students. Their portraits, formal studio photographs, gazed serenely from school catalogs. The superintendents were the school's public face.

None of the superintendents, however, not even Superintendent House, were as emblematic of the school's mission and its place in Indian lives as Lakota disciplinarian Chauncey Yellow Robe. Yellow Robe was born in Montana in 1869, at a time when plentiful buffalo and Lakota military power made reservation boundaries less important than they would later become. As the near-extinction of the buffalo and the burgeoning white presence on the Northern Plains forced a reorientation of Lakota life toward the reservation, Yellow Robe attended and graduated from the Carlisle Indian School. In 1895, he took a position as an industrial teacher at the Santee Agency in eastern Nebraska. First employed at Rapid City in 1904 or 1905, Yellow Robe advanced from industrial teacher to disciplinarian in 1913, a position he held until the short-lived conversion of the school to a tuberculosis sanitarium in 1929.[1]

Yellow Robe thus represented both the Indian past, rooted in political and economic dependence, and one possible future, economic and social assimilation.[2] He served at Rapid City under superintendents House, Young, and Mote, outlasting both Indian and white contemporaries at the school. As disciplinarian from 1913 to 1929, Yellow Robe was a fixture at the school and more prominent in the lives of male students, at least, than the superintendents. His career at Rapid City and his struggles to retain his position at the school while raising his daughters as a single parent demonstrate that there was not one community at Rapid City, but two: staff and students. The community of staff was one with its own rules and relationships, separate from yet in close interaction with students. As was the case with students, Indian staff played a significant role at the Rapid City Indian School, but were not in a position to alter the purposes of the institution.

Indian boarding schools of the early twentieth century trained students for lives on allotments as farmers or housewives. Boarding school graduates without allotments or with allotments that could not be profitably farmed due to climate, BIA leasing policies, or lack of capital faced a difficult and uncertain future. For what had their educations prepared them? As Lomawaima notes in *They Called It Prairie Light*, boarding schools taught Indian students to work in boarding schools. But going back to work for the school was neither the only nor even necessarily the most obvious choice for boarding school graduates. The rhetoric of BIA schooling, after all, pointed students outward, toward a future they would face on their own, without government assistance. As Lomawaima points out, the ethic of self-sufficiency and the habits students learned as they labored in boarding school work details directed graduates toward an alternative: manual labor. Digging potatoes in Nebraska, putting up hay for a Pennington County rancher, or doing a Rapid City household's laundry was very much like the work students did at school, for it was hard, minimally skilled, and supervised, requiring neither an investment in tools or other capital nor much knowledge of the economy. Entry requirements, therefore, were low. So were prospects for advancement. And manual labor had the additional disadvantage that much of it was seasonal, often concentrated in summer or early fall. On the Northern Plains, where hunting and trapping economies had collapsed in the nineteenth century, seasonal work was likely to mean yearly uncertainty.[3]

Employment at the Indian School should be viewed in the context of the economic alternatives available to Indians in the early twentieth century. Work at the school was year-round; as a government institution with a stable budget, the school offered its work force, whites and Indians alike, a level of job security unknown in the private sector. Indians were quick to take advantage of the opportunity. By 1912, out of a total of thirty-one employees at the Rapid City Indian School, nine were Indian. Thomas Standing Elk, Benjamin Prairie Hen (later Black Fox), Earl Heddrick, Lizzie Williams, Lizzie Allen, and Maggie Good Voice filled assistant positions at annual salaries of $300. Julia DeCora, thirty-nine, earned $540 as the school seamstress; Louis Goings, thirty-six, $660 as shoe and harness maker; and Chauncey Yellow Robe, forty, $660 as industrial teacher. Except for DeCora, a Winnebago, school records listed all the Indian employees as Sioux. DeCora's salary was identical to that of the cook, baker, and laundress, all white, and Yellow Robe and Goings received pay equal to or greater than three of the four teachers, the financial clerk, and the physician. House's salary in 1912 was $1,800, the clerk received $900, one of the four teachers $800, and matron E. O. Stilwell $720. If they could escape the low-paying assistant positions, Indian employees could earn salaries equal to white employees of the same grade, although the better-paying positions usually went to older, more experienced employees, not to recent boarding school graduates.[4]

The exceptions were Indian employees with clerical skills. Jennie Larson, a Chippewa graduate of the Hayward Indian School in Wisconsin, took the business course at Haskell, finishing four years' work in only two years' time. Rapid City hired the eighteen-year-old Larson as assistant clerk in 1913 at $720 annual salary. After an automobile accident on August 24, 1914, in Lead, South Dakota, cut short Larson's promising life, Florence V. Summers, nineteen, replaced her, but started at only $600. In the early 1920s, Rapid City employed Thomas W. Killer and Frances D. Adams as assistant clerks at $720 and $600, respectively. Killer, a Lakota from Pine Ridge, served in the army and married Rapid City graduate Ida Tyon, also from Pine Ridge, before being appointed to the school. Adams had graduated from high school and completed the Haskell business course. He worked in the Stenographic Section at BIA headquarters in Washington, D.C., before his appointment to Rapid City. Although the BIA abolished the assistant clerk positions in 1923, Adams stayed on as stenographer and property clerk.[5]

Another Indian employee of the BIA, George A. Day, took over as chief clerk in 1924, starting at $1,680. Day's position at Rapid City was second only to that of the superintendent. Superintendent Mote, who lauded Day's conscientious, accurate work, considered him fully capable of managing the school in his own absence. Day had considerable experience in business, having worked for such firms as the North Western Fuel Company and the E. I. duPont deNemours Powder Company in his native Wisconsin before entering the BIA as an assistant lease clerk at Rosebud Agency, South Dakota, in 1915. By 1930, Day earned $2,300 a year at the Rapid City Indian School—a handsome salary for any worker in a nation descending into the Great Depression.[6]

Day had the advantage of an extensive business education, pursued at Gordon's Business College in Ashland, Wisconsin, and through the Extension Division of the University of Wisconsin. For young men and women with no more education than could be gained at an ordinary Indian boarding school, without transferring to the Haskell Institute or other advanced school, the Indian Service offered a career path with far less potential for advancement, but also much lower barriers to entry: employment at an Indian school as an assistant. As discussed in chapter 3, the BIA reserved these unskilled or semiskilled positions for Indians. Initially, pay appears to have been the distinction between Indian assistant and non-Indian assistant jobs; the distinctions as expressed in job titles were unclear. In 1910, Rapid City employed Anna Williams, Benjamin Prairie Hen, Benjamin Stead, and John Lone Dog as assistants at yearly salaries of $300. Whites Hattie E. Smith and Theresa C. Kaufman, employed as assistant matrons, earned $540. In 1924, however, Indians filled six of seven assistant positions, and the inequities in pay had disappeared. Victoria Fickle, white, earned $600 as assistant seamstress. Albert Russell, unassigned assistant, and Margaret Benoist, assistant laundress, also earned $600. Hattie Hall, assistant matron, earned $780. Benjamin Black Fox (formerly Prairie Hen), assistant engineer, and Thomas W. Killer and Frances D. Adams, assistant clerks, earned $1,140. For comparison, Super-intendent Young earned $2,400 in 1924, and teachers at the school earned $1,200. While assistant positions became more closely identified with Indians over time, pay improved dramatically as Indians took the higher-paying, nonmenial jobs.[7]

The menial assistant positions were not civil service, and in keeping with their entry-level nature, applicants did not have to take qualifying examinations. Until 1924, Indians were also eligible for appointment without examination to better-paying positions, such as disciplinarian or dairyman, which did not require extensive education and for which boarding school training presumably fitted them. The application form for Indian applicants made clear the BIA's expectations, which were both gendered and reflective of boarding school curricula. One question asked female applicants if they had "been trained in the usual household duties, such as cooking, sewing, laundering, and care of the household generally." Another asked female applicants if they understood "butter making, care of milk, canning, drying, pickling, and preserving fruits, curing meats, and preparing household delicacies and necessities as usually understood by thrifty, intelligent housewives in farming communities." Male applicants were asked if they were "accustomed to the duties of a farmer and a stockgrower" and if they were "handy with ordinary farm tools and implements; able to make repairs of buildings, vehicles, harness, fences, and do rough carpenter work." All applicants, male and female, had to state whether or not they used or had ever been addicted to alcohol, tobacco, or opiates and whether or not they would be willing to pledge themselves to abstain from alcohol and narcotics while in the Indian Service. The application forms constituted a sort of follow-up exam for boarding school graduates, designed to keep them on the straight and narrow path of BIA expectations.[8]

Lazarus W. Adams, a graduate of the Chamberlain Indian School, fully met those expectations when he applied for the position of dairyman at Rapid City in 1924. Asked on his personnel record forms to list any special qualifications he might have for a position in the Indian Service, Adams wrote that "[b]eing an Indian I am interested in Indians and I feel I am better able to understand Indian boys." He also had twelve years' experience farming, most of it on land leased in the vicinity of Veblen, South Dakota. Eight local citizens, including two bankers, the blacksmith, and a county commissioner, signed a letter attesting to Adams's skill as a farmer, noting that he "was especially good in the raising and keeping of live-stock" and that "[n]o better horses could be found in the country than those kept by Lazarus Adams." Though Superintendent Young had hoped to hire Adams without examination, a change in BIA policy in late 1924 made it necessary for him to take a noncompetitive examination. The examination certified his fitness for the position of dairyman, but did not rank him in relation to other candidates. Rapid City hired Adams at a salary of $1,200.[9]

The requirement that Indian job applicants take noncompetitive civil service examinations brought BIA hiring practices for Indians into closer conformity with those for non-Indians. The BIA employed non-Indians under civil service rules, which required that applicants take competitive examinations administered by the United States Civil Service Commission. A notice from the commission announcing examinations for matron and seamstress in the Indian Service details the process. Published on May 21, 1924, the notice advertised examinations for matron to be given July 9 and September 3 and examinations for seamstress to be given on July 10 and September 4, 1924. The matron examination covered the positions of matron, assistant matron, housekeeper, field matron, and female industrial teacher. The seamstress examination was more specific, given only for the position of seamstress. An attached form listed examination sites in all forty-eight states, the District of Columbia, Alaska, Hawaii, and Puerto Rico. Examination sites were plentiful, even in the West: applicants could choose from a list of twenty cities and towns in Nebraska, eleven in Montana, nine in Wyoming, and eighteen in South Dakota, including Rapid City. At most testing locations, applicants could pick up an application blank from the local secretary of the U.S. Civil Service Board at the post office. At some of the smaller towns, such as Lander, Wyoming, and Lemmon, South Dakota, the local secretary could be addressed care of the U.S. Land Office. Boards of Pension Examining Surgeons, from whom applicants could secure the required medical certificate, were located in most of the listed towns and cities.[10]

Though the examination announcement did not detail the tests in their entireties, it stated fields to be covered and the weights given to each in the scoring. For matron, whose duties included acting "in the capacity of a mother to children in her care," subjects included home management, meal planning, child care, and training and experience. Of the 100 points possible on the examination, training and experience counted for 40, far outweighing any other field. Training and experience were worth 35 points out of 100 in the seamstress examination; other fields were knowledge of materials, plain hand and machine sewing, and pattern making and clothing construction. Each seamstress applicant was to bring needle, scissors, thread, and an 8 by 12 inch piece of white muslin to the examination, to demonstrate hand sewing. Both tests lasted four and a half hours, and all applicants were to bring recent photographs of themselves, to be entered into their personnel files if they passed their examinations.[11]

The examination announcement provided not only examination dates and testing fields, but information about conditions of employment in the Indian Service as well. Applicants for the positions of matron and seamstress were to be between the ages of twenty-one and forty-five, unless they were the spouses of persons already employed, entitled to preference because of military service, or Indians. The Indian Service required applicants to state whether or not they had dependents who would require accommodation. Most of the positions filled from the matron and seamstress examinations were for boarding schools, where quarters were restricted to one room, so applicants without dependents received preference. "As the Commission has had difficulty in securing sufficient eligibles without dependents for these positions," the announcement noted, "qualified persons without dependents are urged to apply." Those who received appointments would get furnished quarters, heat, and light at no charge. Boarding school employees ate at a common mess; their meals were furnished at cost. Such living arrangements were best suited for single persons, with no outside attachments.[12]

Applicants who passed their civil service examinations went on a list of eligibles from which the BIA made appointments. Eligibles learned in greater detail what the BIA expected of its employees and just how demanding it could be. From the dates of their appointments to their arrivals at their duty assignments, new employees were on their own, for the BIA expected them to pay their own transportation and expenses, however remote their places of employment might be. Prepared employees brought their own sheets and towels, and the unfortunate might find themselves bunked two to a room. "[E]mployees with families," the BIA warned, "must content themselves with the quarters that may be available." Average cost of board at schools with an employees' mess was $30 per month in 1910 and $15 per month for children under twelve. At $14 per month for adults in the same period, board at Rapid City was far below average cost.[13]

Upon arriving and entering their duties, civil service employees went on probationary status for six months, after which their appointments automatically became permanent if the BIA found their service satisfactory. In addition to the regular duties of their positions, the BIA noted that employees might find themselves required to fill in for ill or absent co-workers: a teacher might be assigned the duties of a matron, for example, or a farmer the responsibilities of a disciplinarian. Even if a supervisor did not assign employees to additional tasks outside their positions, the work of an Indian Service employee was hard and long. As Superintendent House told a prospective teacher in 1912, the hours of work at an Indian school were not as well defined as at a public school. Teachers worked from 8:00 or 8:30 until 11:30 in the morning, from 1:15 to 4:30 in the afternoon, and from 7:00 to 8:00 in the evening. Teachers also taught classes in Sunday school and assisted in church functions on Sunday afternoons. There was clearly no place for non-Christians at Rapid City, nor for those used to leisure: "[v]ery little service is required on Saturdays," House stated, but the only days off teachers could count on were their thirty days' leave, taken during summer vacation.[14]

Teacher workloads remained an issue at the Rapid City Indian School throughout its years of operation. In 1925, Superintendent Young noted to former Rapid City principal George E. Peters, then principal of the Haskell Institute in Lawrence, Kansas, that "[s]ome of our teachers have the idea that they are being seriously over-worked." To still criticism of the workload, Young wanted to compare evening duties at Rapid City and Haskell. At Rapid City, aside from participation in a school assembly on Sunday evenings, teachers worked either two or three evenings a week. Rapid City had night school Tuesday and Wednesday nights, and at other times teachers participated in the various student literary societies and socials, though Young had discontinued detailing teachers to any of the socials except those involving music. "I confess that I can not see where overwork comes in under these circumstances," he said.[15]

Because Haskell was a much larger school than Rapid City and organized differently, Peters was not sure a valid comparison of workloads could be made. Haskell had a larger corps of teachers and many assisting personnel, allowing greater specialization. Teachers at Haskell worked the same hours in the morning and evening as at Rapid City, but not all of their class periods were recitation periods; some were study periods. Haskell students had three study hour evenings per week, but the number of teachers and the availability of student officers to supervise meant that teachers worked the study periods only one night a week. Chapel exercises and entertainments were not compulsory for Haskell students and thus required less effort from teachers, whose participation was voluntary. Peters's attitudes toward teachers' workloads and social lives were, however, revealing: while acknowledging that teachers at Haskell were "very, very busy," he said that "considering that they live at the school and should, to a large extent, have their social life there instead of in the city or outside places, I do not feel that they are over-burdened as a rule." Workloads in the Indian Service were reasonable if one meant to make the service one's life.[16]

Teachers were not the only Rapid City employees whose hours were long and duties diverse. As the workers most directly responsible for the health and welfare of students, matrons and disciplinarians, in particular, spent most of their waking hours on duty, with students. Explaining the duties of matron to applicant Edith M. Triggs in 1914, Superintendent House noted that the school's Home 2, where the position was open, housed thirty to forty girls. The matron of the building, classed as assistant matron in the school hierarchy, was "supposed to look after [the girls] and maintain order and discipline and do all she can to develop the best in the girls under her care. She is also expected to be interested in the general welfare of the school, and assist in the general exercises, and instruct the girls in social duties and restraints. The matron of this building has also been the president of the YWCA, though this is not a compulsory duty." He added that the work required both physical strength and emotional balance, since working with the children would at times be very trying to the matron's patience.[17]

To a greater extent than for any other Rapid City staff, the presence of family complicated the work of matrons and disciplinarians. Triggs hoped to bring her two daughters, ages eight and two, to Rapid City if she won appointment as assistant matron. House strongly discouraged her. While there were parents who could care for their own children and the students as well, he thought it more likely that the burdens of child care would leave matrons with too little time for the students under their supervision. To avoid dissatisfaction among the students, a matron's children would have to be under student discipline as well. Triggs, who was probably a widow, made no mention of accommodations for a husband, thus avoiding another potential problem: matrons had to live in the girls' buildings, and the service strongly discouraged overnight visits by their husbands. Sex, even when blessed by the sacrament of marriage, had no place in BIA dormitories.[18]

Superintendent House not only avoided hiring women with children, but also preferred not to employ parents who had children attending the school. "Parents naturally want to exercise authority over their own children, and resent in a measure the authority exercised by a school, if same is done in their immediate presence," he stated to the commissioner of Indian affairs in 1912. "Where parents are employed and see the discipline and rigor applied to their own children, it is quite frequently a cause of trouble between them and the other employees who come into contact with their children." House discussed the issue in reference to the employment applications of a Mr. and Mrs. Benjamin McBride, allottees from the Yankton Agency, South Dakota, who lived in Rapid City and sent their children to the Indian School. The McBrides were very nice people, House said, and were well educated, but he was particularly averse to employing a mother with children at the school.[19]

Despite his unwillingness to employ single parents with children or parents with children attending the school, House was more flexible in accommodating the children of current employees than were his superiors in the BIA. Supervisor E. E. Newton, inspecting the school in 1913, criticized the work of domestic science teacher Francis E. Roberts, who had given birth to twins six weeks before Newton's visit. In her report, Newton remarked that she was "unable to see how Mrs. Roberts can do her work with the added care of two small babies." Assistant Commissioner E. B. Meritt suggested that House recommend Roberts's dismissal. House instead defended her, stating that her work was fully up to usual standards. Roberts, whose husband was the school farmer, did not shoulder the entire burden of caring for her twins, since she hired one or two small girls from among the students to help her. "The little girls like this work very much," House said, "and the larger ones of the class also receive some very good instruction in the care of infants, as Mrs. Roberts is a very intelligent woman along these lines." House, himself a parent, expected Roberts to resign whenever she felt that the care of her children interfered with her duties as domestic science teacher. She planned to resign when her children became older and needed more of her attention, but neither Roberts nor House believed her resignation was yet necessary. Whether or not pressure from Meritt hastened Roberts's departure, she and her husband had left the school by 1916.[20]

Chauncey Yellow Robe struggled under similarly adverse circumstances to retain employment at the school while caring for his two daughters. When Superintendent House recommended that he be promoted from industrial teacher to disciplinarian in 1913, he noted that Yellow Robe, as a married man with family at the school, would be unable to stay in the boys' building at night, as was expected of disciplinarians. Lest the boys be left unsupervised, House suggested Yellow Robe's replacement as industrial teacher be a single man of good character and some ability as a disciplinarian, who could room in the boys' building and keep an eye on them in Yellow Robe's absence.[21]

Despite Yellow Robe's family attachments, the BIA approved his promotion to disciplinarian. By all accounts, he was an excellent disciplinarian, a man of forceful character who commanded the respect of students and who worked well within the organization of the school. In addition to his duties as disciplinarian, Yellow Robe sponsored the Sons of Pahasapa, a boys' society at the school. By the 1920s, however, advancing age and the death of his wife placed increasing burdens on Yellow Robe, and he never succeeded in establishing a rapport with Superintendent Mote, who began to find fault with his work. In 1927, in Yellow Robe's fourteenth year as disciplinarian, Mote lauded his dignity and courage, but thought he was losing the vigor necessary to control a large group of boys. He was also forgetting things and absenting himself from work and going to Rapid City without first notifying Mote.[22]

While Mote and Yellow Robe apparently reached an understanding regarding the disciplinarian's comings and goings, Mote was harshly critical of his continued failure to control the movements and actions of the boys in his charge. On his way back from a trip to Underwood, South Dakota, at 1:00 A.M. on a Sunday morning, Mote saw four boys returning from Rapid City to the school. At noon on the same day, at a time when students should be on the grounds, he spotted three boys walking to town. Over the next few days, three boys ran away from the school and were on trains out of Rapid City before anyone called attention to their absence from the dormitory. Mote, who knew that Yellow Robe seldom called roll anymore, urged him to have his student officers call roll four times daily and keep a particularly close eye on the boys as departure times neared in the evenings for the 8:00 and 10:30 trains out of town.[23]

Criticism of Yellow Robe from District Superintendent James H. McGregor focused not on his age, which Mote thought to be a strike against him, but on the fact that Yellow Robe lived in a separate cottage, distant from the boys' building. McGregor told Mote that the "large red-blooded Americans that you have in your large boys' dormitory require a mature hand in the building to stay a natural inclination to boisterousness" and that he believed it would be much safer if the disciplinarian lived in the building. The issue quickly became Yellow Robe's care of his daughters. Mote agreed that it would be better to have a disciplinarian in the building, but said that Yellow Robe could not care for his daughters after the death of his wife if forced to live in the boys' building. McGregor retorted that while Yellow Robe's daughters were without a parent, so were the boys in the dormitory if Yellow Robe could not fulfill the duties for which the BIA paid him.[24]

Marginal comments on McGregor's letters reveal something of the nature and tone of Mote's relationship with Yellow Robe. Mote marked correspondence to be forwarded to school employees for their comment by writing their names in the upper corners. McGregor's first letter bears the notes "Mr. Robe," written in Mote's hand in the upper left corner and underlined, and " 'Can't move me' " in the lower left, in a hand that may not be Mote's but certainly is not Yellow Robe's. It is probable that Yellow Robe saw the letter and that "Can't move me" was the gist of his reply. If he chose to dig in his heels, he had the advantage of long service at Rapid City. In 1928 he was also, as McGregor commented in a second letter, a potential candidate for Congress and had been a great hit as an entertainer during President Calvin Coolidge's trip to the Black Hills. Yellow Robe nevertheless conceded, after Mote forwarded McGregor's second, more emphatic letter on the disciplinarian's duties, and promised to send his girls away and move into the boys' dormitory the following fall.[25]

Despite the difficulties employees with families faced at the Rapid City Indian School, employees' children became a tolerated if not always welcomed presence at the school. Not surprisingly, it was their misdeeds that drew attention. In 1927, Superintendent Mote complained that boys were destroying squashes and pumpkins in one of the school orchards and rolling large pumpkins into Rapid Creek. Children were also picking apples from trees, taking one or two bites, and then throwing them away. He suspected that employees' children were as much at fault as students and asked employees to keep their children out of the orchards. Francis Goings, son of Indian employee Louis H. Goings, shoe and harness maker, drew Mote's ire when he held a noisy Saturday night party in the family quarters with visiting friends that lasted until 3:00 in the morning. Mote demanded the names of Francis's guests and told the elder Goings he would be responsible for any future disturbances in his home. Mote may not have been any more easily irritated than previous superintendents, but he was much more likely than House or Young to make a written record of his displeasure.[26]

Mote's correspondence with two employees, matron Ema D. Russell and baker Maye I. Peck, preserves the parents' reactions to disciplinary action he took against their sons. The school provided transportation to town for the children of employees attending school in Rapid City, a service that Mote believed no other Indian school provided. Controlling twenty to twenty-five children riding in a makeshift bus made from a small truck tried the patience of the drivers, and Dallas DeCory had enough when boys started throwing mud. Mote responded by taking Alfred E. "Sonny" Walters, Jr., Russell's son by her deceased first husband, Alfred E. Walters, and Edward Peck off the truck for a week. Both mothers protested that their sons did not start the mud throwing and that in any case they could enforce more effective punishments than making their sons walk to and from school. Russell claimed that DeCory had kicked the two boys and asked Mote to tell DeCory to "keep his feet on the ground." Mote let the punishments stand and chastised the parents for not cooperating with the maintenance of good order on the truck. Race appeared to have played no role in Mote's decision: Edward Peck was white, and Sonny Walters was of white and Lakota parentage.[27]

Mote's insistence that employees control the behavior of their children was but part of a larger set of expectations governing employee behavior at the school. As discussed in chapter 3, Indian assistants lived under the same discipline as students at the Rapid City Indian School. Other employees, though not subjected to the rigor of student discipline, lived under exacting standards of conduct that prized loyalty to superiors and conformity of thought and expression. What Rapid City's superintendents expected of employees can be gleaned from an undated document filed with an employees' calendar from the 1909–18 period. The document, an unsigned carbon copy, listed ten beliefs that made up an employees' creed:

1. I believe in purpose, in a goal higher than salary, higher than fine examination records, higher than a wedding outfit-goal that touches the stars—a goal that I can never touch, but that shines before me like a beacon light.
2. I believe in loyalty, first to the great profession which I have embraced, next to the system of which I am a unit.
3. I believe in growth, in gaining from year to year a wider outlook upon the world and its people, as well as a deeper insight, a more thorough knowledge of myself, my powers and limitations.
4. I believe in sympathy, first with the children, and the homes from which they come, next with my fellow-workers, whose joys and sorrows are like my own.
5. I believe in earnestness, in putting my heart into my work.
6. I believe in faithfulness, in doing unasked the regular duties and cheerfully adding those which are irregular.

7. I believe in honesty, in acknowledging a blunder, being proud of a success, in trying to make successes many and blunders few.

8. I believe in system, in forming and possessing orderly habits of work and play.

9. I believe in cheerfulness, in radiating sunshine, then watching for reflections.

10. I believe that the Great Good Power will help me to live up toward my belief.

There is nothing to indicate that this creed was ever posted or circulated among employees. It articulates, however, a set of expectations that guided relationships within the school. Reams of correspondence between the superintendents and employees attest to the importance the superintendents placed on these beliefs. When they chastised employees for not possessing the proper attitude, failing to manifest a spirit of loyalty, or lacking industry and system, they acted in accordance with normative values corresponding to the creed.[28]

In response to specific incidents, Rapid City's superintendents spoke more directly to their expectations of employee behavior. They believed wholeheartedly that employees were examples for the students, and they consequently discouraged actions that conflicted with Victorian notions of propriety. Superintendent House, for example, frowned on card playing in public places on Sundays and the display of poker chips or anything else that might indicate gambling. Learning that employees were playing cards on Sundays in the sitting room of the employees' club and that cards and chips were left about, House ordered the cards and chips taken to his office. The owners could retrieve them by calling at his office, but he made it clear in a memorandum to employees that there should be no more evidence of card playing on Sundays. No general card parties could be held without his express permission. House did not forbid employees from playing cards in their rooms, but expected that employees would not "congregate in any individual room to the annoyance or to the detriment of the best interests of the school."[29]

Superintendent House similarly discouraged smoking and profanity among Rapid City staff. Annoyed at the amount of smoking by staff in the presence of students, whose use of tobacco the BIA tried with limited success to discourage, he forbade smoking in public places on campus and in school shops and buildings. House allowed smoking only in employees' private rooms and ordered strict enforcement of the ban on student smoking. He was even less tolerant of public profanity, particularly in the presence of students: if employees persisted in using profane or obscene language, he would request their resignations. There is no evidence that House ever dismissed an employee for improper language, but that he made the threat at all demonstrates the lengths to which he would go to enforce propriety on the campus. In keeping with the tenets of the employees' creed, House concluded his directives on smoking and profanity by stating that "[a] cheerful and hearty cooperation in these matters is desired and expected."[30]

Fornication was a rather more serious offense than smoking or profanity at the school, one for which Superintendent House forced the resignations of two employees. The alleged offense took place the afternoon of January 1, 1915, when many of the employees and students were in town, watching movies for the holiday. Some of the boys remained at the school, as did white industrial teacher Lee Hayes, who had been dividing his attentions between one of the teachers and Indian cook Cora A. Hawk. Hayes met Hawk in her room, where he stayed for an hour. What happened between the two was a matter of dispute. Though Hayes later disclaimed any impropriety, the half-dozen boys in the attic, observing through a hole in the room's ceiling, thought they had seen something note-worthy and promptly spread the tale when their friends returned from Rapid City.[31]

Within hours, rumors that boys had observed Hayes and Hawk in a compromising position reached House. The next morning, he called Hayes to his office and told him of the rumor. Not satisfied with Hayes's denials, House said that he would bring the boys in for questioning on January 4 and that Hayes could examine the boys and present evidence in his favor at that time. Shortly before the hearing, Hayes and Hawk resigned. House questioned the students anyway and obtained from Harden Smith, Fred Schmidt, and Harvey Langdeau a signed statement that they had observed Hayes and Hawk in the latter's room, in bed together and in a partly undressed condition.[32]

Forwarding the employees' resignations to the BIA, House said nothing of the circumstances of their resignations, but recommended that Hawk be barred from reinstatement. Pressed by Assistant Commissioner E. B. Meritt for a specific cause for his adverse recommendation, House relayed his account of the entire incident as well as the signed statement of the three students. House recommended against Hawk's reinstatement, but said nothing of Hayes, because only Hawk had violated school regulations by entertaining a gentleman caller in her room. The gentleman caller apparently faced no comparable sanctions, revealing a clear double standard in regard to men's and women's sexuality.[33]

Overt conflicts over sexual behavior of the sort that led Hayes and Hawk to resign were rare at the Rapid City Indian School. Conflict more often focused on work performance, where the values expressed in the employees' creed played a central role. Josiah Bird, for example, did not impress Superintendent House with his energy and initiative and in his relationships with other employees fell far short of the collegiality House expected. Bird arrived at Rapid City after a stint at the Pierre Indian School, whose superintendent refused to recommend him for further employment. House nevertheless hired Bird as an Indian assistant. To his annoyance, Bird took days off for illnesses House thought were very minor. When

House refused to give him all Saturday afternoons off, Bird complained that he was doing all the work at the school. House lectured him "that if he felt that way that he had better leave as I did not want any employee to feel that he was doing it all and if he was unable to see that other people were at work that he probably had overlooked something and advised him that if he wished to stay in the position here he should attend to the work assigned him and be willing to take his share of the responsibility etc." Instead, Bird left. When he asked Charles E. Dagenett, supervisor of Indian employment, to help him find work in an automobile factory in Detroit, Dagenett checked with House, who declined at length to recommend him.[34]

Superintendent Young and white teacher Lee Roy Willis had a rather more serious clash over standards of performance and conduct. Young found Willis so unsatisfactory that he took his complaints to the commissioner of Indian affairs soon after taking charge of the Rapid City Indian School in 1922. Willis, who taught the seventh and eighth grades, had neither the confidence nor the respect of his pupils. His standards, Young believed, were far too low; in history recitations, Willis let students answer questions with their books open in front of them. Moreover, he made the mistake of telling students that "he did not care whether they learned or not since his salary went on just the same."[35]

Nor did Willis's personal conduct meet with Superintendent Young's approval. Despite repeated admonishments, Willis frequently made unkind and discourteous remarks to other employees in the shared dining room. He was opinionated and not properly receptive to Young's suggestions. Perhaps most seriously, Willis made two or three boys his special pets, took them for rides in his automobile, and often had them in his room late into the night. Though Young did not make any suggestions of sexual impropriety, he was worried enough about this aspect of Willis's behavior to make it the subject of a personal discussion with the teacher and took what was for him the rare step of sending him a special disciplinary letter.[36]

Because Willis went on staff at the school in the last few months of House's tenure as superintendent, Young submitted his letter through House and invited the latter's comment. House seconded Young's estimation of Willis's character, stating that "his peculiarities, and lack of energy and indifference to the general success of the school, make him, in my opinion, unfit for the position of teacher." House further recommended against Willis's transfer to another school or transfer to a different position in the Indian Service. The proper course, he believed, would be to ask Willis to resign. If he did not, "specific charges should be formulated with a view to his dismissal." House clearly understood the limitations Civil Service regulations placed on a superintendent's ability to dismiss unsatisfactory employees. Just as clear was his determination to see Willis go.[37]

In the end, Willis resigned, though not without a parting shot at Superintendent Young and several Rapid City employees. In a letter to the BIA that came to the attention of Chief Supervisor of Education Peairs, Willis accused Rapid City personnel of a number of improprieties. School engineer Walter G. Peck, white, and industrial teacher Alfred E. Walters, Indian, were common gamblers, he charged, playing cards for money on Sundays at the Elks Lodge in Rapid City. Carpenter Earl G. Kelsey, white, was cruel and abusive in his treatment of the boys who worked in his department and struck student Dewey Matt in the head with a hatchet, sending the boy to the hospital. Superintendent Young and Principal George E. Peters knew of the attack, Willis alleged, and thought nothing of it. Peairs passed on to Young a summary of Willis's allegations against Young and white teacher Maude Hopkins: that Young was "over-bearing, deceitful, that you go to church every Sunday and sit in the front pew with a long, pious face, in order to fool people; that you openly state that while the school is primarily for Indians, all of the privileges and advantages belong to the white people; that Miss Hopkins is a gossip and that she carries all sorts of news to you and Mrs. Young which is afterwards used by you in persecuting employees."[38]

Peairs did not believe the charges against Young and Hopkins warranted an official investigation, but those against Peck, Walters, and Kelsey were more serious. Not wanting to risk the harm to the school that might result from an open investigation, he suggested that Young make a quiet and thorough inquiry. Young should consider his letter "official but confidential, and make a confidential report" back to Peairs. "I would suggest that this letter should not go into your regular files because, if read by others, it might cause trouble or disturbance," Peairs concluded. Following these suggestions, Young kept the matter quiet and confined his inquiries to a few older employees he trusted. His report to Peairs denied Willis's allegations, and Peairs let the matter die.[39]

As discussed in chapter 5, Young forced Earl G. Kelsey to resign in 1924 for striking students on his detail, lending some belated support to at least one of Willis's allegations. Kelsey, like Willis, was unpopular with other employees, a dislike occasioned by his outbursts of temper. In terms of the employees' creed, the carpenter violated articles four, five, and nine, for he showed little sympathy for students and fellow employees, shirked work when he could, and made no effort to radiate sunshine. Volatile, resentful of criticism or suggestions, inclined to disobey instructions, Kelsey caused Young "more worry and annoyance than all the rest of the employee force together." Young judged him "temperamentally unfit to render service at an Indian school."[40]

Superintendent Young did not mention any possible alternatives, but perhaps Kelsey would have been better off at one of the BIA's other units, such as an agency or hospital, away from children. The superintendents of such units, however, preferred not to take employees like Kelsey who were used to working at a school with a detail of student workers. As discussed in chapter 3, student work details were a poor means of teaching trades. Instead of receiving useful, hands-on instruction in a variety of skills, students simply served as unpaid labor, doing whatever menial work was necessary to keep the school functioning. Kelsey's carpenters, for example, were more likely to learn the work of a handyman, doing small repairs under the instructor's supervision, than to learn the confidence, initiative, and range of skills necessary to build a complete house or barn. The system of work details—gang labor, really—had equally adverse effects on the employees supervising. They performed poorly when they had no students to order about and had to do the work themselves.[41]

In the final week of May 1933, Superintendent Raymond E. Staley learned that the Rapid City Indian School would close by June 30. As the school year drew to an end, Staley tried to make plans for Rapid City's students. They could not stay at the school, but few could afford to go home: as the Depression entered a fourth dry, dusty year on the Plains, families could not pay their children's transportation. A few students, orphans cared for by the school, had no homes. Staley arranged transfers for some of the students to the Pierre and Flandreau boarding schools and struggled to find money in his budget to send the other children home.[42]

Students, however, were not the only ones in danger of being stranded. In the chaos of the school's closing, Staley tried to find jobs for Rapid City staff, who would soon be both unemployed and homeless. Staley contacted Pine Ridge's Superintendent James H. McGregor to plead the cases of Lakota employees George R. Brown, Albert L. Russell, Jesse H. Rouillard, Benjamin Black Fox, and Mary Primeau, all from Pine Ridge. The five needed jobs, and Staley was sure they would do their best in any position McGregor gave them. The four men, Staley pointed out, were members of the school's employees' orchestra, "no doubt the best orchestra in the Indian Service." Despite their need, their musical ability, and their long years of service, McGregor could promise the employees from

Pine Ridge little. He might be able to help one or two find work, but dozens of men and women asked him for work daily. McGregor was "sorry that so many of the Pine Ridge people were caught in the 'wreck,' " but he could give them nothing definite.[43]

The closing of the Rapid City Indian School took from Indians an employment resource that offered steady jobs at good wages, an alternative to seasonal, manual labor. The school also provided educated Indians, particularly those with clerical training, a place to utilize their skills. Opportunities were not equal: the best-paying staff positions, such as chief clerk, went to men, and the superintendents were all white men. Those perhaps most in need of employment, single women with children, found it difficult or impossible to get positions at Rapid City. The burdens of child care fell heavily on women, for the superintendents expected women to resign when motherhood conflicted with their duties at the school. Except for those in clerical positions, such as Indian clerks Jennie Larson and Lottie G. Brown, women's work at Rapid City was an enlargement of the role of women in middle-class households of the early twentieth century: they baked, sewed, laundered, raised children, and taught. All but the last were duties for which Rapid City prepared its female students. The work of Indian men at the school, again excepting clerical workers, was similarly based on the farming, carpentry, and other skills taught at BIA boarding schools. Yellow Robe's work as disciplinarian was not the anomaly it might have seemed, for the system of student officers at many boarding schools prepared students for just such positions of authority.

That Yellow Robe held a position of considerable authority at the school for so many years demonstrates the significance of Indian employees. Indian assistants did much of the manual labor of the school. Indians in better-paying positions, such as cook, laundress, and farmer, not only contributed to the maintenance of the institution, but instructed students as well. Whites usually filled the teaching and supervisory positions, though Sarah E.

Bradley, a Cherokee from North Carolina, taught at Rapid City during the 1926–27 school year before transferring to Pipestone, Minnesota. A measure of the importance of Indian employees at Rapid City may be gleaned from the school's payroll. In 1910, Indians accounted for $3,660, or 19 percent of $19,580 total payroll expenses. In 1924, $9,960, or 30 percent of $33,720 authorized for payroll, went to Indian employees.[44]

As the payroll numbers demonstrate, the role of the Rapid City Indian School in providing jobs for Indians should not be understated. It should be noted, however, that while employment in the Indian Service brought wages and housing benefits, it did not always foster the maintenance of community. Applicants for positions had to go where the jobs were, and relocations were a fact of life for career personnel. Yellow Robe's long years of service at an institution close to his home reservation were exceptional. More typical were the Rapid City personnel who, like Larson and Day, transferred from other BIA jurisdictions and for whom Rapid City might be far from home and family. Long hours of work, the difficulties of bringing family to the school, and the superintendents' expectations that employees would focus their lives on the school reinforced employees' isolation.

The degree to which Indian employees could create an Indian community at the school reflective of any values differing from those of the superintendents and white employees was severely limited. Rapid City's superintendents wielded an authority at the school that no employees, Indian or white, could match. Even Chauncey Yellow Robe, well entrenched as he was by the late 1920s, had to concede to Superintendent Mote on the issue of residence in the boys' dormitory. The employees' creed, stressing as it did loyalty to the BIA and a cheerful obedience to superiors, expressed normative values that when heeded bound employees tightly to the assimilative mission of the school. Charting an independent course was not possible at the Rapid City Indian School, as white employees Lee Roy Willis and Earl G. Kelsey learned.

The employees most successful at the school were those who, like Indian clerk George A. Day, internalized the values and mission of the school. Recommending Day for a raise in pay, Superintendent Mote remarked that the clerk "works long hours, many times not leaving the office in the evening till after 6:00 o'clock and returning again after supper. He shoulders much responsibility, not only in the office but in connection with other activities. . . . He is extremely accurate in his work, loyal to all his superiors, and to the policies of the Bureau." If Chauncey Yellow Robe's career pointed the way toward a future of economic and social assimilation for Indians, George A. Day, conscientious clerk and devout Christian, demonstrated the degree to which that future could be achieved at the Rapid City Indian School.[45]

CHAPTER 7

EXTENDING THE REACH
OF THE BUREAU

In its role as a school, the Rapid City Indian School directly affected the lives of Indian students and their families. As an institution of the Bureau of Indian Affairs, however, it had broader functions, and its authority extended beyond the classroom. Leaving the reservations did not change the legal status of Indians on agency rolls, but it did take them out of the realm of reservation officials, who did not have the resources to keep tabs on and supervise the lives of Indians scattered among off-reservation towns. Going to town, even for a short visit, also distanced Indians from the resources available to them through the BIA, which the BIA routed through the reservations.

For differing reasons, reservation employees and sojourning Indians both looked for off-reservation intermediaries, through whom necessary items of business could be conducted. By virtue of their location near Rapid City and responsible rank in the Indian Service, the superintendents of the Rapid City Indian School found themselves called on to perform a number of duties that were important to the overall mission of the BIA or to the lives of individual Indians, yet were often wholly unrelated to the educational function of the school. The school superintendents extended many of the services of the reservations, as well as the interference in

Indian lives practiced by reservation superintendents and their employees, to Indians in and around Rapid City. In turn, Indians seeking aid used the superintendents as intermediaries with the BIA.

Much of the work devolving on superintendents of the Rapid City Indian School concerned Sioux Benefits. "Senator Dawes's Sioux Bill," passed in 1889 to strip land from the Great Sioux Reserve in the western Dakotas and divide the remainder into the Standing Rock, Cheyenne River, Crow Creek, Rosebud, and Pine Ridge Reservations, included provisions for the allotment of the new reservations. The bill also provided for Sioux Benefits, consisting of issues of stock and farming implements meant to give allottees the chance to establish viable farms on their homesteadlike allotments. Some allottees tried to have the benefits modified to suit their needs and cultural preferences: Superintendent House noted that Rapid City students sometimes asked that half their benefits be in cash, with the rest in heifers, or that they be issued only horses.[1]

As Superintendent John R. Brennan of the Pine Ridge Agency, South Dakota, explained to House in 1916, there were three basic benefits packages: "Regular Benefits, consisting of two mares, two cows, with calves, a wagon, set of harness, plow, harrow, axe, pitchfork and $50.00 in cash; Heifers and Cash,—10 head of heifers and about $40.00 in cash; or all Cash amounting to $515.27." Brennan preferred not to break up the packages. Heifers and cash were acceptable if he believed the recipient to be capable of caring for the cattle; but anyone wishing additional horses would have to take cash and buy the horses on the open market.[2]

Young people became eligible for benefits at the age of eighteen. Reflecting the BIA's definitions of proper gender roles, Brennan thought that single women in that stage of their lives should be setting up households. Consequently, he recommended that they take cash unless early marriage or other circumstances made it possible for them to make use of the regular benefits or to take proper care of the heifers. The property contained in the regular benefits would only bring hardship to single women, he said, clearly indicating a belief that farming was men's work. In keeping with that bias, young men were to receive regular benefits or heifers and cash unless they could demonstrate to the superintendent's satisfaction that an all-cash award would be of more use through investment in education or business.[3]

Other superintendents shared Brennan's biases, although not always his unwillingness to break up the benefits packages. For example, the superintendent of the Crow Creek Agency, South Dakota, recommended that Victoria Carpenter, a student of his agency attending the Rapid City Indian School, apply for two mares and two cows and the balance of her benefits in cash. Carpenter's father had "been quite successful in handling stock, and she would have no use for the implements and tools." The superintendent thus assumed, correctly or not, that Victoria Carpenter's property would be added to that of her father and that she would not take up farming on her own.[4]

By contrast, a different set of assumptions governed Cook B. Moccasin's benefits. The Crow Creek superintendent thought the young man should take the regular benefits if he were in good health, even if making use of the stock and implements meant giving up his schooling. As a possible alternative, the superintendent suggested that Moccasin could hire someone else to look after his stock and implements, with the unwritten assumption that Moccasin would return to his allotment and take up the work himself on completion of his schooling.[5]

Neither women nor men received the cash portions of their benefits directly. Cash went into BIA accounts as Individual Indian Moneys, which could be spent only under departmental supervision. The exceptions were when applicants for benefits had left wardship status through receipt of patents in fee for their allotments or when applicants, men or women, had demonstrated competence, as determined by the BIA, to manage their own affairs.[6]

Reservation authorities called on school superintendents to supervise both Sioux Benefits and expenditures of Individual Indian Moneys. Livestock or property transferred to Indians as Sioux Benefits could not be sold without departmental permission. The bill of sale forms used for Indian purchases specified that the items bought could not be sold without the permission of the responsible reservation superintendent.[7]

Reservation officials kept close enough watch on allottees to be able to enforce the regulations. In February 1917, Superintendent Brennan wrote to Superintendent House to request his assistance in recovering allotment benefits allegedly sold by Charles Black Horse, Jr. Issued a team, harness, and wagon in July 1917, Black Horse allegedly sold them in the vicinity of Rapid City. Brennan and his employees located the team at Keystone, South Dakota, and the harness at Fruitdale and tried to have a U.S. deputy marshal recover the property. Brennan thought the wagon was still in Rapid City and wanted House to send the school farmer, Judson Shook, to talk to Black Horse's wife and mother-in-law, who lived near town and allegedly knew the location of the wagon. If Shook could spot the wagon, he would take it to the school until weather permitted its return to Pine Ridge. Brennan wanted the team kept at the school, too, where the animals could be stabled without expense to the BIA. Shook did not find the wagon, but Brennan recovered the team and harness and thanked House for his assistance. Black Horse served a ninety-day sentence in the Sioux Falls penitentiary for selling government property.[8]

Reservation authorities also exercised control over the movements of Indians they believed were not using government benefits properly, again calling on the school for assistance. In May 1919, W. P. Marshall, a government farmer on the Cheyenne River Reservation, asked Superintendent House to look into the actions of James Red Bull. Marshall had heard that Red Bull gambled in

Rapid City and dealt in BIA livestock for other Indians. While House heard little good about Red Bull from other Indians, he could find no evidence of wrongdoing and reported that Red Bull and his wife stayed in Rapid City "principally for the purpose of being near their children in school. Mrs. Red Bull seems to be very much devoted to the children and they come here to the school almost every day to see their children; sometimes a little annoying."[9]

The superintendent's duties went beyond keeping tabs on individuals reservation officials distrusted. At certain times of the year, particularly fall and spring, many Indians camped near Rapid City to work for local ranchers, farmers, and businesses, an economic strategy that did not always please reservation officials. On February 19, 1920, Michael V. Wolf, boss farmer of the Cherry Creek district of the Cheyenne River Reservation, wrote Superintendent House to ask him to send Indians from the Cherry Creek district back to their allotments. The people were in camp at Rapid City, and Wolf wanted them back at their homes by March 1 so they could care for their livestock, which had been left "at the mercy of the four winds." Furthermore, he had heard that the men were "gambling and leading lives of immorality." He planned to ask the city authorities to make arrests of any men caught gambling and apparently expected House to pass the word along to the Indians.[10]

Reservation officials clearly believed that Indians misused benefits. They therefore tried to regulate Indian economic activity, imposing rules that were tediously time-consuming for Indians and school personnel alike. For example, in March 1919, Pine Ridge's Superintendent H. M. Tidwell asked Superintendent House to detail school farmer Judson Shook to look into an application by allottee Jessie Weasel, then working in Rapid City, to purchase horses and stock worth $400. On a previous occasion, Weasel's family had purchased saddles and tents with money approved for a lumber purchase, and Tidwell refused to release Weasel's money for a livestock purchase unless the stock could first be inspected and branded, to deter unauthorized resale, by a responsible BIA employee.[11]

Superintendent House sent Lakota employees Francis B. Wages and Chauncey Yellow Robe to investigate Weasel's application. Speaking to Henry Weasel, Jessie Weasel's husband, they found that the family had both a need for a team and cow and the hay and pasturage to maintain them. Wages and Yellow Robe checked Henry Weasel's employment history, too, and learned he had been working for several years for John J. Farrar, president of the Rapid City Gypsum, Lime, and Portland Cement Company. Farrar was sure the Weasels could find plenty of work for a team. Henry Weasel "was very reasonable about the matter" and willing to let school employees supervise the purchase or even pick out the stock for him and brand it before purchase.[12]

Jessie and Henry Weasel got their stock, all inspected beforehand by the school farmer, only to find out the following fall that the cow was dry and would give no milk. Henry Weasel took the cow to the school and asked permission to sell or slaughter it, hoping to buy a cow that would give milk. House passed Weasel's request to Tidwell, who turned it down: he would not issue a permit for the sale or slaughter of the cow, but instead wanted it traded for another cow and calf, with the transaction again supervised by the school. To facilitate the transaction, which Tidwell realized was "more or less of an annoyance" to House, he sent along blank bills of sale, which were to be completed in duplicate by the other party to the trade and returned to Pine Ridge for Tidwell's files.[13]

Three months later, the Weasels still did not have a new cow. Superintendent House knew quite well how difficult it would be to trade a dry cow of very little value for a milk cow, currently in short supply. Aware of the impossibility of Tidwell's instructions, House asked that Henry Weasel be allowed to sell the cow and use the money as he wished. He noted that Weasel worked steadily and made a good salary and thought it was "up to [Weasel] to take care of himself." Faced with the burden of managing the Weasels' affairs under unrealistic constraints, House reminded Tidwell of the ostensible purpose of allotment: to promote Indian self-reliance through the exercise of responsibility. Here was a clear example of one BIA official willing to give up control of an Indian family's economic decisions, and another unwilling to do so—even though the Weasels apparently had more business sense than Tidwell, their ostensible guardian.[14]

This interference to which Jessie and Henry Weasel were subjected was unusual only in its complications. The staff of the Rapid City Indian School oversaw a wide range of Indian economic activity. School personnel routinely supervised purchases, with reservation officials setting the amounts Indians could spend. In one transaction, Superintendent House received a letter from Pine Ridge and authority for Alfred Black Bear to purchase a team of horses for $150, a wagon for $150, and a set of harness for $85. Black Bear, not literate in English, planned to work for hire in Rapid City when not working on his own allotment near Manderson, South Dakota. In another instance, Rosebud Indian Agency's Superintendent W. O. Roberts asked the school, then under Superintendent Raymond E. Staley, to investigate a request by Mrs. William Eagle Tail to purchase $125 of building materials on the account of her husband, serving time for desertion from the military.[15]

Much of the work done by the school concerned transactions associated with allotment or leasing. Reservation officials commonly routed money due tribal members living in Rapid City through the school, mailing the checks to the school along with lists of check numbers, amounts, and the individuals to whom they were to be delivered. The Rosebud superintendent cautioned House to be sure the checks went to the designated recipients, since some were not above forging endorsements and cashing someone else's check. Reservation officials sometimes requested that money from a cashed check be collected from one recipient and given to another individual in payment of a debt. Cash allotments also required action by the school. They came as United States Treasury warrants, which had to be signed by the allottee and then returned to the reservation so the money could be placed in a supervised account. When the recipients lived in Rapid City, the task of securing signatures and mailing back the warrants fell to the school superintendents.[16]

School superintendents also secured signatures on grazing and mineral leases. Leasing regulations in force during World War I required that all lands not being used by allottees be leased, so that food would be produced for the war effort. When the school returned leases on student Susan DeSheuquette's allotment to the office of E. M. Garber, superintendent of the Lower Brule, South Dakota, Indian Agency, without DeSheuquette's signature, Garber promptly sent the leases back to the school. Explaining that regulations required him to sign DeSheuquette's leases if she would not do so herself, Garber asked Superintendent House to once again present the leases to her. Her father, Leon DeSheuquette, favored the lease, Garber wrote, and planned to write his daughter to that effect. If Susan DeSheuquette would sign the lease, Garber wanted the signature witnessed and an acknowledgment signed by House. If she refused to sign, Garber asked that she give her reasons over her signature.[17]

As Garber implied, lessors could refuse to sign leases. In these cases, school superintendents sometimes acted as disinterested intermediaries, articulating to reservation authorities the lessors' objections. In 1922, J. W. C. Killer, government farmer of the White Clay district of the Pine Ridge reservation, forwarded to the Rapid City Indian School grazing leases requiring the signature of Ida Tyon, a student at the school. The leases covered Tyon's allotments and her interest in the allotment of Thomas Tyon, Sr., deceased. Superintendent S. A. M. Young returned the leases unsigned. After he had fully explained the leases to Ida Tyon, Young wrote, she preferred not to sign: the compensation was too low, and the lessee, Thomas Tyon, Jr., had been slow to make payment in the past.

Young gave no indication that he put any pressure on Ida Tyon to sign, suggesting that a school superintendent might possibly intervene to forestall an ill-advised lease.[18]

When lessees were adults living near Rapid City, the school might act as a forwarding point for paperwork. In 1931, L. S. Bonnin of the Cheyenne and Arapaho Agency, Oklahoma, sent three oil and gas mining leases to the school for the signature of James Riley. Riley lived in Belle Fourche, 50 miles from Rapid City. While Bonnin could have mailed the material directly, he did not trust Riley, agent of the Chicago and North Western Railway in Belle Fourche, to execute the leases properly and wanted "the nearest Government Official" to see that all of the twenty-four signatures required (four for each of the three leases and twelve acknowledgment forms) were notarized and in their proper places. Bonnin asked Superintendent Young to order Riley to Rapid City and have him sign the mass of paperwork in Young's presence. Instead, Young simply mailed the leases and acknowledgments to Riley at Belle Fourche, with straightforward instructions on how they were to be completed. Young asked that everything be mailed back to him at Rapid City, where he would forward the material to Bonnin. He apparently saw no reason to supervise a man self-evidently capable of managing his own affairs.[19]

When the lessors were minors, however, students at the school, school and reservation officials sometimes worked together to exercise considerable control over the lessors' financial affairs. The transaction by which Fannie Red Bull, a student at Rapid City Indian School, leased property on the Crow Creek reservation offers a typical case in point. BIA farmer John E. Derby sent the lease to Superintendent House, who had Red Bull sign it and returned the papers to Derby.[20]

After the completion of the lease agreement in May 1917, near the end of the school term, Red Bull did not return home, as she had been ill. By mid-June, she had regained her health, but preferred to remain at the school. House wrote to F. C. Campbell, superintendent of the Cheyenne River Agency, to that effect. As House told the story, Red Bull believed Moses Red Bull and others of the family wanted her home "so as to get the money from her." House, noting that she was "a fine girl and has done well in school," wanted to keep her at the school rather than let the young woman and her money fall into the hands of her reservation relatives. Campbell agreed and thought it in "the best interests of Fannie Red Bull and indirectly to all others concerned that she remain in Rapid City" rather than participate in an ethic of sharing that Campbell, like many others in the BIA, thought encouraged sloth and indolence at the expense of individual advancement.[21]

BIA fears that money would corrupt Indians if acquired by any means other than individual labor and that its recipients would squander cash shaped responses to Indian requests for funds. The Rapid City Indian School sometimes handled requests for funds from Indians who needed the money for immediate use rather than for capital expenditures. In June 1927, Agnes Craven of the Pine Ridge Reservation wrote to Pine Ridge's Superintendent E. W. Jermark asking for emergency funds of $100. Craven had gone to Rapid City with her mother, two brothers, and a sister to pick up two other sisters, who attended the school. The family was in one of the Indian encampments near Rapid City, starving, without food or adequate clothes. Craven requested money to fill the family's immediate needs as well as enough extra money to allow her to buy food and clothing in Rapid City, where prices were lower than on the reservation. Then she planned to return to Pine Ridge, where she had a garden planted.[22]

Jermark sent a copy of Craven's letter to Superintendent Mote, writing in a cover letter that "no doubt, this is a case where the family have gone to Rapid City and would like to have spending money while there." Jermark sent Craven only $25, with instructions to return to Pine Ridge and take up her financial problems with her government farmer and to submit her application for funds through regular channels. In case of an emergency, Craven could contact Mote at the school, who would go over her needs with her and present his assessment to Jermark. Jermark would send additional funds only after consultation with Mote.[23]

Yet in some cases the school reacted with both sympathy and alacrity to the needs of Indians stranded in Rapid City. On October 24, 1916, Reverend I. I. Gorby of the Presbyterian church passed word to Superintendent House that Frank Bear Nose was at the Rapid City railroad station with the body of his daughter and needed assistance. House went to the station with an interpreter and learned that Bear Nose's two-year-old daughter had been killed near Whitewood, South Dakota, when she fell out of a wagon and struck her head on a rock. Whitewood health officers had advised Bear Nose to return immediately by train to Smithwick, South Dakota, the rail station nearest his home, yet had issued him a permit to transport the body of his daughter only to Rapid City, since he did not have the money to go any farther.[24]

On learning that Bear Nose was assigned to the Pine Ridge Agency, House apparently wired Pine Ridge's Superintendent Brennan, asking for funds to use in assisting Bear Nose. Receiving authorization to spend up to thirty-one dollars, House bought train tickets for Bear Nose, gave him five dollars for his expenses at Smithwick, arranged for his daughter's body to be shipped there, and secured a certificate from a local undertaker authorizing the shipment. House kept the receipts and completed all the necessary vouchers for Brennan, allowing Bear Nose to continue his journey with as few complications as possible.[25]

When necessary, the school also took care of reservation residents who fell ill while in Rapid City. In June 1919, Superintendent House had Manuel Romero of the Eagle Nest district of Pine Ridge transferred to the school hospital when the city hospital could no longer keep him. House was prepared to hire a special nurse to care for the aged Romero and arranged funding with Elmer B. Pomeroy, the government farmer overseeing Romero's affairs on the reservation. When Romero died a few days later, House had the body returned to Romero's family and put the undertaker, Carl Behrens, in touch with Pomeroy to settle the bills.[26]

As the Depression took its toll on Indian families living in the Rapid City area, emergencies frequently required the intervention of the Indian School. The school both administered relief to destitute Indians and forwarded requests for funds to their reservations. In January 1932, Rosebud's Superintendent W. O. Roberts wrote Superintendent Young to ask for his assistance in disbursing Red Cross funds. Agency offices had Red Cross money on hand for the use of reservation residents. Roberts observed that while the money was primarily for the more needy on the reservation, "we find it necessary in some instances to give help also to the able-bodied Indians who are not able to obtain any productive work. We are requiring this class of Indian to supply labor in lieu of a handout." While Roberts did not know how many people on Rosebud rolls were in Rapid City, he hoped Young would be able to put some of them to work, thus making them eligible for relief. Roberts proposed that able-bodied Indians in Rapid City be given two days of work per week through January, crediting them $1.50 per person per day. They would be paid not in cash but in purchase orders for groceries issued through the Rosebud offices. He suggested that Young contact Joseph Pawnee, who might need work and who would likely know the names of others in need of employment. Roberts cautioned that he did not intend "to give unlimited assistance to these Indians as we do not have enough allowance to take care of these needy cases on the reservation" and urged Young to be conservative in his assistance to Indians in Rapid City.[27]

Superintendent Young sent out letters to several men in the Rapid City area, explaining the conditions of Roberts's offer and asking the men to report to the school for duty if they wished to work. He employed four men under this arrangement in January, giving each four days of work, allowing them to earn $6 per person for the month. As Young noted to Roberts, he could only give each man four days of work, since Roberts's letter did not reach him until January 14. Still, Young found a way to stretch his authority. Taking the letter as immediate authorization for employment, he gave each man employed two days per calendar week left in the month, thus fitting in four days of work in a week's time. Young wanted to know if the arrangement would be continued, for the letter only authorized work through January, and he thought there would be continuing demand for this form of relief.[28]

Roberts authorized additional work, but only under conditions that placed a considerable administrative burden on Young. Since Roberts had only seventy-five dollars on hand for Indians living in towns off the reservation, he would not authorize relief for anyone who had family members with funds on account at Rosebud Indian Agency. Nor would he issue more than one purchase order per family or living group. He wanted Young to investigate each case and be sure that the applicant had dependents to support and was in genuine need. Those without dependents were on their own. "There are many young, single, able-bodied Indians who have no responsibility and who have always got along in some way," Roberts wrote. "It is not our purpose to maintain and support that class from relief funds." He wanted the money to go only to responsible heads of households and trusted that Young's long experience in the Indian Service would enable him to distinguish between "the worthy cases" and those less deserving of assistance. Young was to fill the role of a welfare case officer, dispensing money according to both material and moral criteria.[29]

Superintendent Young and his successor at the Rapid City Indian School, Raymond E. Staley, also acted as intermediaries for people left destitute by the Depression, writing reservation offices on the behalf of enrolled tribal members living in the vicinity of the city. Young prefaced one such letter to W. F. Dickens, superintendent of the Cheyenne River Agency, with the explanation that members of a family had called on him and asked him to write in their favor and that he did not presume "to interfere in any way with [Dickens's] regular course of business." The care with which Young distanced himself from the requests of the Rousseau family may have been due to his lack of familiarity with their cases. Ellen Beatrice Vosburg, a member of the family who claimed to be one-fourth Indian and a widow, asked for her pro rata share of the Cheyenne Three Per Cent Fund and that she be allowed $25 a month for the support of herself and her five-year-old son, Vance LaVerne Vosburg. She also asked that Dickens look into enrolling her son at Cheyenne River and wanted it known that her last interest check had failed to arrive. Maggie Powell Rousseau and Edward and Dan Rousseau also complained about missing interest checks. Hazel Rousseau Magstadt had applied for her pro rata share and wanted to know if any action had been taken on her request. Although disclaiming any knowledge of the regulations concerning the Rousseaus' requests, Young recommended that they be allowed to withdraw their money, since he thought them "to all intents and purposes white people" and therefore not truly the responsibility of the BIA.[30]

Superintendent Young appeared more sympathetic to Sylvester Garreau, a 1931 graduate of the Rapid City Indian School on tribal rolls at the Cheyenne River reservation. Garreau had married another graduate not long after the close of school, and the young couple soon had a child. Young wrote Dickens that Garreau had "been willing to work at all times," but like so many people during the Depression had been unable to find employment. The couple needed money to pay the doctor and other expenses related to their son's birth. Young passed along Garreau's request that Dickens send Garreau any money he might have to his credit, in whatever amount Dickens saw fit.[31]

Superintendent Staley found the role of letter-writer to be both tiring and embarrassing. In December 1932, he wrote to Dickens detailing the plight of Mrs. Joseph Crane Pretty Voice, who was at one of the semipermanent Indian encampments near Rapid City. The family, with seven children, lived in a tent. County authorities had provided a small amount of short-term relief in the form of food and fuel, but the family was again destitute, and Crane Pretty Voice wanted money that she believed was due her husband. Staley wrote to Dickens that "you will think that I am a professional beggar since it seems that about every other letter I write you it is about somebody's claim or money due them" and explained that the role was one thrust on him by people who "come after me and make all kinds of reports as to the amount of money due, how long it has been due, how long they have written you and all like that." Assuring Dickens that he knew just how annoying his letters must be, Staley asked Dickens to understand that he helped the Indians with their inquiries only because they begged him to do so.[32]

Despite the limited relief funds available to the BIA, local officials tried to hide cases of extreme poverty from the general public. In April 1933, Superintendent James H. McGregor of the Pine Ridge Agency wrote Superintendent Staley, asking him to look for a woman named Nellie Swimmer: he had heard that she was begging on the streets of Rapid City. According to McGregor, Swimmer presented the following typewritten note to those from whom she sought aid:

> To Whom it may concern:
> I am Nellie Swimmer with a Family of eight children to take care of. I cant see to sew, also I have been sick for the past twenty years. I want food and clothing.
> Yours very truly,
> P.S. Nellie wants a Dollar.

McGregor hoped to find out where she lived, though there were Swimmers on a number of the reservations, and asked Staley to look into the case, should she appear again. McGregor thought it unnecessary for Swimmer to be on the street, "as [Indians] can be taken care of in our reservations without begging," and hoped to discourage the practice. Making inquiries, Staley heard that

Swimmer had gone on to Scenic. He asked Rapid City police and welfare workers to notify him if Swimmer returned and promised McGregor he would ask the Indian community at south camp near the city to watch for her as well. Staley's ready cooperation suggests that he shared McGregor's abhorrence of begging.[33]

The social control agendas implied by the effort to locate Nellie Swimmer reflected less the Depression than a continuation of longstanding efforts by the superintendents of the Indian School to police the Indian population of Rapid City. To some extent, the school simply extended the reach of reservation officials intent on supervising the lives of Indians enrolled at their agencies. However, the services of its superintendents were also available to Indians seeking assistance with their own legal problems.

Superintendent Mossman of the Standing Rock Agency, North Dakota, made use of the network of BIA institutions in October 1927, when he sent a letter addressed to "My dear Superintendents" to the Rosebud and Cheyenne River Agencies and the Rapid City Indian School, asking for information on the whereabouts of Bede Dog. Dog had allegedly impregnated a girl at Standing Rock and was under obligation to marry her when he left for Rosebud in the summer of 1927. Mossman had heard that Bede Dog had accompanied his father, Louie Dog, to Rapid City; he wanted to be informed immediately if anyone located the two men. Superintendent Mote could only tell Mossman that Louie Dog had left Rapid City several weeks previously for the Cherry Creek area of the Cheyenne River Reservation.[34]

Superintendent Mote gave a little more assistance to Andrew Bissonette, who first wrote him while in the Pennington County Jail in Rapid City in April 1929. Bissonette, together with an unnamed white man, awaited trial on a grand larceny charge. Just what sort of advice he wanted from Mote is unclear from the letter, but he did not want anyone else to know of his arrest, did not want to talk to the state's attorney, and did not want the authorities to hear the story of his alleged accomplice until he had talked to someone. Since Bissonette did not have the money to hire an attorney, he hoped that Mote, as a member of the Indian Service, could visit him at the jail, hear his story, and advise him.[35]

Mote initially refused to become involved, explaining that his work at the school left him no time to help Bissonette as he requested. He advised Bissonette to tell all the facts of the case to the state's attorney, who would prosecute the case, and trust that the latter would be honest and fair with him if he cooperated fully. Some idea of the value of Mote's advice might be gleaned from Bissonette's second letter, again written from the county jail, while he awaited sentencing after having been found guilty of grand larceny.[36]

This time Bissonette, still protesting his innocence, asked Superintendent Mote to intervene on his behalf with the sentencing judge. Bissonette's family circumstances meant that time in the penitentiary would be particularly burdensome. His father suffered from kidney ailments, and surgery might be necessary. His wife, who had already lost one eye, was losing sight in the other. The couple had three young children who would be without support if their father were put away. Mote, still avoiding contact with Bissonette, forwarded his correspondence to the Office of the Commissioner of Indian Affairs. In reply, Assistant Commissioner J. Henry Scattergood informed Bissonette that the BIA could not help him. The crime of which he was convicted had been committed in territory under state jurisdiction, he had had two competent attorneys to defend him, and he had been convicted in what appeared to Scattergood to be a fair trial. Bissonette thus could expect no assistance from the BIA.[37]

Perhaps because of the limited nature of the request, Superintendent Young proved more helpful when Eva J. Conger Roubideaux wrote him in October 1931, asking for information relating to alleged infidelity on the part of her husband, Roy A. Roubideaux. Young had fired Roy Roubideaux from his job as a painter at the school after an alleged affair with a student. Eva Roubideaux wanted the girl's name and any other facts Young could disclose to buttress her case in a custody dispute over the couple's three young children. "I am a desperate mother fighting for her children," she wrote, "penniless and no relatives, and with my back to the wall." If Young could answer by return mail, Roubideaux promised her undying gratitude.[38]

Young promptly obliged with the details of the case. He had fired Roy Roubideaux after two female students ran away with him. Roubideaux and one of the students "were criminally intimate at the time [the student] ran away," a relationship both Roubideaux and the student allegedly admitted to Young. Young had expelled the student and gave Eva Roubideaux her name, last known location, and home reservation, as well as the name of the other student who participated in the adventure. Under Young's interrogation, the expelled student allegedly stated that she expected to marry Roy Roubideaux, but Young believed her to have had relationships with other men, one of whom he named in his letter to Eva Roubideaux. He apparently felt no need to protect the reputation of an expelled student.[39]

But superintendents' interventions in sexual and marital relationships paled in comparison with the war against liquor and the saloon waged by Superintendent House. In an address titled "The Indians and the Liquor Traffic," he cast alcohol as a threat to the civilizing mission of the school, to the progress of white and Indian education alike, and to the business interests of the city. Claiming intemperance was the greatest threat to Indian progress, House argued that "very much of the earnest effort of the government to bring these people into . . . the community, to make them good citizens, is either thwarted, or in a measure nullified by [the] degradation of the liquor traffic and its resultant vices." Threatening both body and mind, alcohol and the institution of the saloon worked against the development of the good in human nature that education sought to achieve. As such, it threatened school interests, white and Indian, in Rapid City.[40]

House went on to contend that liquor prevented the full development of Rapid City's trade with the residents of nearby reservations. The Indian School brought at least $100,000 to the city. Rapid City's proximity to the Pine Ridge, Rosebud, and Cheyenne River Reservations, "three of the largest Indian Reservations in the United States," made it a center for reservation residents, many of whom traveled to the city to visit their children at the school or to buy supplies or transact other business. "When superintendents of reservations become convinced that the Indians coming to Rapid City will not be in danger of coming under the influence of the saloon, getting drunk, losing their money and degrading themselves," House observed, the superintendents "will be much more willing to encourage [the Indians] to come here, and consequently the interests of both Indians and legitimate business will be enhanced." He was sure the volume of Indian business done in the city could be doubled, to $200,000, and that contact with the city, if the city were dry, would be an uplifting experience for Indian visitors.[41]

House apparently believed that the legal traffic in liquor made enforcement of the prohibition against selling liquor to Indians more difficult to enforce, perhaps by increasing the volume of alcohol on the market and the number of outlets. "I am aware that many people who have not taken any decided stand against the saloon interests strongly condemn the selling or giving [of] intoxicants to Indians," he wrote, "but the fact remains that in many instances they get it and the traffic is responsible." House appealed to business interests: fully half of his address concerned the economic benefits of prohibition, and his reference to "saloon interests" suggested a willingness to intervene in local politics, via the business community, on the liquor issue. Dated April 16, 1915, his address came only four days before an election in which Rapid City went dry on a 49-vote majority.[42]

House had already shown a willingness to use the resources of his office to attack the illegal traffic in alcohol to Indians. In December 1910, he wrote U.S. attorney E. E. Wagner of Sioux Falls, South Dakota, to report an alcohol case generated by the school at the request of an Indian. There had been "considerable drunkenness on the part of Indians" in and around Rapid City, and an older, unallotted man, Two Arrows, complained to House and offered to help locate those selling the alcohol.[43]

Superintendent House sent Two Arrows, Henry Crow, and school employee Yellow Robe to several Rapid City saloons to make what amounted to undercover buys. At one saloon, the three succeeded in purchasing a quart of whiskey from a man who gave the appearance of being a saloon employee, but was not the regular bartender. The three then gave the alcohol to House. Two Arrows, Crow, and Yellow Robe did not know the seller's name, but were sure they could identify the man visually. On that basis, House wanted a John Doe warrant sworn out and a U.S. marshal sent directly to the city to make the arrest. Otherwise, he feared that a preliminary hearing would give the seller time to flee the city, as had happened in a previous case. On learning that Wagner's office could not issue a John Doe warrant without at least a description that could be expected to lead to an identification, House succeeded, with some difficulty, in identifying the John Doe as one Charles Clark.[44]

Undercover buys of the sort ordered by Superintendent House were common enough that Henry A. Larson, chief special officer of the United States Indian Service in charge of liquor enforcement, felt it necessary to issue guidelines in the form of a circular sent to all special officers and deputies. Larson warned against making too many cases, arguing that a few good cases that would stand up in court were more effective in suppressing the liquor traffic than large numbers of poor cases. He also cautioned against improper use of "decoys," as he referred to Indian buyers, to prevent entrapment. Planned buys of alcohol were only to be used when officers had good reason to believe that criminal traffic in liquor existed and evidence could not be secured by any other method. Furthermore, decoys were to be "of such a degree of Indian blood and racial appearance as to place the seller immediately on guard." Larson warned that "[t]he use of light colored decoys will not be tolerated." Nor should the decoys be taken far from their home reservations.[45]

While House's use of planned buys appears to fall within Larson's guidelines, the procedure did not yield many convictions, in part due to a lack of cooperation from the office of the U.S. attorney. While House kept no further correspondence on the case against Charles Clark, a case against one Tom Stevens went badly. House had Stevens arrested for supplying alcohol to students of the Indian school and gave his personal attention to the case. The U.S. attorney for South Dakota knew of the case and promised assistance, but none arrived, and the case went to trial with the local state's attorney prosecuting. The state's attorney made a strong effort, but the defense presented an alibi that satisfied the jury, which acquitted Stevens. The case led House to remark in correspondence that he "very much dislike[d] any connection with such cases," which drew the ire of Assistant Commissioner E. B. Meritt, who demanded an explanation. When House explained that he preferred to leave such cases to those who specialized in them, but would willingly participate when duty demanded that he do so, Meritt let him off with a warning to be more careful in future correspondence.[46]

Despite the difficulties brought on by the Stevens case, Superintendent House persisted in his efforts to control the liquor traffic in Rapid City. In December 1916, after the city had gone dry, House wrote Larson to request the authority and funding to hire his own deputies. In fall and spring, depending on the work available, Rapid City attracted many seasonal laborers from nearby reservations. At these times, and whenever celebrations or other special occasions brought large numbers of Indians to the city, bootlegging flourished. While Larson often supplied officers for these occasions,

House did not think it practical to ask for an officer each time. Furthermore, as special officers became known to the locals, their effectiveness diminished. Larson responded with very nearly the authority House requested: he applied with the BIA to have House appointed a deputy special officer, with the authority to employ posse service for up to five days per month. While Larson did not place funds at House's disposal, as requested, House's commission allowed him to hire personnel subject to the regulations governing posse service, with vouchers to be submitted to Larson.[47]

House's efforts were not entirely successful, for in 1920 he once again requested assistance from Larson, asking that someone unknown in the Rapid City area be sent in to gather information on an Indian he suspected of bootlegging. By then, the ratification of the Eighteenth Amendment and passage of the Volstead Act had made Prohibition the law of the land, and the Rapid City Indian School's crusade against liquor ended with House's departure in 1922.[48]

Even though much of the noneducational activity of the Rapid City Indian School in some way aided sojourning Indians, overall, its efforts were directed toward extending reservation controls to Indians living in the city. When the school brought the paperwork of allotment and benefits to Indians living in and around Rapid City, it performed a valuable service. The possibilities for Indian mobility grew, and restrictions on freedom lessened, when maintenance of trust relationships no longer required Indians' physical presence at their agencies of enrollment. But the superintendents carried out this service under guidelines set by reservation superintendents, which gave priority to the maintenance of control over Indian finances. Standing in for reservation personnel, school superintendents and employees extended the reservation regime to the city.

In other areas, the school extended a supervision that meshed with the interests of school and reservation superintendents alike.

In administering relief work during the Depression, Superintendent Young sought to apply criteria of both need and moral worth to individuals asking for aid. Superintendents' judgments of worth played an unmistakable role in their decisions governing various types of assistance: if Mote avoided involvement with the legal troubles of a man charged with grand larceny, Young gave out information of a highly personal nature to a mother fighting for the custody of her children. House's battle against the liquor traffic in Rapid City represented a moral crusade of the most overt sort, one that he carried into local courts and elections.

None of these activities fell within the educational mission of the Rapid City Indian School. Nor is there any evidence to suggest that the superintendents' activities laid an institutional foundation for further extensions of services to off-reservation Indian communities. Their ad hoc activities were built not on formal statements of mission, but on the culture of the Indian Service, where superintendents of field jurisdictions willingly shared responsibility over each other's wards. Nonetheless, despite the intrusive nature of much of the superintendents' work among off-reservation populations, the Indian School was a valuable resource for Indians in an era when the BIA lacked the institutional structure to provide services to tribal members living off the reservations.

Epilogue

American Indians outlasted the institutions designed to destroy them as tribal peoples. The Carlisle Indian School closed in 1918. The Hampton Institute discontinued its Indian program in 1923. The Rapid City Indian School closed in 1933. The Haskell Institute survives as Haskell Junior College. The reservations from which Rapid City drew its students remain, as do the tribal cultures of their peoples. Instead of dying out or assimilating, Indians in the Northern Plains enjoyed a demographic, political, and cultural renaissance that began in the 1930s and continues today.

As Peter Iverson notes in *The Plains Indians of the Twentieth Century*, "one of the most remarkable features of the modern Plains is that Indians have remained a part of it." How did the Rapid City Indian School contribute to this story of survival and rebirth? Several generations of tribal leadership emerged from Carlisle, Haskell, and other large off-reservation schools offering advanced training. With its more regional base of recruitment, smaller size, and less advanced curriculum, the Indian School played a lesser role. It offered immersion training in English and an introduction to manual labor. An exceptional student like Nancy Schmidt or Robert Emery might go on from Rapid City to graduate from high school and even spend a year at the State Normal School.[1]

Were the benefits of attending the Rapid City Indian School worth the hardship? A Lakota student offered one answer in an encounter with a school employee, years after both had left the school. In her old age, matron Theresa C. Kaufman often thought about how hard she had been on the girls under her supervision. Under Kaufman, the girls' dormitories at Rapid City were legendary in the Indian Service for their cleanliness. Girls took off their shoes when they entered the dormitories, lest they track in dirt. Kaufman detailed older girls to clean up the younger girls then inspected them to be sure every last hair was in place. Details of girls brushed and swept the floors until they shone. Kaufman put girls to work in the freezing cold of winter, scrubbing the dormitories' porches. "It'd be icy from scrubbing," the student said. "That's how clean that woman was. She thought they had to be scrubbed. Everything, the halls, everything; everything was shiny."[2]

"Had she been too hard on the girls? 'You weren't that bad,' the student told Kaufman.'You go downtown [to Rapid City] and you ask who is this girl, who is that girl—it'd be one of your girls that'd be working.' That was quite a while ago. And I said, 'It's your girls that they hire now. We work now because we learned how to work from you, and you taught us how to be clean and neat. And we can get a job because we know how to work.'" Kaufman was "nice and strict," and the student appreciated that. The girls who went to school under Kaufman "were good clean women. [They] [k]new how to clean and keep house." The student saw nothing wrong with the highly gendered curriculum of the school, but in fact valued her training because it imparted lessons of domesticity so thoroughly.[3]

One student's experiences should not be taken as a blanket endorsement of the Rapid City Indian School's goals and methods. They suggest, however, the possibility that students did not necessarily see the school as a hostile institution with agendas wholly foreign to their own wants and needs. Richard Henry Pratt, Thomas J. Morgan, and others of their time saw boarding schools standing in utter opposition to their notions of Indian cultures. Refusing to understand the effort that went into subsistence hunting, they thought Indian men were lazy and imagined them to be averse to work. Unfamiliar with the demands of caring for families or farming, they slighted the skills, attention to detail, and concerns for cleanliness of Indian women. Knowing little of how rigorously Indians trained their children to assume adult roles, they thought Indians unlearned and undisciplined. Having thoroughly misunderstood Indians and Indian cultures, the proponents of off-reservation boarding schools thought the schools would obliterate Indian cultures by introducing new habits of thought and work. The evidence of Indian survival indicates that the concepts taught at Rapid City and other off-reservation boarding schools were more easily incorporated into Indian lives than Morgan and his kind ever imagined possible.

That the Indian School's students were able to make use of their school experiences was a tribute to the endurance and persistence of students and staff alike. Perhaps because of their basic hostility to Indians, Congress and the Bureau of Indian Affairs never devoted to the school the resources it needed. Largely but not entirely because of the lack of money, there were severe flaws in the operation of the school. While food there improved in the 1910s and 1920s, health conditions, particularly the incidence of tuberculosis and trachoma, deteriorated over the life of the school. The system of contract physicians, by which the school hired local doctors to visit regularly, was never satisfactory because the pay the school offered was insufficient for the work required. Before Rapid City even opened, off-reservation boarding schools earned a grisly reputation from the frequent deaths of their students. If students did not die at school, too often they came home sick and died soon after. While Rapid City's superintendents were aware of this reputation and kept obviously sick children out of the school, they were unable to take more positive steps to protect students' health. Rapid City was not the charnel house that Carlisle was in its early years, but neither was it a healthy place for children to spend their childhoods.

Underfunding similarly hampered education at the Rapid City Indian School. Through the 1910s, the school had too few teachers to instruct students in academic subjects. The half-and-half schedule, never conducive to learning, was even less so when a shortage of teachers meant some children could only be in school every other day. Even when the teacher shortage eased in the 1920s, the inability of the school to function without student labor meant the retention of the half-and-half, despite its obvious flaws. Luther Standing Bear, entering Carlisle in its first class in 1879, immediately understood the drawbacks of spending half his time in school and the other half at work. "Now there was one thing I really wanted," he said, "and that was to have all my time in school, instead of working as a tinsmith half the day. I could not see that the trade was going to benefit me any, as the Government was already giving the Indians all the tinware they wanted." Pratt, however, insisted that Standing Bear learn a trade. Though tinsmithing did indeed turn out to be a useless skill, for precisely the reasons Standing Bear anticipated, his work at Carlisle was more educational than the labor many Indian children performed at school. When the "vocational" work of Rapid City did not consist of drudge work to maintain the school, it often had even less practical value than Standing Bear's tinsmithing, as when Agnes Hawkins learned Kitchen Gardening by theory only, because the January weather made it impossible to plant seed.[4]

In other areas, students' families bore the burdens imposed by the Rapid City Indian School's limited resources. Keeping students properly clothed at school was expensive for families, especially in the 1920s. Bringing students home for summer vacations, the only time during the year they could leave the school, proved costly, and again the burden fell on the families. When one considers the changing role of the school in the 1920s, its lack of money for clothes and other necessities such as medical care appears particularly unfortunate. As poverty brought on by allotment and a worsening agricultural economy, followed by the Great Depression, took their toll on Indian families, more turned to the Indian School as a child care provider of last resort. The school could have met the needs of children from impoverished families better if the institution itself had not been so strapped for money.

The successes of the Rapid City Indian School in the face of these problems can best be understood if it is seen as but one institution of the many with which Indians interacted. In an era in which the BIA enforced school attendance with reservation police, the Indian School was one of several schooling alternatives for Indian families. Competing with mission schools, reservation boarding schools, and other off-reservation boarding schools for the enrollment of Indian children, the Rapid City Indian School could not simply round up children to fill its dormitories.

Instead, Rapid City's superintendents had to meet Indian families on the reservations to recruit their children voluntarily. Indian parents used this leverage to effect limited changes in the way their children were schooled. By threatening to withhold future enrollments, they forced Superintendent House to engage in highly unorthodox lobbying to restore their children's summer vacations. If Indian parents had to send their children away for school, they put all their children in one school, despite the BIA's policies in favor of a gradated system, where only the oldest and most advanced pupils would attend off-reservation boarding schools. Rapid City thus enrolled students in the first three grades, after the BIA had officially eliminated those grades at off-reservation schools. Other parents and children simply preferred Rapid City to the other schools available and bent the rules accordingly. Some preferred its teaching to that available at other schools, and by the 1920s Rapid City offered a wide variety of sports and other student activities, making it more attractive to students.

Parents sent children to Rapid City for other reasons as well. The Indian School was part of a network of BIA jurisdictions with which Indians interacted. Indian employees of the school enrolled their children and their relatives there. Beset by reservation poverty or family crisis, Indian parents used the school to help care for their children. When reservation officials and Indian judges deemed it necessary to remove children from their parents, they worked with Rapid City superintendents to transfer the children to the school. It thus became a provider of child welfare services, although welfare placements strained the school's meager resources of dormitory space, clothing, and medical care. For Indians living in or near Rapid City, the school offered a link to services usually available through reservation superintendents, such as the provision of Sioux Benefits or lease money. In a less welcome role, superintendents also extended the interference of reservation supervision to Indians living near the school.

After weighing these Indian-white interactions, it is clear that the model of action-response, with the school continually impinging on Indian lives and Indians responding, is not an accurate characterization of relationships at the Rapid City Indian School. The school was only one of many elements that made up the environment of Indians in the Northern Plains. In an era when they faced assaults on their lands and their customs, demographic threats from diseases, and environmental and economic changes over which few in the region, Indian or white, had any control, Indians often sought out the school and initiated interactions with it in pursuit of their own goals. Whether they saw in the school a way to prepare their children for an uncertain future or the means to carry on a feud with a reservation superintendent, the school had something to offer.

The superintendents and employees of the Rapid City Indian School mirrored attitudes prevalent in the BIA as a whole, and indeed in the larger society. They did not realize how much Indians had to offer the school. This lack of recognition may be considered Rapid City's greatest failure. Beginning with Pratt at Carlisle, proponents of off-reservation boarding schools assumed the hostility of Indian parents to schooling. Even when Indians showed themselves willing to send their children to BIA or mission schools, there remained a distrust of Indian parents and a conviction that to be successful schooling had to separate children from their parents, culturally if not necessarily physically.

One may speculate about what might have been. Had the BIA been less suspicious of Indian parents, would it have built any boarding schools, much less off-reservation schools? Superintendent House saw advantages in educating children at Rapid City, without reference to the commonly stated goal of physically separating children from family and tribal influences. Because of its proximity to a public high school, a business college, and the State School of Mines, Rapid City offered, he concluded, a better educational environment than could be found on isolated reservations. With the school's advantages linked to positive opportunities, and not merely taking children away from their reservations, its rationale would not have been undermined had it invited greater parental involvement.

Had their involvement been allowed and encouraged, Indian parents might have played very different roles at the Indian School. Superintendent House preferred not to employ Indian parents whose children attended the school because he thought they might object to attempts to discipline their children. But had parents been more of a presence at the school, perhaps employed as house mothers and house fathers, would the school's strict regimentation of its students have been necessary? To the extent that it was justified at all, the military discipline of the school was needed because there were so few adults to supervise the children. Increasing the number of adults at Rapid City by employing Indian parents might well have rendered much of the regimentation unnecessary. It certainly would have made it far more difficult for staff to strike or verbally humiliate students or to subject students to the strap and the guardhouse. Involving Indian parents might have made the school safer for their children, without interfering with its teaching mission.

Had the school had the funds and permission to employ more labor, it certainly could have hired more Indian assistants to do the work of maintaining the school. Employing sufficient staff at Rapid City would have lifted from students' shoulders the burden of detail work, allowing more time for both classroom work and recreation by abolishing the half-and-half schedule. Many of the hardships of boarding school life could have been alleviated, and the school's academic program could have been brought up to the standards of comparably sized public institutions enrolling white children. It should be noted, however, that raising academic standards at the school would have required that the BIA put aside the notions of Indian racial inferiority embodied in Estelle Reel's dumbed-down "Course of Study" and the later curriculum of pre-vocational and vocational courses advocated by Cato Sells. The common thread was a conviction on the part of BIA officials that Indians, whether adults or children, were destined for subordinate positions in a country run by Anglo-Saxon whites. If Indian adults could not be trusted with the upbringing of their children, neither could Indian children aspire to be anything more than servants, housewives, or farmers or stock growers on their small allotments.

By allowing such racial ideologies to direct and limit education at the Rapid City Indian School and other boarding schools, the BIA forced Indian education into a mold of Indian-white conflict. Standing Bear went to Carlisle as a volunteer, albeit one who expected to be killed at any moment. When Rapid City opened in 1898, Indian children attended day schools, reservation boarding schools, and off-reservation schools under threat of force, represented by reservation superintendents and Indian police. Hostile to Indian cultures and suspicious of Indian parents, neither officials in Washington nor BIA employees in the field trusted Indian parents and children to see the value of government education. Rather than address Indian concerns and the limitations of the schools and their curriculums, educators enforced their conviction that they knew what was right for Indians with the disciplinarian's strap and the school and agency jails.

That exercise of power over Indian students and their families was a central fact of the Rapid City Indian School, in no small part responsible for its mixed legacy. Recalling the school many years after it closed, Eva Enos said, "That was a good school, I couldn't say nothing bad about it because it was run by good people." That was Rapid City as she knew it. Other students had good experiences, too. To see the better side of Rapid City, one has but to remember Nancy Schmidt's journey from the 1911 graduating class to the Rapid City High School and the State Normal School. Her success, and the successes of Mortimer Hernandez and Albert McGaa at the Pierre Oratory Contest or the Rapid City boys' and girls' basketball teams at the Indian Basketball Tournament in 1929, demonstrated the ability of the staff and especially the students to transcend the expectations of conflict that shaped the school.[5]

But Adolph Cuny's long months in the school jail and his flight across the Pine Ridge Reservation were a reminder of just how bitter that conflict could be. So, too, were Charley DeSheuquette's verbal battle with teacher Daisy Haines and the laundry accident that cost Sadie Plenty Holes the fingers of one hand. The deaths of James Means and Mark Sherman were part of Rapid City's legacy as well, as were the amputations of Paul Loves War's and Henry Bull's lower legs. The Rapid City Indian School was a place of suffering and joy alike, of defeat as well as achievement. That, perhaps, is how it should be remembered—as a place that was both good and bad, or neither, and in the end simply gone, living only in the memories of students who are fewer with each passing year.

NOTES

INTRODUCTION

1. Luther Standing Bear, *My People the Sioux*, ed. E. A. Brininstool, 123–24.

2. Ibid., 124.

3. In the nineteenth and early twentieth centuries, the bureau of the Interior Department that is now the Bureau of Indian Affairs (BIA) was usually known as the Indian Office. I have chosen to use the more recent designation because it is familiar and less likely to confuse.

4. Francis Paul Prucha, *The Great Father: The United States Government and the American Indians, Vol. II*, 632–40; Frederick E. Hoxie, "From Prison to Homeland: The Cheyenne River Indian Reservation before World War I," in Peter Iverson, ed., *The Plains Indians of the Twentieth Century*, 56–58; Frederick E. Hoxie, *Parading through History: The Making of the Crow Nation in America, 1805–1935*, 228–33.

5. Prucha, *The Great Father*, 659–71.

6. Ibid.; Janet A. McDonnell, *The Dispossession of the American Indian, 1887–1934*, 121.

7. Prucha, *The Great Father*, 646–49; Hoxie, "From Prison to Homeland," 59. For a complete discussion of Indian police and judges, see William T. Hagan, *Indian Police and Judges: Experiments in Acculturation and Control*.

8. For an excellent discussion of the development of federal Indian boarding schools, see David Wallace Adams, *Education for Extinction: American Indians and the Boarding School Experience, 1875–1928*.

9. Richard Henry Pratt, *Battlefield and Classroom: Four Decades with the American Indian, 1867–1904*, ed. Robert M. Utley, 104–35, 154–62.

10. Ibid., 191–204, 212–67; Francis Paul Prucha, ed., *Americanizing the American Indians: Writings by the "Friends of the Indian," 1880–1900*, 261; U.S. Congress, Senate, Committee on Indian Affairs, *Conduct and Management of Indian Schools, Etc.*, 57th Congress, 1st session, Senate document 201.

11. Prucha, *The Great Father*, 700–707; *Annual Report of the Commissioner of Indian Affairs, 1909* (hereafter cited as CIA Report), 78.

12. Prucha, *Americanizing the American Indians*, 222–223, 244.

13. Before his military service in the Civil War, Pratt worked as a tinsmith. He demonstrated no inclination later in life to return to the trade.

14. CIA Report, 1909, 78, 80.

15. Paula M. Nelson, *After the West Was Won: Homesteaders and Town-Builders in Western South Dakota, 1900–1917*, 14–23; Prucha, *The Great Father*, 867–70.

16. "The School of the Hills, Rapid City, South Dakota, 1922," Superintendents Subject Correspondence File (hereafter cited as SSCF) Box 9, School Annuals, Graduate Programs, School Paper file, Rapid City Indian School, Record Group 75 (hereafter cited as RG 75), National Archives—Central Plains Region (hereafter cited as NA—CPR).

CHAPTER 1. MANY ROADS TO RAPID

1. Nancy E. Ulargran to Superintendent, Rapid City Indian School, May 17, 1911, SSCF Box 6, Education and Administration 1911—Students Eligible file, Rapid City Indian School, RG 75, NA—CPR.

2. Adams, *Education for Extinction*, 210–11.

3. Brenda J. Child, "A Bitter Lesson: Native Americans and the Government Boarding School Experience, 1890–1940," 45–46.

4. K. Tsianina Lomawaima, *They Called It Prairie Light: The Story of the Chilocco Indian School*, 32–36.

5. In correspondence, Indian Office employees commonly referred to the Rapid City Indian School simply as "Rapid."

6. Standing Bear, *My People the Sioux*, 123–32, 162.

7. Prucha, *The Great Father*, 700–707.

8. Ibid., 815–17; "The Rosebud," *Rapid City Daily Journal*, June 25, 1904 (quotation).

9. Hoxie, "From Prison To Homeland," 59.

10. Though Congress discontinued spending for sectarian contract schools (all Catholic, after the withdrawal of the few Protestant schools from the contract system in 1892) in 1900, the BIA allowed Indian children to attend mission schools as alternatives to BIA schools.

11. Prucha, *The Great Father*, 731–36.

12. "Indian School Pupils," *Rapid City Daily Journal*, September 21, 1898; "Indian School Arrivals," *Rapid City Daily Journal*, September 27, 1898; Ralph P. Collins, Superintendent, "Report of School at Rapid City, S. Dak.," in CIA Report, 1899, 430–31; Sam B. Davis, Superintendent, "Report of School at Rapid City, S. Dak.," CIA Report, 1901, 570–71; David B. Miller, *Gateway to the Hills: An Illustrated History of Rapid City*, 33.

13. W. A. Jones, in CIA Report, 1903, 26–27; Prucha, *The Great Father*, 816–19.

14. Francis E. Leupp, in CIA Report, 1908, 16–17; Prucha, *The Great Father*, 819–20.

15. Francis E. Leupp, Education—Administration Circular No. 295, "Transfer of pupils under 14," May 18, 1909, General Correspondence Files (hereafter cited as GCF) Box 28, Decimal Classification (hereafter cited as DC) 820.2 Enrollment and Attendance—1909 file, Rapid City Indian School, RG 75, NA—CPR.

16. Ibid.

17. Jesse F. House, Superintendent, Rapid City Indian School, to the Commissioner of Indian Affairs (hereafter CIA), July 21, 1909, SSCF Box 2, Buildings and Equipment—Equipment file, School Lands subfile; F. H. Abbott, Acting CIA, to House, August 5, 1909, SSCF Box 6, Education and Administration file; House, "Enrollment of Pupils," to CIA, June 3, 1910, GCF Box 28, DC 820.2 Enrollment and Attendance—1910 file; all Rapid City Indian School, RG 75, NA—CPR.

18. C. M. Schwandt, School Social Worker, to Kirk K. Newport, Principal, Rapid City Indian School, August 9, 1932; Newport to Schwandt, August 12, 1932; both GCF Box 30, DC 820.2 Enrollment and Attendance—1932 file, Rapid City Indian School, RG 75, NA—CPR.

19. John R. Brennan, Agent, Pine Ridge Agency, to House, September 30, 1907; J. J. Duncan, Day School Inspector, Pine Ridge Agency, to Lawson Odle, in charge of Rapid City, October 22, 1907; both GCF Box 28, DC 820.2 Enrollment and Attendance—1907 file, Rapid City Indian School, RG 75, NA—CPR.

20. Adams, *Education for Extinction*, 214; Child, "A Bitter Lesson," 183–86; U.S. Congress, Senate, Committee on Indian Affairs, *Conduct and Management of Indian Schools, Etc.*

21. John A. Buntin, Superintendent, Tongue River Agency, to House, October 11, 1911, GCF Box 90, DC 842 Tongue River Agency file, Rapid City Indian School, RG 75, NA—CPR.

22. Mrs. Joseph Brown to J. R. Brennan, September 27, 1912, Pine Ridge Agency GCF 169, Superintendent's Education Correspondence Box 952, J. R. Brennan Correspondence 1912 file, Pine Ridge Agency; Felix Eagle Feather to House, February 22, 1910, GCF Box 28, DC 820.2 Enrollment and Attendance—1910 file, Rapid City Indian School; Charlie B. Twiss to House, February 12, 1911, SSCF Box 6 Education Administration, 1911—Students Eligible file, Rapid City Indian School; all RG 75, NA—CPR; Eva Enos interview with author, 1998. Brown's daughters were probably Louise and Rosie Brown.

23. Nicholas Ruleau to House, September 12, 1910, SSCF Box 7 Education, a-2-10 "Nicholas Ruleau" 1910 file, Rapid City Indian School; Alfred Black Bear to House, July 29, 1918, Pine Ridge Agency Education Records GCF 196, Box 1150, Correspondence Rapid City, S.D. School, July 9, 1917–Dec. 15, 1917, file, Pine Ridge Agency; A. Hankaas to Superintendent, undated, SSCF Box 7 Education, a-2-68 "Hankass [sic]" 1910 file, Rapid City Indian School; all RG 75, NA—CPR. Black Bear's letter does not mention his daughter's name.

24. F. H. Abbott, Acting CIA, to House, August 6, 1909, SSCF Box 6, Education Administration file, Rapid City Indian School, RG 75, NA—CPR.

25. House to Harvey B. Peairs, Supervisor in Charge of Indian Schools, July 18, 1910; Peairs to House, November 10, 1910; House to Peairs, November 15, 1910; all SSCF Box 7 Education, a-2-56 Education Related Correspondence 1912 file, Rapid City Indian School, RG 75, NA—CPR.

26. Ibid.

27. Correspondence between George E. Peters, Principal, Rapid City Indian School, and House, August 10–18, 1917, GCF Box 12, DC 161 (P–R), "Peters, George E." file, Rapid City Indian School, RG 75, NA—CPR.

28. House to W. C. Dunn, Superintendent, Sisseton Indian Agency, August 31, 1917, GCF Box 12, DC 161 (P–R), "Y. Robe, Chauncey" file; Chauncey Yellow Robe, Disciplinarian, Rapid City Indian School, to House, September 12, 1917, GCF Box 28, DC 820.2 Enrollment and Attendance—1917 file; both Rapid City Indian School, RG 75, NA—CPR.

29. James H. McGregor, Superintendent, Cheyenne River Agency, to House, December 3, 1918, GCF Box 29, DC 820.2 Enrollment and Attendance—1918 file, Rapid City Indian School, RG 75, NA—CPR.

30. House to McGregor, September 26, 1918, Cheyenne River Agency Box 429, Rapid City School Correspondence (1915 to 1920) file, Cheyenne River Agency; House to McGregor, December 10, 1918, GCF Box 29, DC 820.2 Enrollment and Attendance—1918 file, Rapid City Indian School; both RG 75, NA—CPR.

31. Ibid.

32. Ibid.

33. C. D. Munro, Superintendent, Cheyenne River Agency, to S. A. M. Young, Superintendent, Rapid City Indian School, July 24, 1922, GCF Box 29, DC 820.2 Enrollment and Attendance—1922 file; Principal (no name given), Rosebud Boarding School, to Elizabeth Whitehat, August 14, 1924, GCF Box 30, DC 820.2 Enrollment and Attendance—1924 file; both Rapid City Indian School, RG 75, NA—CPR.

34. Young to the Agent, Chicago & North Western Railway Company, October 3, 1922, GCF Box 29, DC 820.2 Enrollment and Attendance—1922 file; Young to Superintendents, September 18, 1923, GCF Box 30, DC 820.2 Enrollment and Attendance—1923 file; both Rapid City Indian School, RG 75, NA—CPR.

35. Susie Battle to House, August 22, 1917, GCF Box 88, DC 842 Pine Ridge Agency 1913–16, Rapid City Indian School, RG 75, NA—CPR; "Catalog and Synopsis of Courses, United States Indian School, Rapid City, South Dakota, 1916–17"; "The School of the Hills, U.S. Indian School, Rapid City, S.D., August, 1923"; both SSCF Box 9, School Annuals, Graduate Programs, School Paper file, Rapid City Indian School, RG 75, NA—CPR. Despite its title, this file contains no school papers. There is no evidence that Rapid City produced a school paper.

36. Frank Bullard to Young, June 1, 1924; Young to Bullard, June 4, 1924; Young to E. W. Jermark, Superintendent, Pine Ridge Agency, February 28, 1925; all GCF Box 6, DC 161 (A–B), "Frank B. Bullard" file; Sophie E. Picard to House, July 2, 1916; House to Picard, July 8, 1916; "Record of Sophie E. Picard"; all GCF Box 12, GCF 161 (P–R), "Picard, Sophie" file, Rapid City Indian School, RG 75, NA—CPR.

37. Reverend Sam Rouillard to Young, August 23, 1922; Young to Rouillard, August 25, 1922; both GCF Box 13, DC 161 (R–S), "Rouillard, Isaac" file, Rapid City Indian School, RG 75, NA—CPR.

38. John J. Farrar to Mr. Blish, Superintendent of Day Schools, Pine Ridge Agency, September 21, 1917, Pine Ridge Agency Education Records GCF 196, Box 1150, Correspondence Rapid City, S.D., School, July 9, 1917–Dec. 15, 1917, file, Pine Ridge Agency; Lucy Cottier to House, August 29, 1910; House to Cottier, September 5, 1910; both SSCF

Box 7, Education, a-2-54 "John Cottier" 1910 file, Rapid City Indian School; all RG 75, NA—CPR.

39. Child, "A Bitter Lesson," 45–50.

40. Nancy E. Ulargran to House, May 17, 1911, SSCF Box 6 Education Administration, 1911—Students Eligible file; "Report of Attendance, Quarter Ending December 31st, 1912," GCF Box 27, DC 820.0 "Quarterly Report Ending December 31st, 1912" file; "Report of Attendance, Quarter Ending December 31st, 1917," GCF Box 27, DC 820.0 "Quarterly Report Ending December 31st, 1917" file; all Rapid City Indian School, RG 75, NA—CPR.

41. W. H. Blish, Day School Inspector, Pine Ridge Agency, April 14, 1922; Young to Blish, April 17, 1922; both GCF Box 29, DC 840.2 Enrollment and Attendance—1922 file, Rapid City Indian School, RG 75, NA—CPR.

42. Julia McGaa to Superintendent, Pine Ridge Agency, July 28, 1930; Josephine Provost to Day School Inspector, August 16, 1930; George A. Day, Senior Clerk and Special Disbursing Agent, Rapid City Indian School, to C. P. Detwiler, Acting Superintendent, Pine Ridge Agency, August 25, 1930; all Pine Ridge Agency General Records, Main Decimal Files Box 687, 806.26 Rapid City 1 of 3 file, Pine Ridge Agency, RG 75, NA—CPR.

43. C. H. Gensler, Superintendent, Lower Brule Agency, to Young, November 2, 1922; Young to Gensler, January 16, 1923; both GCF Box 88, DC 842 Lower Brule Agency file, Rapid City Indian School, NA—CPR.

44. Theodore Sharp, Superintendent, Flathead Agency, to E. B. Meritt, CIA, March 26, 1920; Meritt to Sharp, April 10, 1920; Sharp to House, April 16, 1920; all GCF Box 29, DC 820.2 Enrollment and Attendance—1920 file; "Report of Attendance, Quarter Ending December 31, 1922," GCF Box 27, DC 820.0 "Quarterly Report Ending December 31, 1922" file; all Rapid City Indian School, RG 75, NA—CPR.

45. Henry J. McQuigg, Superintendent, Turtle Mountain Indian Agency, to Young, December 26, 1924; Young to McQuigg, December 29, 1924; both GCF Box 30, DC 840.2 Enrollment and Attendance—1924 file, Rapid City Indian School, RG 75, NA—CPR.

46. McQuigg to Sharon R. Mote, Superintendent, Rapid City Indian School, January 29, 1926, with notes written on the letter by Mote and Theresa C. Kaufman, Matron, Rapid City Indian School, GCF Box 91, DC 842 Turtle Mountain Agency file; Young to the Rice District, United Charities of St. Paul, December 10, 1930, GCF Box 24, DC 710 Sanitation file; Young to Laverne Bonser, December 8, 1931, GCF Box 30, DC 820.2 Enrollment and Attendance—1932 file; all Rapid City Indian School, RG 75, NA—CPR.

47. *Abstract of the Thirteenth Census of the United States*, 74; *Abstract of the Fourteenth Census of the United States*, 65. Census enumerators counted only 81 Indians in Pennington County, in which Rapid City was located, in 1900. By 1930, the total had risen to 300, a number which still was almost certainly low. Lakotas from the Pine Ridge, Rosebud, and Cheyenne River Reservations often camped outside Rapid City on a seasonal basis. *Thirteenth Census of the United States, Vol. III: Population*, 710; *Fifteenth Census of the United States, Vol. III, Part 2: Population*, 844.

CHAPTER 2. PROVIDING FOR THE CHILDREN

1. C. H. Gensler, Superintendent, Lower Brule Agency, to S. A. M. Young, Superintendent, Rapid City Indian School, October 20, 1922, GCF Box 88, DC 842 Lower Brule Agency file, Rapid City Indian School, RG 75, NA—CPR.

2. Young to Gensler, October 25, 1922, GCF Box 88, DC 842 Lower Brule Agency file, Rapid City Indian School, RG 75, NA—CPR.

3. Standing Bear, *My People the Sioux*, 21–23, 139–40; "Government Indian School," *Rapid City Daily Journal*, January 27, 1906. In later years, boys and girls ate at the same tables at the Rapid City Indian School.

4. Interview 008, American Indian Research Project, 8–9.

5. Ibid., 1–2, 10.

6. Jesse F. House, Superintendent, Rapid City Indian School, to Major John R. Brennan, Superintendent, Pine Ridge Agency, November 25, 1911, Pine Ridge Agency Education Records GCF 196, Box 1150, Correspondence Rapid City Indian School, "Oct. 18, 1910–June 21, 1912" file, Pine Ridge Agency, RG 75, NA—CPR.

7. Undated, handwritten menu, placed with materials dating from 1913–14, SSCF Box 8, Curriculum 1909–18 file, Rapid City Indian School, RG 75, NA—CPR.

8. Interview 719, American Indian Research Project, 1. Sara Buffalo does not appear on school rosters of the period; presumably she adopted her husband's last name.

9. Menu for week of March 10 to March 16, 1929, GCF Box 26, DC 781 Menus file, Rapid City Indian School, RG 75, NA—CPR; Lewis Meriam et al., *The Problem of Indian Administration* (hereafter cited as Meriam Report), 328.

10. Meriam Report, 328; E. W. Jermark, Superintendent, Pine Ridge Agency, to Sharon R. Mote, Superintendent, Rapid City Indian School,

November 20, 1928, Pine Ridge Agency General Records Main Decimal File Box 687, 806.26 Rapid City 2 of 3 file, Pine Ridge Agency, RG 75, NA—CPR.

11. Basil H. Johnston, *Indian School Days*, 25–26, 32–40, 49.

12. Memorandum, Sharon R. Mote, Superintendent, to Theresa C. Kaufman, Matron, February 20, 1928, GCF Box 26, DC 871 Memos file, Rapid City Indian School, RG 75, NA—CPR.

13. "Milk Lunch Pupils.—January, 1926," Mote, January 13, 1926, GCF Box 26, DC 781 Menus file; Memorandum, Mote, September 5, 1928, GCF Box 3, DC 102 Memoranda file; both Rapid City Indian School, RG 75, NA—CPR.

14. "RAPID CITY INDIAN SCHOOL, Rapid City, South Dakota," Carl Stevens, Supervisor of Schools, January 3–10, 1924, 2, SSCF Box 1, Administration and Control file, "Carl Stevens" subfile; Mote to CIA, February 5, 1928, GCF Box 14, DC 161 (S–T), "District Superintendent" file; both Rapid City Indian School, RG 75, NA—CPR.

15. "RAPID CITY INDIAN SCHOOL, Rapid City, South Dakota," Stevens, January 3–10, 1924, 2, 6; "RAPID CITY INDIAN SCHOOL, Rapid City, South Dakota," Stevens, January 6–12, 1925, 2; both SSCF Box 1, Administration and Control file, "Carl Stevens" subfile, Rapid City Indian School, RG 75, NA—CPR; Meriam Report, 328.

16. "RAPID CITY INDIAN SCHOOL, Rapid City, South Dakota," Stevens, January 3–10, 1924, 2, 5; "RAPID CITY INDIAN SCHOOL, Rapid City, South Dakota," Stevens, January 6–12, 1925, 6; both SSCF Box 1, Administration and Control file, "Carl Stevens" subfile, Rapid City Indian School, RG 75, NA—CPR.

17. "RAPID CITY INDIAN SCHOOL, Rapid City, South Dakota," Stevens, January 6–12, 1925, 6, SSCF Box 1, Administration and Control file, "Carl Stevens" subfile, Rapid City Indian School, RG 75, NA—CPR.

18. Robert A. Trennert, Jr., *The Phoenix Indian School: Forced Assimilation in Arizona, 1891–1935*, 115.

19. "Catalog and Synopsis of Courses, United States Indian School, Rapid City, South Dakota, 1916–1917," SSCF Box 9, School Annuals, Graduate Programs, School Paper file, Rapid City Indian School, RG 75, NA—CPR; Trennert, *The Phoenix Indian School*, 106, 108, 117–18, 121–22; Lomawaima, *They Called It Prairie Light*, 90–92; Eva Enos interview, Warm Valley Historical Project, 30–31.

20. Lomawaima, *They Called It Prairie Light*, 95–97; Eva Enos interview, Warm Valley Historical Project, 30–31.

21. Michael C. Coleman, *American Indian Children at School, 1850–1930*, 80–83; House to Mrs. Charles N. Snyder (no other name give), September 4, 1911, GCF Box 28, DC 820.2 Enrollment and Attendance—1911 file, Rapid City Indian School, RG 75, NA—CPR; Eva Enos interview, Warm Valley Historical Project, 29.

22. F. A. Andersen, Clerk, to Olson & Co., December 11, 1911, GCF Box 9, DC 161 (H–K), "Kills Plenty, Silas" file, Rapid City Indian School, RG 75, NA—CPR.

23. Jesse F. House, Superintendent, to Paul R. Vincent, November 5, 1917, GCF Box 28, DC 820.2 Enrollment and Attendance—1917 file; H. M. Tidwell, Superintendent, Pine Ridge Agency, to House, October 14, 1920, GCF Box 89, DC 842 Pine Ridge Agency 1917–21 file; both Rapid City Indian School, RG 75, NA—CPR.

24. House to H. M. Tidwell, Superintendent, Pine Ridge Agency, October 20, 1920, GCF Box 89, DC 842 Pine Ridge Agency 1917–21 file, Rapid City Indian School, RG 75, NA—CPR.

25. Lomawaima, *They Called It Prairie Light*, 90–92; Eva Enos interview, Warm Valley Historical Project, 29–30.

26. House to John B. Brown, Superintendent, Phoenix Indian School, October 30, 1919, GCF Box 85, Agencies and Schools Not Otherwise Classified file, Rapid City Indian School, RG 75, NA—CPR.

27. Superintendent Sharon R. Mote to the Sigmund Eisner Company, December 1, 1925, DC 826 Rotary Club, Boy Scouts, etc., file; Mote to the Lewis Company, October 24, 1925, DC 826.1 Student Activities Association file; both GCF Box 85, Rapid City Indian School, RG 75, NA—CPR.

28. Mote to W. E. Dunn, Superintendent, Crow Creek Agency, October 2, 1925, GCF Box 86, DC 842 Crow Creek Agency file, Rapid City Indian School, RG 75, NA—CPR.

29. Mote to the Lewis Company, October 24, 1925, GCF Box 85, DC 826.1 Student Activities Association file, Rapid City Indian School, RG 75, NA—CPR.

30. "RAPID CITY INDIAN SCHOOL, Rapid City, South Dakota," Stevens, January 6–12, 1925, SSCF Box 1, Administration and Control file, "Carl Stevens, Supervisor" subfile, Rapid City Indian School, RG 75, NA—CPR.

31. E. D. Mossman, Superintendent, Standing Rock Agency, to Other Superintendents, July 27, 1927, GCF Box 90, DC 842 Standing Rock Agency 1926–27 file, Rapid City Indian School, RG 75, NA—CPR.

32. Ibid.

33. Memorandum, Mote to Theresa C. Kaufman and Lottie Cornelius, March 27, 1929, GCF Box 3, DC 102 Memoranda 1929 file, Rapid City Indian School, RG 75, NA—CPR.

34. Hoxie, *Parading through History*, 171–74.

35. Adams, *Education for Extinction*, 131–35.

36. U.S. Congress, Senate, Committee on Indian Affairs, *Conduct and Management of Indian Schools, Etc.*

37. Mote to Robe and Wold, October 13, 1927, GCF Box 1, DC 040 Publicity file, Rapid City Indian School, RG 75, NA—CPR.

38. CIA Report, 1901, 570.

39. Julius Henke, Day School Inspector, Rosebud Agency, to House, August 19, 1912; House to Henke, August 22, 1912; both GCF Box 28, DC 820.2 Enrollment and Attendance—1912 file, Rapid City Indian School, RG 75, NA—CPR.

40. "Form of Proposal for Employment as Contract Physician in the United States Indian Service," undated; Order of Employment, Chief, Division of Appointments, Department of the Interior, to H. J. T. Ince, December 23, 1926; both GCF Box 9, DC 161 (H–K), "Ince, H. J. T." file, Rapid City Indian School, RG 75, NA—CPR.

41. House to CIA, September 30, 1921; E. B. Meritt, CIA, to Young, April 6, 1922; Young to Meritt, April 25, 1922; all GCF Box 9, DC 161 (H–K), "Ince, H. J. T." file, Rapid City Indian School, RG 75, NA—CPR.

42. William H. McNeill, *Plagues and Peoples*, 255.

43. House to Henry M. Tidwell, Superintendent, Pine Ridge Agency, October 5, 1918; House to CIA, October 5, 1918; E. B. Meritt, Assistant CIA, to House, October 8, 1918; all SSCF Box 10, Spanish Influenza Epidemic—1918 file, Rapid City Indian School, RG 75, NA—CPR.

44. L. L. Culp, Special Physician, to CIA, November 11, 1918; House to W. P. Marshall, November 11, 1918; both SSCF Box 10, Spanish Influenza Epidemic—1918 file, Rapid City Indian School, RG 75, NA—CPR.

45. Culp to CIA, November 11, 1918; House to Marshall, November 11, 1918; C. J. Crandall, Superintendent, Pierre Indian School, to House, October 23, 1918; Crandall to House, October 31, 1918; all SSCF Box 10, Spanish Influenza Epidemic—1918 file, Rapid City Indian School, RG 75, NA—CPR.

46. House to CIA, December 2, 1919; House to CIA, December 5, 1919; House to CIA, December 12, 1919; House to CIA, December 16, 1919; all SSCF Box 10, "Reports ECT. [*sic*] Epidemic of Smallpox & Scarlet Fever—1919" file, Rapid City Indian School, RG 75, NA—CPR.

47. F. J. Austin, Health Officer, Pennington County, South Dakota, to Raymond E. Staley, March 23, 1933, GCF Box 24, DC 700 Health and Social Relations 1930–33 file; Mote to all employees, "Health Week," February 12, 1926; "Health Songs," undated; Isabel Rouillard, "Health Record," February 22–28, no year given; GCF Box 24, DC 700 Sanitation file, Rapid City Indian School, RG 75, NA—CPR.

48. Mote to Jacob Breid, Superintendent, Sac and Fox Sanitarium, March 25, 1926; Mote to Breid, March 3, 1927; GCF Box 90, DC 842 Sac and Fox Agency; Mote to CIA, April 26, 1927, GCF Box 24, DC 700 Health and Social Relations 1925–29 file; Rapid City Indian School, RG 75, NA—CPR.

49. Emil Krulish, District Medical Director, "Rapid City Indian School, South Dakota," April 12, 1927, GCF Box 14, DC 161 (S–T), "District Medical Officer Dr. Emil Krulish" file; Krulish, "Rapid City Indian School, South Dakota, Report on Medical Services," March 26, 1928, GCF Box 24, DC 700 Health and Social Relations—1925–29 file; Mote to Dr. H. J. T. Ince, April 11, 1927, GCF Box 9, DC 161 (H–K), "Ince, H. J. T." file; Rapid City Indian School, RG 75, NA—CPR.

CHAPTER 3. CURRICULUM

1. Atkins quoted in Prucha, *Americanizing the American Indians*, 203.

2. Ibid., 201–4.

3. Lawrence A. Cremin, *The Transformation of the School: Progressivism in American Education, 1876–1957*, 66–73.

4. Ibid., 23–34.

5. Larry Cuban, *How Teachers Taught: Constancy and Change in American Classrooms, 1880–1990*, 24, 122. Cuban uses the definition of rural schools as schools in districts outside cities or towns of 4,000 or more population. One-room schools and one-teacher schools were not necessarily identical categories, for one-room schools might employ more than one teacher. A one-teacher school, though, would almost necessarily have been a one-room school.

6. Ibid., 24–26, 122–26.

7. Albert H. Kneale, *Indian Agent*, 25–26, 32–37, 39, 43–44, 47–48, 52–53. The BIA hired Albert Kneale to teach school and Edith to serve as housekeeper, a common arrangement for married employees.

8. CIA Report, 1898, 26; Ralph P. Collins, Superintendent, Rapid City Indian School, "Report of School at Rapid City, S. Dak.," CIA Report, 1899,

396–97; "The Indian School," *Rapid City Daily Journal*, October 2, 1898; "A Fine Institution," *Rapid City Daily Journal*, February 15, 1900; Cuban, *How Teachers Taught*, 24.

9. Sam B. Davis, Superintendent, Rapid City Indian School, "Report of School at Rapid City, S. Dak.," CIA Report, 1901, 570; "A Model School," *Rapid City Daily Journal*, November 15, 1901; "At the Indian School," *Rapid City Daily Journal*, August 13, 1903; J. F. House, Superintendent, "Report of School at Rapid City, S. Dak.," CIA Report, 1905, 434; "Government Indian School," *Rapid City Daily Journal*, January 27, 1906; "Catalog and Synopsis of Courses, United States Indian School, Rapid City, South Dakota, 1916–17," SSCF Box 9, School Annuals, Graduate Programs, School Paper file, Rapid City Indian School, RG 75, NA—CPR.

10. Peyton Carter, Supervisor, to CIA, February 1, 1921, SSCF Box 1 Administration and Control, "Carl Stevens, Supervisor" file; "The School of the Hills, Rapid City, South Dakota, 1922," SSCF Box 9, School Annuals, Graduate Programs, School Paper file; both Rapid City Indian School, RG 75, NA—CPR.

11. K. Tsianina Lomawaima, "Education for Domesticity: Formation of a Standardized Curriculum in B.I.A. Schools," unpublished paper presented at the American Society for Ethnohistory Meeting, November 13, 1992, 4–5. This article will be published in a forthcoming education issue of the *Journal of American Indian Education*.

12. Ibid., 6–10; Estelle Reel, Superintendent of Indian Schools, "Course of Study for Indian Schools," CIA Report, 1901, 419.

13. Frederick E. Hoxie, *A Final Promise: The Campaign to Assimilate the Indians, 1880–1920*, 190–204; Reel, "Course of Study," 419.

14. Reel, "Course of Study," 426–27.

15. Ibid., 439.

16. Cuban, *How Teachers Taught*, 6–8.

17. Reel, "Course of Study," 418–57; Cuban, *How Teachers Taught*, 38–45.

18. Cuban, *How Teachers Taught*, 142–45; Hoxie, *A Final Promise*, 198–206.

19. "Conference between Superintendent House and Mr. McBrien," undated but probably 1916, GCF Box 3, DC 112 Circulars file; "Report on Supervision of Individual Instructors," November 5, 1914, GCF Box 6, DC 161 (A–B), "Bishop, Elizabeth R." file; both Rapid City Indian School, RG 75, NA—CPR.

20. "Report on Supervision of Individual Instructors," March 15, 1916, GCF Box 14, DC 161 (S–T), "Turner, Olive Miss" file, Rapid City Indian School, RG 75, NA—CPR.

21. "Conference between Superintendent House and Mr. McBrien," undated, GCF Box 3, DC 112 Circulars file; Robert B. Irons, Superintendent, Rapid City Public Schools, Rapid City, South Dakota, to United States Indian School, March 19, 1917, GCF Box 28, DC 820.2 Enrollment and Attendance—1916 file; both Rapid City Indian School, RG 75, NA—CPR.

22. Willis E. Johnson, President, Northern Normal and Industrial School, Aberdeen, South Dakota, to House, September 14, 1917; Superintendent (name illegible), Rosebud Agency, to House, September 20, 1917; Superintendent (name illegible), Rosebud Agency, to CIA, September 20, 1917; Johnson to House, October 9, 1917; Nancy Schmidt to House, October 23, 1917; all GCF Box 13, DC 161 (R–S), "Schmidt, Nancy" file, Rapid City Indian School, RG 75, NA—CPR.

23. Schmidt to House, October 23, 1917; "Record of Nancy Arrow" (employee record), May 22, 1926; both GCF Box 13, DC 161 (R–S), "Schmidt, Nancy" file; Arthur T. Arrow to S. A. M. Young, Superintendent, Rapid City Indian School, June 11, 1923, GCF Box 88, DC 842 Haskell Institute file; Sharon R. Mote, Superintendent, Rapid City Indian School, to Harvey B. Peairs, General Superintendent, October 4, 1926, GCF Box 14, DC 161 (S–T), "Gen. Supt. H. B. Peairs" file; "Record of Arthur T. Arrow" (employee record), August 14, 1926; Charles H. Burke, CIA, to Mote, January 27, 1927; both GCF Box 14, DC 161 (S–T), "Arthur Arrow" file; Raymond E. Staley, Superintendent, Rapid City Indian School, to W. O. Roberts, Superintendent, Rosebud Agency, June 3, 1933, GCF Box 90, DC 842 Rosebud Agency 1932–33 file; all Rapid City Indian School, RG 75, NA—CPR. Arthur T. Arrow was dismissed from his job as clerk at the Pipestone Agency on charges of misconduct. Examining Arrow's books after his departure, the BIA alleged that he had embezzled about $460 and referred the case to the Justice Department, which apparently took no action. On learning that Arrow was employed at the Rapid City Indian School, CIA Burke ordered him fired and later expelled from employee housing and barred from the campus, which probably ended Nancy Arrow's employment, too. She died in the winter of 1932–33.

24. "News Item," Department of the Interior, Office of Indian Affairs, undated, SSCF Box 8, Curriculum 1909–18 file, Rapid City Indian School, RG 75, NA—CPR.

25. "Catalog and Synopsis of Courses, United States Indian School, Rapid City, South Dakota, 1916–17," 12, SSCF Box 9, School Annuals, Graduate Programs, School Paper file; "Conference between Superintendent House and Mr. McBrien," undated, GCF Box 3, DC 112 Circulars

file; House to Charles F. Peirce, Superintendent, Pierre Indian School, May 31, 1921, GCF Box 87, DC 842 Flandreau Indian School file; all Rapid City Indian School, RG 75, NA—CPR.

26. Carl Stevens, Supervisor of Schools, "Report, Rapid City Indian School, Rapid City, South Dakota," January 6–12, 1925, SSCF Box 1 Administration and Control, "Carl Stevens Supervisor" file; Mary Stewart to CIA, May 11, 1927; telegram, E. B. Meritt, Assistant CIA, to Mote, August 23, 1927; both GCF Box 13, DC 161 (R–S), "Stewart, Mary" file; all Rapid City Indian School, RG 75, NA—CPR. Assistant Commissioner E. B. Meritt transferred Stewart to Haskell on August 23, 1927.

27. Meriam Report, 374–77.

28. Pratt, *Battlefield and Classroom*, 116–27.

29. Ibid., 190–204; Adams, *Education for Extinction*, 44–48; David Wallace Adams, "Education in Hues: Red and Black at Hampton Institute, 1878–1893," *South Atlantic Quarterly* 76:2 (Spring 1977): 159–76; Donal F. Lindsey, *Indians at Hampton Institute, 1877–1923*, 51–53, 70–76, 107.

30. Adams, "Education in Hues," 159–76; Robert A. Trennert, Jr., "Educating Indian Girls at Nonreservation Boarding Schools, 1878–1920," *Western Historical Quarterly* 13:3 (July 1982): 271–90.

31. Coleman, *American Indian Children at School*, 105–15; Trennert, "Educating Indian Girls at Nonreservation Boarding Schools," 271–90; Lomawaima, *They Called It Prairie Light*, 65–67, 81–82.

32. "A Fine Institution," *Rapid City Daily Journal*, February 15, 1900.

33. "Catalog and Synopsis of Courses, United States Indian School, Rapid City, South Dakota, 1916–1917," SSCF Box 9, School Annuals, Graduate Programs, School Paper file, Rapid City Indian School, RG 75, NA—CPR.

34. Ibid.; House to O. H. Lipps, Superintendent, Carlisle Indian School, February 10, 1916; "Vocational Course at Rapid City Indian School," House to Cato Sells, CIA, April 4, 1916; both SSCF Box 8, Curriculum 1909–18 file, Rapid City Indian School, RG 75, NA—CPR.

35. Circular No. 1069, "Directions: New Course of Study for Indian Schools," January 13, 1916, SSCF Box 8, Curriculum 1909–18 file; "Catalog and Synopsis of Courses, United States Indian School, Rapid City, South Dakota, 1916–1917," SSCF Box 9, School Annuals, Graduate Programs, School Paper file; both Rapid City Indian School, RG 75, NA—CPR.

36. Sells to House, March 31, 1916, SSCF Box 8, Curriculum 1909–18 file, Rapid City Indian School, RG 75, NA—CPR.

37. "Course of Study, Rapid City Indian School," House to Sells, April 8, 1916; "Vocational Course at Rapid City School," House to Sells, April 4,

1916; both SSCF Box 8, Curriculum 1909–18 file, Rapid City Indian School, RG 75, NA—CPR.

38. Sells to House, April 20, 1916; "Course of Study, Rapid City Indian School," House to Sells, April 8, 1916; both SSCF Box 8, Curriculum 1909–18 file, Rapid City Indian School, RG 75, NA—CPR.

39. "Farm Carpentry," May 22–27 (no year), GCF Box 12, DC 161 (P–R), "Rasque, George M." file, Rapid City Indian School, RG 75, NA—CPR.

40. "Vocational Record Card. Subject: Sewing," GCF Box 8, DC 161 (F–H), "Hawkins, Agnes" file, Rapid City Indian School, RG 75, NA—CPR.

41. "Report of Attendance, Quarter Ending December 31, 1922," GCF Box 27, DC 820.0 "Quarterly Report Ending—December 31, 1922" file; "Vocational Record Card. Subject: Sewing"; "Vocational Record Card. Subject: Kitchen Gardening"; both GCF Box 8, DC 161 (F–H), "Hawkins, Agnes" file; all Rapid City Indian School, RG 75, NA—CPR.

42. Margaret P. Coverston, Seamstress, "Work for Sewing and Mending Room," May 8, 1916, GCF Box 7, DC 161 (C–E), "Coverston, Margaret P." file; F. L. Hoyt, Principal, "Report on Class in Nursing," May 5, 1916, SSCF Box 8, Curriculum 1909–18 file; both Rapid City Indian School, RG 75, NA—CPR.

43. Eva Enos interview with author, 1998; House to Major John R. Brennan, Superintendent, Pine Ridge Agency, April 17, 1910, SSCF Box 9, Miscellaneous Student Matters 1910–14 file; Honorable Harry L. Gandy, Member of Congress, to House, May 25, 1915; House to Gandy, May 26, 1915; "Claim for Compensation to Injured Employee," March 25, 1915; GCF Box 12, DC 161 (P–R), "Provost, Alma" file; Rapid City Indian School, RG 75, NA—CPR. Congressman Gandy, in Rapid City at the time, made inquiry to House after hearing of the injuries to Provost and Blackman.

44. Meriam Report, 374–76.

45. Lomawaima, 18–19; Meriam Report, 383; C. F. Hawke, Chief Clerk, BIA, to House, October 9, 1909; Chief Education Division (name illegible) to House, January 19, 1910; both SSCF Box 6, Education Administration file, Rapid City Indian School, RG 75, NA—CPR.

46. C. F. Hawke, Second Assistant Commissioner, BIA, to House, July 14, 1910, GCF Box 6, DC 161 (A–B), "Brown, Edward" file; "Sioux-Form 4," January 15, 1912; "Persons of Indian Blood Employed at Rapid City School, S.D.," March 31, 1912; GCF Box 22, DC 226.6 Salaries 1911–24 file; House to J. J. Duncan, Day School Inspector, Pine Ridge Agency, January 15, 1915, GCF Box 88, DC 842 Pine Ridge Agency file; all Rapid City Indian School, RG 75, NA—CPR.

47. "Record of Margaret Clifford," April 1, 1915, GCF Box 7, DC 161 (G–E), "Miss Margaret Clifford" file; "Record of Jessie Bissonette," August 18, 1916, GCF Box 14, DC 161 (S–T), "Twiss, Jessie B." file; "Efficiency Report," Jessie Bissonette, SSCF Box 5, Officers and Employees—Misc. ER's 1917; "Record of Mrs. Mary Primeau," July 1, 1921, GCF Box 12, DC 161 (P–R), "Mrs. Mary Primeau" file; "Efficiency Report," Mary Primeaux [sic], November 6, 1920, SSCF Box 5, "Officers & Employees—Misc. ER's 1920"; Superintendent Raymond E. Staley to James H. McGregor, Superintendent, Pine Ridge Agency, June 5, 1933, GCF Box 89, DC 842 Pine Ridge Agency 1930–33 file; all Rapid City Indian School, RG 75, NA—CPR.

48. Samuel Eagle Shield to House, January 1, 1916, GCF Box 28, DC 820.2 Enrollment and Attendance—1916 file; "Record of Benjamin Black Fox," undated, GCF Box 10, DC 161 (A–B), "Black Fox, Benjamin" file; Superintendent Raymond E. Staley to James H. McGregor, Superintendent, Pine Ridge Agency, June 5, 1933, GCF Box 89, DC 842 Pine Ridge Agency 1930–33 file; all Rapid City Indian School, RG 75, NA—CPR.

49. "Record of Jesse H. Rouillard," December 1, 1924; Rouillard to Mote, September 27, 1926; Young to Mote, March 30, 1928; all GCF Box 13, DC 161 (R–S), "Rouillard, Jesse H." file; Superintendent Raymond E. Staley to James H. McGregor, Superintendent, Pine Ridge Agency, June 5, 1933, GCF Box 89, DC 842 Pine Ridge Agency 1930–33 file; all Rapid City Indian School, RG 75, NA—CPR.

50. "Conference between Superintendent House and Mr. McBrien," undated but probably 1916, GCF Box 3, DC 112 Circulars file, Rapid City Indian School, RG 75, NA—CPR.

51. Sara Buffalo interview, Tape 719, American Indian Research Project, 2; Winnie St. Clair interview, Warm Valley Historical Project, 20–21.

CHAPTER 4. CYCLES OF DAYS AND YEARS

1. "Council of Nations," *Rapid City Daily Journal*, June 25, 1904; "Indians Coming," *Rapid City Daily Journal*, June 29, 1904; "July Fourth Celebration," *Rapid City Daily Journal*, June 30, 1904; "The Indian Camp," *Rapid City Daily Journal*, July 1, 1904.

2. Giant powder was a type of explosive used in mining. Rapid City's economy was closely linked to Black Hills mining, and explosives were more easily acquired for the Fourth of July salutes than the traditional cannon.

3. "July Fourth Celebration," *Rapid City Daily Journal*, June 30, 1904; "Independence Day," *Rapid City Daily Journal*, July 6, 1904.

4. "Independence Day," *Rapid City Daily Journal*, July 6, 1904; "Long Drawn Out," *Rapid City Daily Journal*, July 7, 1904.

5. "Independence Day," *Rapid City Daily Journal*, July 6, 1904; "The Indian Camp," *Rapid City Daily Journal*, July 1, 1904; "Indian Celebration," *Rapid City Daily Journal*, July 4, 1903; "An Interesting Visit," *Rapid City Daily Journal*, July 8, 1903.

6. J. J. Duncan, Day School Inspector, Pine Ridge Reservation, to Jesse F. House, Superintendent, Rapid City Indian School, September 28, 1909, SSCF Box 1 Administration and Control, "J. J. Duncan–Pine Ridge Day School Inspector" file, Rapid City Indian School, RG 75, NA—CPR.

7. C. C. Covey, Superintendent, Rosebud Agency, to Farmers and Day School Teachers, August 30, 1917, GCF Box 28, DC 820.2 Enrollment and Attendance—1917 file; J. J. Duncan, Principal and Day School Inspector, Cheyenne River Agency, to House, September 22, 1917, GCF Box 85, DC 842 Cheyenne River Agency 1913–18 file; both Rapid City Indian School, RG 75, NA—CPR.

8. House to J. L. McBrien, Special Officer, Interior Department, October 30, 1916, GCF Box 28, DC 820.2 Enrollment and Attendance—1916 file; House to Charles F. Peirce, Superintendent, Flandreau Indian School, July 25, 1919, GCF Box 87, DC 842 Flandreau Indian School file; "The School of the Hills: U.S. Indian School, Rapid City, S.D., August, 1923"; "Annual Calendar, 1927–1928, U.S. Indian Boarding School, Rapid City, South Dakota"; both SSCF Box 9, School Annuals, Graduate Programs, School Paper file; all Rapid City Indian School, RG 75, NA—CPR.

9. Eva Enos interview, Warm Valley Historical Project, 28–29.

10. Sharon R. Mote, Superintendent, Rapid City Indian School, to Charles Eggers, Superintendent, Fort Peck Agency, September 8, 1927; C. F. Hawke, Acting Assistant CIA, to Eggers, October 14, 1927; Mote to CIA, October 24, 1927; E. B. Meritt, Assistant CIA, to Mote, December 2, 1927; all GCF Box 87, DC 842 Fort Peck Agency file, Rapid City Indian School, RG 75, NA—CPR.

11. Mote to Superintendent, Fort Peck Agency, August 17, 1928; J. M. Schwartz, Principal and Day School Inspector, Fort Peck Agency, to Mote, September 3, 1928; both GCF Box 87, DC 842 Fort Peck Agency file; George Day, Senior Clerk and Supply Disbursing Agent, Rapid City Indian School, to C. P. Detwiler, Acting Superintendent, Pine Ridge Indian Agency, August 27, 1930, GCF Box 26, DC 806.3 Catholic Mission file; S. A. M. Young, Superintendent, Rapid City Indian School, to C. C. Hickman,

Superintendent, Yankton Agency, GCF Box 91, DC 842 Yankton Agency file; all Rapid City Indian School, RG 75, NA—CPR.

12. Coleman, *American Indian Children at School*, 79–84.

13. "Report of Attendance, Quarter Ending December 31, 1917," GCF Box 27, DC 820.0 "Quarterly Report Ending—December 31, 1917" file; "Report of Attendance, Quarter Ending December 31, 1927," GCF Box 28, DC 820.0 "Quarterly Report Ending December 31, 1927" file; both Rapid City Indian School, RG 75, NA—CPR; Enos interview, 27.

14. Coleman, *Indian Children at School*, 86–87; C. F. Hawke, Second Assistant CIA, to House, November 13, 1914; House to CIA, November 25, 1914; "Daily Program"; all correspondence SSCF Box 8, Curriculum 1909–18 file, Rapid City Indian School, RG 75, NA—CPR.

15. Enos interview, 27; Sara Buffalo interview, Tape 719, American Indian Research Project, 1. Coleman discusses the phenomenon of experienced students coaching new students, and other forms of mediation, in chapter 7, "Peers and Mediation," in *Indian Children at School*.

16. For a description of the daily lives of residential school students, see Johnston, *Indian School Days*, 28–47. In "A Day in the Life of Spanish," Johnston describes the daily routine at St. Peter Claver's Indian Residential School in Spanish, Ontario. Though the experiences of Canadian Indian students of a Catholic residential (boarding) school and those of students at a U.S. government boarding school differed in important respects (Canadian schools were run under government contract by Christian denominations and not by government employees, as was the case in the United States), the daily schedules were remarkably similar.

17. "Catalog and Synopsis of Courses, United States Indian School, Rapid City, South Dakota, 1916–17," SSCF Box 9, School Annuals, Graduate Programs, School Paper file; George E. Peters, Principal, Rapid City Indian School, to Charles F. Peirce, Superintendent, Flandreau Indian School, October 10, 1917, GCF Box 87, DC 842 Flandreau Indian School file; both Rapid City Indian School, RG 75, NA—CPR.

18. "Pleasing Exercises," *Rapid City Daily Journal*, December 2, 1906; "Catalog and Synopsis of Courses, United States Indian School, Rapid City, South Dakota, 1916–17," SSCF Box 9, School Annuals, Graduate Programs, School Paper file; "Thanksgiving Program," November 28, 1928, GCF Box 85, DC 826.1 Student Activities Association file; latter two Rapid City Indian School, RG 75, NA—CPR.

19. Mote to Pathe Exchange, Inc., July 16, 1929; Mote to Ludwig Film Exchanges, January 9, 1926; "License for F. B. O. Pictures (Standard Exhibition Contract)," September 18, 1928; all GCF Box 25, DC 751

"Amusements and Atheletics [sic], Moving Pictures, Supplies, etc." file, Rapid City Indian School, RG 75, NA—CPR.

20. "Annual Calendar, 1927–1928, U.S. Indian Boarding School, Rapid City, South Dakota," SSCF Box 9, School Annuals, Graduate Programs, School Paper file; "Committees for Hallowe'en Social, Saturday evening, Oct. 30," undated, GCF Box 85, DC 826.1 Student Activities file; both Rapid City Indian School, RG 75, NA—CPR.

21. "Annual Calendar, 1927–1928, U.S. Indian Boarding School, Rapid City, South Dakota," SSCF Box 9, School Annuals, Graduate Programs, School Paper file; "Statement of the Students' Activities Association, December 15, 1925"; "Inventory of the Store, December 15, 1925"; both GCF Box 85, DC 826.1 Student Activities Association file, Rapid City Indian School, RG 75, NA—CPR; Enos interview, 33.

22. "Indian School Minstrels," advertisement, *Rapid City Daily Journal*, December 12, 1914; Albert L. Hurtado and Peter Iverson, eds., *Major Problems in American Indian History: Documents and Essays*, 373–74.

23. "The Pioneer's Papoose, A Light Opera in Two Acts," undated program, SSCF Box 9, School Annuals, Graduate Programs, School Paper file, Rapid City Indian School, RG 75, NA—CPR. The cast of characters consisted of students present at the school in the 1910s, but no later than 1918.

24. "The Indian Princess," December 6, 1925, GCF Box 26, DC 815 Academic Training file, Rapid City Indian School, RG 75, NA—CPR.

25. "Lelawala, The Maid of Niagara," undated program, GCF Box 26, DC 805 Commencements, Closing and Opening Dates, Vacation file, Rapid City Indian School, RG 75, NA—CPR. Comparison of this program with material on closing exercises dates it to 1929.

26. Robert F. Berkhofer, Jr., *The White Man's Indian: Images of the American Indian from Columbus to the Present*, 86–101.

27. Carl E. Wilcox, Principal, Rapid City Indian School, "To Those Concerned," April 12, 1927; "Declamation Contest," April 18, 1927; both GCF Box 91, DC 864 Inspection Reports 1925–28 file; "Annual Banquet, Rapid City Indian School," May 14, 1927, GCF Box 26, DC 781 Menus file; all Rapid City Indian School, RG 75, NA—CPR.

28. Adams, *Education for Extinction*, 181–90.

29. "Indian Boys Defeated," *Rapid City Daily Journal*, March 13, 1904; "Indian Boys Successful," *Rapid City Daily Journal*, May 22, 1904; "School of Mines Victorious," *Rapid City Daily Journal*, October 30, 1904; "Basket Ball," *Rapid City Daily Journal*, December 31, 1904; "Indian Boys Successful," *Rapid City Daily Journal*, January 8, 1905; "Indian Boys Beaten," *Rapid City Daily Journal*, March 12, 1905.

30. "The Spearfish Trip," *Rapid City Daily Journal*, May 27, 1905.

31. "Catalog and Synopsis of Courses, United States Indian School, Rapid City, South Dakota, 1916–17," SSCF Box 9, School Annuals, Graduate Programs, School Paper file, Rapid City Indian School, 10, RG 75, NA—CPR.

32. Mote to R. E. Hanley, Director of Athletics, Haskell Institute, September 29, 1925, GCF Box 88, DC 842 Haskell Institute 1923–25 file, Rapid City Indian School, NA—CPR.

33. Mote to R. E. Rawlins, Superintendent of Schools, Pierre, South Dakota, September 2, 1926, GCF Box 25, DC 752 Football file; R. E. Rawlins, Secretary-Treasurer, South Dakota High School Athletic Association, Board of Control, September 13, 1926, GCF Box 25, DC 750 Amusements and Athletics file; "Basket Ball Schedule for season of 1925–1926"; "Basket Ball Schedule, 1927," handwritten; GCF Box 25, DC 754 Basketball file; all Rapid City Indian School, RG 75, NA—CPR.

34. Mote to Superintendent, Murdo High School, September 22, 1927, handwritten reply by name illegible in the margin; Mote to Superintendent, Sundance High School, September 22, 1927, handwritten reply by L. G. Crouch, Superintendent, Sundance High School, in the margin; Mote to Lieutenant Greeg, Manager, Football Team, Fort Meade, October 24, 1926; Dan O. Root, Director of Physical Education, Spearfish Normal School, September 29, 1926; Mote to Euclid Cobb, Football Coach, Rapid City High School, October 7, 1927; "Indian Day Homecoming Football!" flyer; all GCF Box 25, DC 752 Football file, Rapid City Indian School, RG 75, NA—CPR.

35. Fred C. Basler, Faculty Secretary-Treasurer, Student Activities Association, form letter to season ticket buyers, October 27, 1928; Mote, "Memorandum to All Employees," October 31, 1928; Basler, handwritten list of season ticket purchasers, November 23, 1928; all GCF Box 26, DC 758 Season Tickets file; Mote to O. C. Upchurch, District Superintendent, Flandreau Indian School, January 31, 1927, GCF Box 15, DC 161 (T–Z), "Gen. Supt. O. C. Upchurch" file; all Rapid City Indian School, RG 75, NA—CPR.

36. "Statement of Student Activities Association, April 1, 1928," GCF Box 25, DC 750 Amusements and Athletics file; Mote, Memorandum, "To Any Employee Who Has a Car," January 20, 1928, GCF Box 25, DC 754.6 Basketball Tournament file; both Rapid City Indian School, RG 75, NA—CPR.

37. Mote to R. W. Skinner, Principal, Rapid City High School, May 5, 1927, GCF Box 26, DC 755.0 Track Meet file; Mote to C. R. Whitlock, Superintendent, Pierre Indian School, January 18, 1928; J. W. Balmer,

Superintendent, Pipestone Indian School, to Mote, January 27, 1928; Principal (name illegible), Rosebud School, to C. M. Ziebach, Superintendent, Rosebud Agency, February 7, 1928; Carl Stevens, Superintendent, Wahpeton Indian School, to Mote, February 11, 1928; W. J. Birmingham, S.J., St. Francis Mission, to Mote, February 12, 1928; GCF Box 25, DC 750 Amusements and Athletics file; all Rapid City Indian School, RG 75, NA—CPR.

38. James H. McGregor, District Superintendent, to the Heads of Mission and Government Indian Schools, February 25, 1928; C. R. Whitlock, Superintendent, Pierre Indian School, to C. B. Dickinson, Superintendent, Bismarck Indian School, April 29, 1928; both GCF Box 26, DC 755.0 Track Meet file; "Declamatory and Oratorical Contest, Rapid City Indian School," April 30, 1928; "Indian School Meet, May 11–12, 1928, Program," both GCF Box 26, DC 757 "School Plays, Entertainment, ect. [sic]" file; all Rapid City Indian School, RG 75, NA—CPR.

39. Mote, unaddressed letter, December 10, 1928; McGregor to Mote, December 14, 1928; GCF Box 25, DC 754 Basketball file; Mote to Dickinson, February 21, 1929; Balmer to Mote, February 25, 1929; Mote to Dr. C. C. O'Harra, President, South Dakota School of Mines, March 19, 1929; GCF Box 25, DC 754.6 Basketball Tournament file; all Rapid City Indian School, RG 75, NA—CPR.

40. "Inter-Indian School Tournament, Rapid City, S.D. March 15 & 16, 1929," entry sheets, girls' and boys' teams; Mote to O'Harra, March 19, 1929; McGregor to CIA, March 30, 1929; GCF Box 25, DC 754.6 Basketball Tournament file, Rapid City Indian School, RG 75, NA—CPR.

41. "Greatest Show on Record," *Rapid City Daily Journal*, June 21, 1904; "Closing Exercises," *Rapid City Daily Journal*, June 27, 1905; "Commencement Entertainment, Rapid City Indian School, June 22, 1911," SSCF Box 8, "Atheletic [sic] & Entertainment Programs, 1909–1921" file; "Program of the Commencement Exercises of the United States Indian School, Rapid City, So. Dak., June 20th, 1916," SSCF Box 9, School Annuals, Graduate Programs, School Paper file; Rapid City Indian School, RG 75, NA—CPR.

42. House, "General Order," June 20, 1912, SSCF Box 8, "Atheletic [sic] & Entertainment Programs, 1909–1921" file, Rapid City Indian School, RG 75, NA—CPR; "Indians Would Go Home," *Rapid City Daily Journal*, August 9, 1905.

43. Ibid.

44. Adams, *Education for Extinction*, 57–58; Acting Chief Clerk (name illegible), BIA, to House, May 25, 1909; C. F. Hawke, Chief Clerk, to House, June 30, 1909; both SSCF Box 6, Education Administration file; House to CIA, May 19, 1910; Hawke to House, May 28, 1910; GCF Box 28, DC 820.2

Enrollment and Attendance—1912 file, Rapid City Indian School, RG 75, NA—CPR.

45. House to Thomas J. King, Superintendent, Cheyenne River Agency, May 24, 1911, GCF Box 28, DC 840.2 Enrollment and Attendance—1911 file; House to His Roan Horse, June 2, 1910, Box 7 Education, a-2-35 "His Roan Horse" 1910 file; both Rapid City Indian School, RG 75, NA—CPR.

46. Lomawaima, *They Called It Prairie Light*, 78–79; "Efficiency, Scientific Management at Indian School, Get Results," *Rapid City Daily Journal*, September 4, 1915; Child, "A Bitter Lesson," 133–35.

47. "To go on Chicago, Milwaukee & St. Paul Ry. Wednesday evening," SSCF Box 6 Education, 1925—Students Eligible file, Rapid City Indian School; Charles F. Peirce, Superintendent, Flandreau Indian School, to J. R. Brennan, Superintendent, Pine Ridge Agency, April 27, 1915, Pine Ridge Agency education records Box 1148, Various Off-reservation Schools, March 29, 1912–June 24, 1915, file, Pine Ridge Agency; RG 75, NA—CPR.

48. House to C. J. Crandall, Superintendent, Pierre Indian School, July 17, 1919, GCF Box 89, DC 820.2 Enrollment and Attendance—1919 file, Rapid City Indian School, RG 75, NA—CPR; Lomawaima, *They Called It Prairie Light*, 79.

49. C. L. Davis, Supervisor in Charge, Rosebud Agency, to House, November 17, 1916; House to Agnes Yellow Robe, June 7, 1917; both Rosebud Agency GCF General School Correspondence Box A-420, "Rapid City Indian School 1915 + Prior 1916–1917" file 1, Rosebud Agency; E. D. Mossman, Superintendent, Fort Peck Agency, to House, June 28, 1921, GCF Box 88, DC 842 Haskell Institute file, Rapid City Indian School; all RG 75, NA—CPR. There is some confusion about the names of Edith and her mother. Correspondence variously listed Edith as Edith Anderson Cloud and Edith Cloud and Agnes as Agnes Yellow Cloud or Agnes Yellow Robe.

50. Child, "A Bitter Lesson," 135–43.

51. House, "General Order No. 1, Schedule for Summer Months," July 8, 1919, Rapid City Indian School, RG 75, NA—CPR.

52. Enos interview, 31–36.

CHAPTER 5. DISCIPLINE, PUNISHMENT, AND VIOLENCE

1. Adams, *Education for Extinction*, 55–59; "Conference between Superintendent House and Mr. McBrien," 10, GCF Box 3, DC 112 Circulars file, Rapid City Indian School, RG 75, NA—CPR.

2. "Catalog and Synopsis of Courses, United States Indian School, Rapid City, South Dakota, 1916–17," 4–7, SSCF Box 9, School Annuals, Graduate Program, School Paper file, Rapid City Indian School, RG 75, NA—CPR.

3. Coleman, *American Indian Children at School*, 80–88; Tape 719, American Indian Research Project, 1.

4. Pratt, *Battlefield and Classroom*, 118–20, 155–64, 181–204; Lindsey, *Indians at Hampton Institute*, 28–29, 125–27.

5. Coleman, *American Indian Children at School*, 87; Adams, *Education for Extinction*, 118–19.

6. Coleman, *American Indian Children at School*, 87; Adams, *Education for Extinction*, 118–19; William H. McNeill, *The Pursuit of Power: Technology, Armed Force, and Society since A.D. 1000*, 125–30.

7. Sharon R. Mote to Agnes Greiner, handwritten note; Greiner to Mote, handwritten reply in margins of Mote to Greiner; February 24, 1926, GCF Box 1, DC 040 Publicity file, Rapid City Indian School, RG 75, NA—CPR.

8. Ibid.

9. Kirk K. Newport to Margaret Hannan, undated handwritten note, GCF Box 8, DC 161 (F–H), "Hannan, Margaret" file, Rapid City Indian School, RG 75, NA—CPR; Trennert, *The Phoenix Indian School*, 117. The girls' dormitory was not easy to enter and leave quickly, for housekeeping regulations required girls to take their shoes off on entering the building.

10. Memorandum, Mote to Benjamin Fox, Jess Rouillard, and Fred Basler, December 15, 1925, GCF Box 12, DC 161 (P–R), "Y. Robe, Chauncey" file, Rapid City Indian School, RG 75, NA—CPR.

11. Memorandum, Mote to Emerson Hill, November 18, 1927, GCF Box 1, DC 040 Publicity file, Rapid City Indian School, RG 75, NA—CPR.

12. "Changes in Employees," GCF Box 5, DC 160.5 Changes in Employees July 1924–June 1925 file, Rapid City Indian School, RG 75, NA—CPR.

13. Memorandum, Mote to Fred Basler, December 13, 1927; Mote to "Ottipoby," December 27, 1928; Mote to All Employees, November 6, 1928; Mote to Employees Concerned, December 23, 1927; Mote to Netwal, Robe, Basler, Calhoun, March 8, 1928; Mote to Emerson Hill, November 18, 1927; all GCF Box 1, DC 040 Publicity file, Rapid City Indian School, RG 75, NA—CPR.

14. House to Daniel Ross, February 27, 1911, SSCF Box 7 Education, a-2-96 "Watchman" 1911 file; House to CIA, "Depredation by Pupils," June 22, 1915, SSCF Box 8 "Education pupils, Destruction of Property by Pupils" file; both Rapid City Indian School, RG 75, NA—CPR.

15. S. A. M. Young to Robe and Walters, October 23, 1923, GCF Box 12, DC 161 (P–R), "Y. Robe, Chauncey" file; Mote to Audrey Carr, August 18, 1928, GCF Box 7, DC 161 (C–E), "Carr, Audrey" file; both Rapid City Indian School, RG 75, NA—CPR.

16. Frances Masden to Mote, handwritten note, January 7, 1926, GCF Box 10, DC 161 (L–M), "Masden, Miss Frances" file, Rapid City Indian School, RG 75, NA—CPR.

17. Russell to Mote, handwritten note, April 30, 1929, GCF Box 15, DC 161 (T–Z), "Walters, Mrs. A. E." file, Rapid City Indian School, RG 75, NA—CPR. Russell's identity is unclear. She may have been the "Ema D. Walters, Matron," who was widowed by the death of Alfred Edwin Walters, an Indian employee of the school, in 1924.

18. Charley DeSheuquette, "My Part," handwritten note, undated, GCF Box 8, DC 161 (F–H), "Haines, Miss Daisy M." file, Rapid City Indian School, RG 75, NA—CPR. References to Superintendent House (1904–22), Principal George E. Peters, and Ada B. Shuck (class of 1921) indicate that DeSheuquette wrote the note sometime between 1917 and 1921.

19. Ibid.

20. Ibid.

21. Mitchell Desersa to House, January 21, 1910, GCF Box 28, DC 820.2 Enrollment and Attendance—1910 file, Rapid City Indian School, RG 75, NA—CPR.

22. Philomine Bierly to Young, September 30, 1924; Young to Bierly, October 5, 1924; both GCF Box 87, DC 842 Flathead Agency file, Rapid City Indian School, RG 75, NA—CPR.

23. House to Maggie F. Porter, Cook, May 27, 1913, SSCF Box 1, Administration & Control file, Superintendent Jesse House subfile, Rapid City Indian School, RG 75, NA—CPR.

24. Young to CIA, November 4, 1924; Young to Earl G. Kelsey, March 30, 1923; Kelsey to Young, March 30, 1923; Young to Kelsey, October 10, 1924; all GCF Box 9, DC 161 (H–K), "Kelsey, Earl G." file, Rapid City Indian School, RG 75, NA—CPR.

25. "Indian School Pupils," *Rapid City Daily Journal*, September 21, 1898; "A Serious Case of Nostalgia," *Rapid City Daily Journal*, January 12, 1899; "Deserters," May 24, 1920, SSCF Box 9, "Runaways" 1920–21 file, Rapid City Indian School, RG 75, NA—CPR.

26. Don Rickey, Jr., *Forty Miles a Day on Beans and Hay: The Enlisted Soldier Fighting the Indian Wars*, 28–30, 153.

27. Interview 008, 10–12, American Indian Research Project.

28. Child, "A Bitter Lesson," 259–61; Adams, *Education for Extinction,* 223–24.

29. Mote to Charles Roach, October 23, 1928, Box 443 (518431), Misc. Correspondence Rapid City School 1923–28 file, Cheyenne River Agency, RG 75, NA—CPR.

30. John R. Brennan, Superintendent, Pine Ridge Agency, to House, December 31, 1909, SSCF Box 1 Administration and Control, "John R. Brennan Superintendent Pine Ridge" file; "Artificial Feet for Pupils," House to CIA, May 19, 1910, SSCF Box 8, a-7-1 "Artificial Feet for Pupils" 1910 file; all Rapid City Indian School, RG 75, NA—CPR.

31. House to Brennan, "Death of James Means & Mark Sherman," October 19, 1910; "Statement of James Cottier in regard to the death of Mark Sherman and James Means," November 17, 1910; both SSCF Box 9, "Student Deaths" 1910–11 file, Rapid City Indian School, RG 75, NA—CPR.

32. Child, "A Bitter Lesson," 266–67.

33. W. O. Roberts, Superintendent, Rosebud Indian Agency, to Young, October 21, 1930; Young to Roberts, October 24, 1930; Young to Roberts, November 3, 1930; all GCF Box 90, DC 842 Rosebud Agency 1930–31 file, Rapid City Indian School, RG 75, NA—CPR.

34. George R. Brown to House, May 4, 1910, SSCF Box 7 Education, a-2-11 "George Brown" 1911 file, Rapid City Indian School, RG 75, NA—CPR.

35. Memorandum, Mote to Chadsey and Robe, February 20, 1928; Mote to E. E. Benjamin, February 27, 1928; Benjamin to Mote, February 29, 1928; S. S. Long, Superintendent, Chicago and North Western Railway Company, Black Hills Division, Bulletin No. 34, March 5, 1928; all GCF Box 30, DC 820.2 Enrollment and Attendance 1928 file, Rapid City Indian School, RG 75, NA—CPR.

36. E. E. McKean, Superintendent, Rosebud Indian Agency, to Mote, October 6, 1928, GCF Box 90, DC 842 Rosebud Agency 1928–29 file, Rapid City Indian School, RG 75, NA—CPR.

37. Mote to McKean, October 15, 1928, GCF Box 90, DC 842 Rosebud Agency 1928–29 file, Rapid City Indian School, RG 75, NA—CPR.

38. House to J. J. Duncan, Day School Inspector, Pine Ridge Agency, December 2, 1914, GCF Box 88, DC 842 Pine Ridge Agency 1913–16 file; House to Major John R. Brennan, Superintendent, Pine Ridge Agency, May 4, 1912, SSCF Box 9, a-17-4 "Runaways" 1910 file; Rapid City Indian School, RG 75, NA—CPR.

39. House to J. J. Duncan, January 7, 1912; Mrs. Charles Cuny to House, February 24, 1912; both Pine Ridge Agency Education Records GCF 196, Box 1150, Correspondence Rapid City School, "Oct. 18, 1910–June 21, 1912" file, Pine Ridge Agency, RG 75, NA—CPR; House to Brennan, May 27, 1912; Brennan to House, June 19, 1912; House to Brennan, June 21, 1912; Brennan to House, July 16, 1912; House to Brennan, July 19, 1912; all GCF Box 28, DC 820.2 Enrollment and Attendance—1912 file, Rapid City Indian School, RG 75, NA—CPR.

40. House to Brennan, May 4, 1912, SSCF Box 9, a-17-4 "Runaways" 1910 file; House to Superintendents, May 28, 1918, GCF Box 29, DC 820.2 Enrollment and Attendance—1918 file; House to Parents, May 28, 1918, GCF Box 29, DC 820.2 Enrollment and Attendance—1918 file; all Rapid City Indian School, RG 75, NA—CPR.

41. Francis C. Goings, Chief of Police, Pine Ridge Agency, to House, November 23, 1920, GCF Box 29, DC 820.2 Enrollment and Attendance—1920 file, Rapid City Indian School, RG 75, NA—CPR.

42. House to H. M. Tidwell, Superintendent, Pine Ridge Agency, May 24, 1920, SSCF Box 9, "Runaways" 1920–21 file, Rapid City Indian School, RG 75, NA—CPR.

43. Young to C. H. Gensler, Superintendent, Lower Brule Agency, November 21, 1922, GCF Box 88, DC 842 Lower Brule Agency file, Rapid City Indian School, RG 75, NA—CPR.

44. Young to H. B. Peairs, Chief Supervisor of Education, December 29, 1922, GCF Box 88, DC 842 Haskell Institute file, Rapid City Indian School, RG 75, NA—CPR.

45. Peairs to Young, January 4, 1922, GCF Box 88, DC 842 Haskell Institute file, Rapid City Indian School, RG 75, NA—CPR.

46. Charles H. Burke, CIA, to Young, January 23, 1923; Young to Burke, January 29, 1923; E. B. Meritt, Assistant CIA, to Eugene D. Mossman, Superintendent, Standing Rock Indian School, February 3, 1923; Burke to Mossman, February 13, 1923; all GCF Box 86, DC 842 Crow Agency file, Rapid City Indian School, RG 75, NA—CPR.

47. House to F. T. Mann, Superintendent, Pipestone Indian School, December 10, 1915, GCF Box 89, DC 842 Pipestone Agency file; Mote to Robe, January 10, 1928, GCF Box 3, DC 102 Memoranda 1928 file; both Rapid City Indian School, RG 75, NA—CPR.

48. R. W. Hunt to House, November 18, 1919; House to Hunt, December 5, 1919; GCF Box 6, DC 161 (A–B), "Avery, Mr. Sewell V." file; Young to Peairs, December 29, 1922, GCF Box 88, DC 842 Haskell Institute file; Rapid City Indian School, RG 75, NA—CPR.

49. Mote to E. W. Jermark, Superintendent, Pine Ridge Agency, September 23, 1926, General Records Main Decimal File Box 687, 806.26 Rapid City file, Pine Ridge Agency, RG 75, NA—CPR.

50. Memorandum, Jermark to Mote, November 19, 1928, General Records Main Decimal File Box 687, 806.26 Rapid City 2 of 3 file, Pine Ridge Agency, RG 75, NA—CPR.

51. Brennan to House, December 31, 1909, SSCF Box 1 Administration and Control, "John R. Brennan Superintendent Pine Ridge" file; House to Willard Standing Bear, April 23, 1910; House to Standing Bear, April 26, 1910; GCF Box 28, DC 820.2 Enrollment and Attendance—1910 file; all Rapid City Indian School, RG 75, NA—CPR; Memorandum, Jermark to Mote, November 19, 1928, General Records Main Decimal File Box 687, 806.26 Rapid City 2 of 3 file, Pine Ridge Agency, RG 75, NA—CPR. Much correspondence concerning runaways can be reconstructed from telegrams contained in GCF Box 4, DC 143 Telegrams files, Rapid City Indian School, RG 75, NA—CPR.

52. C. H. Asbury, Superintendent, Crow Agency, to O. H. Lipps, Superintendent, Chemawa Indian School, September 15, 1928, GCF Box 30, DC 820.2 Enrollment and Attendance—1928 file; Mote to C. B. Lohmiller, Superintendent, Tongue River Agency, October 12, 1925, GCF Box 90, DC 842 Tongue River Agency file; Rapid City Indian School, RG 75, NA—CPR.

53. House to John R. Brennan, Superintendent, Pine Ridge Agency, April 2, 1915, Pine Ridge Agency Records GCF 196, Box 1150, "Rapid City Boarding School Correspondence Aug. 14, 1914–June 18, 1915" file, Pine Ridge Agency, RG 75, NA—CPR; F. F. Jewett to Cleophus Jewett, January 20, 1920; Chauncey Yellow Robe, Disciplinarian, Rapid City Indian School, to Superintendent, Cheyenne River Agency, February 26, 1920; Superintendent to Yellow Robe, March 3, 1920; all Box 597, Rapid City School—School 3 file, Cheyenne River Agency, RG 75, NA—CPR.

54. House to H. M. Tidwell, Superintendent, Pine Ridge Agency, July 7, 1919, GCF Box 89, DC 842 Pine Ridge Agency 1917–21 file, Rapid City Indian School, RG 75, NA—CPR; Tape 713, 4, American Indian Research Project; Telegraph correspondence between House and Covey, Griegold (or Giegoldt) at Fort Yates, North Dakota, and House and J. W. Housworth at Isabel, South Dakota, from February 1 to March 22, 1917, GCF Box 4, DC 143 Telegrams—1917 file, Rapid City Indian School, RG 75, NA—CPR.

55. Superintendent to Whom It May Concern, December 5, 1917, GCF Box 85, DC 842 Cheyenne River Agency 1913–18 file; Ralph Old Horse to House, March 14, 1920; House to Old Horse, March 17, 1920; GCF Box 89,

DC 842 Pine Ridge Agency 1917–21 file; all Rapid City Indian School, RG 75, NA—CPR.

56. Mote to Mark Spotted Horse, November 9, 1927, GCF Box 16, DC 162 Applications for Position file, Rapid City Indian School, RG 75, NA—CPR.

57. Carl E. Wilcox, Principal, Rapid City Indian School, to Chauncey Yellow Robe, Disciplinarian, June 28, 1927, GCF Box 13, DC 161 (R–S), "Rouillard, Isaac" file; H. E. Mosher, Additional Farmer, Cherry Creek Station, to House, January 3, 1910, GCF Box 28, DC 820.2 Enrollment and Attendance—1910 file; "Employees at Rapid City Indian School, Rapid City, S.D.," March 31, 1910, SSCF Box 1 Administration and Control, Charles H. Dickson—Supervisor file; Rapid City Indian School, RG 75, NA—CPR.

58. Meriam Report, 406.

59. House to J. J. Duncan, February 9, 1910, Pine Ridge Agency GCF 169, Correspondence of Day School Inspector J. J. Duncan, Box 951, "J. J. Duncan Correspondence" 1910 file, Pine Ridge Agency, RG 75, NA—CPR.

CHAPTER 6. EMPLOYEES

1. "Record of Chauncey Y. Robe," GCF Box 12, DC 161 (P–R), "Y. Robe, Chauncey" file, Rapid City Indian School, RG 75, NA—CPR.

2. Chauncey Yellow Robe married a white woman and had two daughters, whom he raised after his wife's death. In correspondence, the superintendents and other Rapid City staff addressed him as Mr. Robe or Chauncey Y. Robe, never as Yellow Robe.

3. Lomawaima, *They Called It Prairie Light*, 18–19, 65–66.

4. "Sioux-Form 4," January 15, 1912; "Persons of Indian Blood Employed at Rapid City School, S.D.," March 31, 1912; "Rapid City Indian School, South Dakota" (salary list), 1912; all GCF Box 22, DC 226.6 Salaries 1911–24 file, Rapid City Indian School, RG 75, NA—CPR.

5. "Efficiency Report," Jennie Larson, May 1, 1914, SSCF Box 5, Officers & Employees—Misc. ER's 1914 file; "Record of Jennie Larson," December 15, 1913; "Death of Miss Larson Assistant Clerk," House to CIA, August 30, 1914; Superintendent (name illegible), Hayward Training School, Hayward, Wisconsin, to House, September 5, 1914; GCF Box 10, DC 161 (L–M), "Jennie Larson—deceased" file; "Efficiency Report," Florence Summers, November 28, 1914, SSCF Box 5, Officers & Employees—Misc. ER's 1914 file; "Efficiency Report," Thomas W. Killer, May 1, 1923; "Efficiency

Report," Frances D. Adams, May 1, 1923; both SSCF Box 5, Officers and Employees—Misc. ER's 1923 file; H. M. Tidwell, Superintendent, Pine Ridge Agency, to S. A. M. Young, Superintendent, Rapid City Indian School, January 27, 1923, GCF Box 9, DC 161 (H–K), "Thomas W. Killer" file; all Rapid City Indian School, RG 75, NA—CPR.

6. "Record of George A. Day," December 24, 1924; Mote to CIA, May 24, 1926; "Efficiency Record," George A. Day, April 1, 1930; all GCF Box 7, DC 161 (C–E), "Day, George A." file, Rapid City Indian School, RG 75, NA—CPR.

7. "Positions, Salaries & Employees—Rapid City School, S.D.," October 31, 1910, SSCF Box 7 Education, Education Related Correspondence 1912 file; "Changes in Employees," GCF Box 5, DC 160.5 Changes in Employees July 1924–June 1925 file; all Rapid City Indian School, RG 75, NA—CPR.

8. "Application for Appointment in the United States Indian School Service," GCF Box 10, DC 161 (L–M), "Mewhirter, Margaret B." file, Rapid City Indian School, RG 75, NA—CPR.

9. E. B. Meritt, Assistant CIA, to Samuel A. M. Young, June 2, 1924; "Record of Lazarus W. Adams," July 1, 1924; Meritt to Young, October 10, 1924; G. F. Anderson et al., "To Whom It May Concern," December 17, 1923; all GCF Box 6, DC 161 (A––B), "Adams, Lazarus" file, Rapid City Indian School, RG 75, NA—CPR.

10. "United States Civil Service Examinations," May 21, 1924, GCF Box 10, DC 161 (L–M), "Mewhirter, Margaret B." file, Rapid City Indian School, RG 75, NA—CPR.

11. Ibid.

12. Ibid.

13. "Condition of Employment in the Indian Field Service," GCF Box 16, DC 162 a-28-10 Applications for Positions 1910–13 file; House to Bessie Andersen, March 14, 1912, GCF Box 6, DC 162, 9-28-10 Applications for Positions 1910–13 file; all Rapid City Indian School, RG 75, NA—CPR.

14. Ibid.

15. Young to George E. Peters, January 26, 1925, GCF Box 12, DC 161 (P–R), "Peters, George E." file, Rapid City Indian School, RG 75, NA—CPR.

16. Peters to Young, January 29, 1925, GCF Box 12, DC 161 (P–R), "Peters, George E." file, Rapid City Indian School, RG 75, NA—CPR.

17. House to Edith M. Triggs, February 25, 1914, GCF Box 16, DC 163 Appointments & Transfers—EM file, Rapid City Indian School, RG 75, NA—CPR.

18. House to Edith M. Triggs, February 25, 1914, GCF Box 16, DC 163 Appointments & Transfers—EM file; Superintendent Mote to DeCory, Arrow, and Mewhirter, September 5, 1928, GCF Box 3, DC 102 Memoranda 1928 file; both Rapid City Indian School, RG 75, NA—CPR.

19. F. H. Abbott, Acting CIA, to Benjamin McBride, December 11, 1912; House to CIA, December 23, 1912; both GCF Box 16, DC 162 a-28-10 Applications for Positions 1910–13 file, Rapid City Indian School, RG 75, NA—CPR.

20. E. B. Meritt, Assistant Commissioner, to House, January 24, 1914; House to Meritt, February 4, 1914; both GCF Box 12, DC 161 (P–R), "Roberts, Francis E." file, Rapid City Indian School, RG 75, NA—CPR. Neither precise dates nor details of the resignations of Francis Roberts and her husband are available. Unsympathetic supervisor E. E. Newton was, indeed, a woman.

21. House to CIA, September 23, 1913, GCF Box 12, DC 161 (P–R), "Y. Robe, Chauncey" file, Rapid City Indian School, RG 75, NA—CPR.

22. Superintendent Mote to CIA, June 28, 1927, GCF Box 11, DC 161 (M–P), "Sharon R. Mote—Superintendent" file; C. Y. Robe to Mote, June 29, 1927; Mote to Yellow Robe, June 29, 1927; both GCF Box 12, DC 161 (P–R), "Y. Robe, Chauncey" file; all Rapid City Indian School, RG 75, NA—CPR.

23. "Memorandum," Mote to Robe, February 24, 1928; "Memorandum," Mote to Robe, February 27, 1928; "Memorandum," Mote to Robe, February 27, 1928; all GCF Box 12, DC 161 (P–R), "Y. Robe, Chauncey" file, Rapid City Indian School, RG 75, NA—CPR.

24. James H. McGregor, District Superintendent, to Mote, January 26, 1928; Mote to McGregor, February 20, 1928; McGregor to Mote, March 1, 1928; all GCF Box 12, DC 161 (P–R), "Y. Robe, Chauncey" file, Rapid City Indian School, RG 75, NA—CPR.

25. Ibid.

26. Memorandum, Mote to employees, 12 September 12, 1927, GCF Box 1, DC 040 Publicity file; Mote to Louis H. Goings, December 10, 1928, GCF Box 30, DC 820.2 Enrollment and Attendance—1928 file; both Rapid City Indian School, RG 75, NA—CPR.

27. Ema D. Russell to Mote, March 30, 1928; Mote to Russell, March 20, 1928; Maye I. Peck to Mote, March 21, 1928; all GCF Box 3, DC 102 Memoranda 1928 file, Rapid City Indian School, RG 75, NA—CPR. In this correspondence, Russell is identified only as "Mrs. Russell," and other materials do not provide a fuller identification. Nor does Russell positively identify Sonny Walters as her son. The content and tone of her note do

suggest, however, that he was indeed her son, in which case "Mrs. Russell" is probably the former Ema D. Walters, previously married to Lakota Alfred E. Walters, a Rapid City industrial teacher who died of a heart attack in 1924. Maye I. Peck was married to engineer Walter G. Peck; both were white.

28. Undated, unsigned document, SSCF Box 8, Curriculum 1909–18 file, Rapid City Indian School, RG 75, NA—CPR.

29. House, "To Members of School Club and Others Interested," December 20, 1920, GCF Box 3, DC 112 Circulars file, Rapid City Indian School, RG 75, NA—CPR.

30. House, "General Order No. 2, 1919–1920, Profanity & Smoking," August 29, 1919, GCF Box 3, DC 112 Circulars file, Rapid City Indian School, RG 75, NA—CPR.

31. E. B. Meritt, Assistant CIA, to House, January 14, 1915; House to Meritt, January 19, 1915; "Statement Made by Harvey Langdeau, Fred Schmidt, Harden Smith," January 4, 1915; all GCF Box 8, DC 161 (F–H), "Hayes, Lee" file, Rapid City Indian School, RG 75, NA—CPR.

32. Ibid.

33. Ibid.

34. Charles E. Dagenett, Supervisor of Indian Employment, to House, November 26, 1917; House to Dagenett, December 3, 1917; both GCF Box 6, DC 161 (A–B), "Bird, Josiah" file, Rapid City Indian School, RG 75, NA—CPR.

35. Young to CIA, March 28, 1922, GCF Box 15, DC 161 (T–Z), "Lee Roy Willis" file, Rapid City Indian School, RG 75, NA—CPR.

36. Ibid.

37. Young to CIA, March 28, 1922; House to CIA, March 28, 1922; both GCF Box 15, DC 161 (T–Z), "Lee Roy Willis" file, Rapid City Indian School, RG 75, NA—CPR.

38. H. B. Peairs, Chief Supervisor of Indian Education, to Young, September 21, 1922, GCF Box 15, DC 161 (T–Z), "Lee Roy Willis" file, Rapid City Indian School, RG 75, NA—CPR.

39. H. B. Peairs, Chief Supervisor of Indian Education, to Young, September 21, 1922; Young to Peairs, September 24, 1922; both GCF Box 15, DC 161 (T–Z), "Lee Roy Willis" file, Rapid City Indian School, RG 75, NA—CPR.

40. Young to CIA, November 4, 1924, GCF Box 9, DC 161 (H–K), "Kelsey, Earl G." file, Rapid City Indian School, RG 75, NA—CPR.

41. Raymond E. Staley, Superintendent, Rapid City Indian School, to Dr. Emil Krulish, BIA Medical Director, October 12, 1929, GCF Box 7,

DC 161 (C–E), "Calhoun, Walter B." file, Rapid City Indian School, RG 75, NA—CPR.

42. Staley to Charles E. Coe, Superintendent, Flathead Agency, May 29, 1933; Coe to Staley, June 2, 1933; Staley to Coe, June 6, 1933; Coe to Staley, June 9, 1933; all GCF Box 87, DC 842 Flathead Agency file, Rapid City Indian School, RG 75, NA—CPR. Staley sent letters to the reservation superintendents announcing the school's closure on May 29. Presumably he informed the reservation superintendents within days of receiving word himself.

43. Staley to James H. McGregor, Superintendent, Pine Ridge Agency, June 5, 1933; McGregor to Staley, June 26, 1933; both GCF Box 89, DC 842 Pine Ridge Agency 1930–33 file, Rapid City Indian School, RG 75, NA—CPR.

44. "Persons of Indian Blood Employed at Rapid City Indian School, S.D.," March 31, 1912; "Rapid City Indian School, South Dakota," undated salary list; both GCF Box 22, DC 226.6 Salaries 1911–24 file; "Changes in Employees," undated, GCF Box 5, DC 160.5 Changes in Employees July 1924–June 1925 file; all Rapid City Indian School, RG 75, NA—CPR.

45. Mote to CIA, September 19, 1925; Mote to CIA, May 24, 1926; both GCF Box 7, DC 161 (C–E), "Day, George A." file, Rapid City Indian School, RG 75, NA—CPR. In 1925, Day requested a ten-month furlough so he could work as a missionary among Indians. The Office of the CIA apparently turned down his request.

CHAPTER 7. EXTENDING THE REACH OF THE BUREAU

1. Prucha, *The Great Father*, 636–40; Jesse F. House, Superintendent, Rapid City Indian School, to John R. Brennan, Superintendent, Pine Ridge Indian Agency, February 29, 1916, GCF Box 88, DC 842 Pine Ridge Agency 1913–16 file, Rapid City Indian School, RG 75, NA—CPR.

2. Brennan to House, March 3, 1916, GCF Box 88, DC 842 Pine Ridge Agency 1913–16 file, Rapid City Indian School, RG 75, NA—CPR.

3. Brennan to House, April 28, 1917, GCF Box 12, DC 161 (P–R), "Red Bull, Fannie" file; Brennan to House, March 3, 1916, GCF Box 88, DC 842 Pine Ridge Agency 1913–16 file; both Rapid City Indian School, RG 75, NA—CPR.

4. Superintendent (name illegible), Crow Creek Agency, to House, December 11, 1912, GCF Box 28, DC 820.2 Enrollment and Attendance—1912 file, Rapid City Indian School, RG 75, NA—CPR.

5. Ibid.

6. Ibid.

7. "Bill of Sale," filed with correspondence, H. M. Tidwell, Superintendent, Pine Ridge Agency, to House, November 25, 1919, GCF Box 89, DC 842 Pine Ridge Agency 1917–21 file, Rapid City Indian School, RG 75, NA—CPR.

8. Brennan to House, February 13, 1917; Brennan to House, June 18, 1917; both GCF Box 88, DC 842 Pine Ridge Agency 1913–16 file, Rapid City Indian School, RG 75, NA—CPR.

9. W. P. Marshall, Farmer, Cheyenne River Agency, to House, May 12, 1919; House to Marshall, May 17, 1919; both GCF Box 85, DC 842 Cheyenne River 1919–21 file, Rapid City Indian School, RG 75, NA—CPR.

10. Michael V. Wolf to House, February 19, 1920, GCF Box 85, DC 842 Cheyenne River 1919–21 file, Rapid City Indian School, RG 75, NA—CPR.

11. Tidwell to House, March 8, 1919, GCF Box 89, DC 842 Pine Ridge Agency 1917–21 file, Rapid City Indian School, RG 75, NA—CPR.

12. Handwritten note to Chauncey Yellow Robe, in margins of Tidwell to House, March 8, 1919; House to Tidwell, March 14, 1919; both GCF Box 89, DC 842 Pine Ridge Agency 1917–21 file, Rapid City Indian School, RG 75, NA—CPR.

13. House to Tidwell, November 24, 1919; Tidwell to House, November 25, 1919; both GCF Box 89, DC 842 Pine Ridge Agency 1917–21 file, Rapid City Indian School, RG 75, NA—CPR.

14. House to Tidwell, February 28, 1920, GCF Box 89, DC 842 Pine Ridge Agency 1917–21 file, Rapid City Indian School, RG 75, NA—CPR.

15. House to Alfred Black Bear, June 13, 1921, GCF Box 89, DC 842 Pine Ridge Agency 1917–21 file; W. O. Roberts, Superintendent, Rosebud Indian Agency, to Raymond H. Staley, Superintendent, Rapid City Indian School, March 16, 1933, GCF Box 90, DC 842 Rosebud Agency 1932–33 file; both Rapid City Indian School, RG 75, NA—CPR.

16. Marshall to House, May 12, 1919, GCF Box 85, DC 842 Cheyenne River 1919–21 file; Tidwell to House, September 30, 1920, GCF Box 89, DC 842 Pine Ridge Agency 1917–21 file; both Rapid City Indian School, RG 75, NA—CPR; Rosebud Superintendent to House, January 6, 1922, GCF General School Correspondence (1908–23) Box A-420, Rapid City Indian School 1918–23 file, Rosebud Agency, RG 75, NA—CPR.

17. "Allot. #181," E. M. Garber, Superintendent, Lower Brule, South Dakota, December 18, 1918, GCF Box 88, Lower Brule Agency file, Rapid City Indian School, RG 75, NA—CPR.

18. J. W. C. Killer, Farmer, White Clay District, Pine Ridge Agency, to S. A. M. Young, Superintendent, Rapid City Indian School, April 5, 1922; Young to Killer, April 7, 1922; both GCF Box 9, DC 161 (H–K), "(Tyon Ida) Killer Miss Ida" file, Rapid City Indian School, RG 75, NA—CPR.

19. L. S. Bonnin, Cheyenne and Arapaho Agency, Concho, Oklahoma, to Young, January 28, 1931; Young to James Riley, February 7, 1931; both GCF Box 85, DC 842 Agencies and Schools Not Otherwise Classified file, Rapid City Indian School, RG 75, NA—CPR.

20. John E. Derby, Farmer, Cherry Creek, South Dakota, to House, May 8, 1917; House to Derby, May 14, 1917; both GCF Box 12, DC 161 (P–R), "Red Bull, Fannie" file, Rapid City Indian School, RG 75, NA—CPR.

21. House to F. C. Campbell, Superintendent, Cheyenne River Agency, South Dakota, June 12, 1917; Campbell to House, June 16, 1917; both GCF Box 12, DC 161 (P–R), "Red Bull, Fannie" file, Rapid City Indian School, RG 75, NA—CPR.

22. Agnes Craven to E. W. Jermark, Superintendent, Pine Ridge Agency, June 7, 1927, GCF Box 89, DC 842 Pine Ridge Agency 1925–27 file, Rapid City Indian School, RG 75, NA—CPR.

23. Jermark to Craven, June 11, 1927; Jermark to Sharon R. Mote, Superintendent, Rapid City Indian School, June 11, 1927; both GCF Box 89, DC 842 Pine Ridge Agency 1925–27 file, Rapid City Indian School, RG 75, NA—CPR.

24. House to Brennan, October 24, 1916, GCF Box 88, DC 842 Pine Ridge Agency 1913–16 file, Rapid City Indian School, RG 75, NA—CPR.

25. Ibid.

26. House to Elmer B. Pomeroy, Farmer, Eagle Nest District, Pine Ridge Agency, June 4, 1919; Pomeroy to House, June 6, 1919; House to Pomeroy, June 9, 1919; all GCF Box 89, DC 842 Pine Ridge Agency 1917–21 file, Rapid City Indian School, RG 75, NA—CPR.

27. Roberts to Young, January 8, 1932, GCF Box 90, DC 842 Rosebud Agency 1932–33 file, Rapid City Indian School, RG 75, NA—CPR.

28. Young to Mitchell Desersa, January 14, 1932; Young to Joseph Pawnee, January 14, 1932; Young to Roberts, January 26, 1932; all GCF Box 90, DC 842 Rosebud Agency 1932–33 file, Rapid City Indian School, RG 75, NA—CPR.

29. Roberts to Young, January 27, 1932, GCF Box 90, DC 842 Rosebud Agency 1932–33 file, Rapid City Indian School, RG 75, NA—CPR.

30. Young to W. F. Dickens, Superintendent, Cheyenne River Agency, March 9, 1932, GCF Box 86, DC 842 Cheyenne River Agency 1930–33 file, Rapid City Indian School, RG 75, NA—CPR.

31. Young to Dickens, March 14, 1932, GCF Box 86, DC 842 Cheyenne River Agency 1930–33 file, Rapid City Indian School, RG 75, NA—CPR.

32. Raymond E. Staley, Superintendent, Rapid City Indian School, to Dickens, December 15, 1932, GCF Box 8, DC 842 Cheyenne River Agency 1930–33 file, Rapid City Indian School, RG 75, NA—CPR.

33. James H. McGregor, Superintendent, Pine Ridge Agency, to Staley, April 12, 1933; Staley to McGregor, April 17, 1933; both GCF Box 89, DC 842 Pine Ridge Agency 1930–33 file, Rapid City Indian School, RG 75, NA—CPR.

34. E. D. Mossman, Superintendent, Standing Rock Agency, to Superintendents, Rosebud and Cheyenne River Agencies, Rapid City Indian School, October 20, 1927; Mote to Mossman, October 24, 1927; both GCF Box 90, DC 842 Standing Rock Agency 1926–27 file, Rapid City Indian School, RG 75, NA—CPR.

35. Andrew Bissonette to Mote, April 18, 1929, GCF Box 89, DC 842 Pine Ridge Agency 1928–29 file, Rapid City Indian School, RG 75, NA—CPR.

36. Mote to Bissonette, May 1, 1929; Bissonette to Mote, June 18, 1929; both GCF Box 89, DC 842 Pine Ridge Agency 1928–29 file, Rapid City Indian School, RG 75, NA—CPR.

37. Bissonette to Mote, June 18, 1929, GCF Box 89, DC 842 Pine Ridge Agency 1928–29 file; J. Henry Scattergood, Assistant CIA, to Bissonette, July 16, 1929, GCF Box 90, DC 842 Standing Rock Agency 1927–29 file; both Rapid City Indian School, RG 75, NA—CPR.

38. Eva J. Conger Roubideaux to Young, October 21, 1931, GCF Box 90, DC 842 Rosebud Agency 1930–31 file, Rapid City Indian School, RG 75, NA—CPR.

39. Young to Roubideaux, October 21, 1931, GCF Box 90, DC 842 Rosebud Agency 1930–31 file, Rapid City Indian School, RG 75, NA—CPR. I have withheld the names of the students mentioned in Young's letter.

40. "The Indians and the Liquor Traffic," House, April 16, 1915, SSCF Box 10, Policy & Liquor Control 1909–21 file, Rapid City Indian School, RG 75, NA—CPR.

41. Ibid.

42. Ibid.; House to Henry A. Larson, Chief Special Officer, United States Indian Service, Denver, Colorado, April 21, 1915, SSCF Box 10, Policy & Liquor Control 1909–21 file, Rapid City Indian School, RG 75, NA—CPR.

43. Correspondence between House and E. E. Wagner, U.S. Attorney, Sioux Falls, South Dakota, December 14, 1910, through January 11, 1911,

all SSCF Box 10, Policy & Liquor Control 1909–21 file, Rapid City Indian School, RG 75, NA—CPR.

44. Ibid.

45. "Circular #4. Operations," Larson, October 17, 1912, SSCF Box 10, Policy & Liquor Control 1909–21 file, Rapid City Indian School, RG 75, NA—CPR.

46. House to Larson, November 19, 1914; Correspondence between House and E. B. Meritt, Assistant CIA, January 14, 1915, through February 23, 1915; all SSCF Box 10, Policy & Liquor Control 1909–21 file, Rapid City Indian School, RG 75, NA—CPR.

47. House to Larson, December 5, 1916; Larson to House, December 15, 1916; both SSCF Box 10, Policy & Liquor Control 1909–21 file, Rapid City Indian School, RG 75, NA—CPR.

48. House to Larson, November 24, 1920, SSCF Box 10, Policy & Liquor Control 1909–21 file, Rapid City Indian School, RG 75, NA—CPR.

EPILOGUE

1. Iverson, *The Plains Indians of the Twentieth Century*, 4–5.

2. Tape 008, American Indian Research Project, 13–14.

3. Ibid.

4. Standing Bear, *My People the Sioux*, 175–76.

5. Eva Enos interview with author, 1998.

BIBLIOGRAPHY

GOVERNMENT DOCUMENTS

Abstract of the Thirteenth Census of the United States. Washington, D.C.: Government Printing Office, 1913.

Abstract of the Fourteenth Census of the United States. Washington, D.C.: Government Printing Office, 1923.

Annual Report of the Commissioner of Indian Affairs, 1898. Washington, D.C.: Government Printing Office, 1898.

Annual Report of the Commissioner of Indian Affairs, 1899. Washington, D.C.: Government Printing Office, 1899.

Annual Report of the Commissioner of Indian Affairs, 1901. Washington, D.C.: Government Printing Office, 1901.

Annual Report of the Commissioner of Indian Affairs, 1903. Washington, D.C.: Government Printing Office, 1903.

Annual Report of the Commissioner of Indian Affairs, 1905. Washington, D.C.: Government Printing Office, 1905.

Annual Report of the Commissioner of Indian Affairs, 1908. Washington, D.C.: Government Printing Office, 1908.

Annual Report of the Commissioner of Indian Affairs, 1909. Washington, D.C.: Government Printing Office, 1909.

Annual Report of the Commissioner of Indian Affairs, 1920. Washington, D.C.: Government Printing Office, 1920.

Thirteenth Census of the United States, Vol. III: Population. Washington, D.C.: Government Printing Office, 1913.

Fifteenth Census of the United States, Vol. III, Part 2: Population. Washington, D.C.: Government Printing Office, 1932.

U.S. Congress. Senate. Committee on Indian Affairs. *Conduct and Management of Indian Schools, Etc.* 57th Congress, 1st session, Senate document 201.

ARCHIVAL COLLECTIONS

American Indian Research Project. South Dakota Oral History Center. Pierre and Vermillion, South Dakota.

Records of the Cheyenne River Agency. Bureau of Indian Affairs. Record Group 75. National Archives and Records Administration. National Archives—Central Plains Region, Kansas City, Missouri.

Records of the Pine Ridge Agency. Bureau of Indian Affairs. Record Group 75. National Archives and Records Administration. National Archives—Central Plains Region, Kansas City, Missouri.

Records of the Rapid City Indian School. Bureau of Indian Affairs. Record Group 75. National Archives and Records Administration. National Archives—Central Plains Region, Kansas City, Missouri.

Records of the Rosebud Agency. Bureau of Indian Affairs. Record Group 75. National Archives and Records Administration. National Archives—Central Plains Region, Kansas City, Missouri.

Records of the Standing Rock Agency. Bureau of Indian Affairs. Record Group 75. National Archives and Records Administration. National Archives—Central Plains Region, Kansas City, Missouri.

Warm Valley Historical Project. Shoshone Episcopal Mission. Fort Washakie, Wyoming.

NEWSPAPERS

Rapid City Daily Journal (Rapid City, South Dakota).

BOOKS AND ARTICLES

Primary Sources

Johnston, Basil H. *Indian School Days.* Norman: University of Oklahoma Press, 1989.

Kneale, Albert H. *Indian Agent*. Caldwell, Idaho: Caxton Printers, 1950.

Meriam, Lewis, et al. *The Problem of Indian Administration*. Baltimore: Johns Hopkins University Press, 1928.

Pratt, Richard Henry. *Battlefield and Classroom: Four Decades with the American Indian, 1867–1904*. Edited by Robert M. Utley. New Haven: Yale University Press, 1964; reprint, Lincoln: University of Nebraska Press, 1987.

Standing Bear, Luther. *My People the Sioux*. Edited by E. A. Brininstool. New York: Houghton Mifflin, 1928; reprint, Lincoln: University of Nebraska Press, 1975.

Secondary Sources

Adams, David Wallace. *Education for Extinction: American Indians and the Boarding School Experience, 1875–1928*. Lawrence: University Press of Kansas, 1995.

———. "Education in Hues: Red and Black at Hampton Institute, 1878–1893." *South Atlantic Quarterly* 76:2 (Spring 1977): 159–76.

Berkhofer, Robert F., Jr. *The White Man's Indian: Images of the American Indian from Columbus to the Present*. New York: Knopf, 1978.

Coleman, Michael C. *American Indian Children at School, 1850–1930*. Jackson: University Press of Mississippi, 1993.

Cremin, Lawrence A. *The Transformation of the School: Progressivism in American Education, 1876–1957*. New York: Random House, 1961.

Cuban, Larry. *How Teachers Taught: Constancy and Change in American Classrooms, 1880–1990*. 2nd ed. Research on Teaching Series. New York: Teachers College Press, 1993.

Ellis, Clyde. *To Change Them Forever: Indian Education at the Rainy Mountain Boarding School, 1893–1920*. Norman: University of Oklahoma Press, 1996.

Hagan, William T. *Indian Police and Judges: Experiments in Acculturation and Control*. Lincoln: University of Nebraska Press, 1980.

Hoxie, Frederick E. *A Final Promise: The Campaign to Assimilate the Indians, 1880–1920*. Cambridge: Cambridge University Press, 1984.

———. *Parading through History: The Making of the Crow Nation in America, 1805–1935*. Cambridge: Cambridge University Press, 1995.

Hurtado, Albert L., and Peter Iverson, eds. *Major Problems in American Indian History: Documents and Essays*. Lexington, Mass.: D. C. Heath, 1994.

Hyer, Sally. *One House, One Voice, One Heart: Native American Education at the Santa Fe Indian School*. Santa Fe: University of New Mexico Press, 1990.

Iverson, Peter. *Carlos Montezuma and the Changing World of American Indians*. Albuquerque: University of New Mexico Press, 1982.

———, ed. *The Plains Indians of the Twentieth Century*. Norman: University of Oklahoma Press, 1985.

Kraut, Alan M. *The Huddled Masses: The Immigrant in American Society, 1880–1921*. American History Series. Arlington Heights, Ill.: Harlan Davidson, 1982.

Kvasnicka, Robert M., and Herman J. Viola, eds. *The Commissioners of Indian Affairs, 1824–1977*. Lincoln: University of Nebraska Press, 1979.

Lindsey, Donal F. *Indians at Hampton Institute, 1877–1923*. Urbana: University of Illinois Press, 1995.

Lomawaima, K. Tsianina. *They Called It Prairie Light: The Story of the Chilocco Indian School*. Lincoln: University of Nebraska Press, 1994.

McBeth, Sally J. *Ethnic Identity and the Boarding School Experience of West-Central Oklahoma American Indians*. Washington, D.C.: University Press of America, 1983.

McDonnell, Janet A. *The Dispossession of the American Indian, 1887–1934*. Bloomington: Indiana University Press, 1991.

McNeill, William H. *Plagues and Peoples*. New York: Doubleday, 1977.

———. *The Pursuit of Power: Technology, Armed Force, and Society since A.D. 1000*. Chicago: University of Chicago Press, 1982.

Mihesuah, Devon A. *Cultivating the Rosebuds: The Education of Women at the Cherokee Female Seminary, 1851–1909*. Urbana: University of Illinois Press, 1993.

———. "Too Dark to Be Angels: The Class System among the Cherokees at the Female Seminary." *American Indian Culture and Research Journal* 15:1 (1991): 29–52.

Miller, David B. *Gateway to the Hills, An Illustrated History of Rapid City*. Northridge, Calif.: Windsor Publications, 1985.

Nelson, Paula M. *After the West Was Won: Homesteaders and Town-Builders in Western South Dakota, 1900–1917*. Iowa City: University of Iowa Press, 1986.

Prucha, Francis Paul. *The Great Father: The United States Government and the American Indians*. Lincoln: University of Nebraska Press, 1984.

———, ed. *Americanizing the American Indians: Writings by the "Friends of the Indian," 1880–1900*. Cambridge, Mass.: Harvard University Press, 1973; reprint, Lincoln: University of Nebraska Press, 1978.

Rickey, Don, Jr. *Forty Miles a Day on Beans and Hay: The Enlisted Soldier Fighting the Indian Wars*. Norman: University of Oklahoma Press, 1963.

St. Pierre, Mark. *Madonna Swan: A Lakota Woman's Story*. Norman: University of Oklahoma Press, 1991.

Szasz, Margaret. *Education and the American Indian: The Road to Self-Determination since 1928*. Albuquerque: University of New Mexico Press, 1977.

Trennert, Robert A., Jr. "Educating Indian Girls at Nonreservation Boarding Schools, 1878–1920." *Western Historical Quarterly* 13:3 (July 1982): 271–90.

———. "From Carlisle to Phoenix: The Rise and Fall of the Indian Outing System, 1878–1930." *Pacific Historical Review* 52 (November 1983): 267–91.

———. *The Phoenix Indian School: Forced Assimilation in Arizona, 1891–1935*. Norman: University of Oklahoma Press, 1988.

DISSERTATIONS AND UNPUBLISHED PAPERS

Adams, David Wallace. "The Federal Indian Boarding School: A Study of Environment and Response, 1879–1918." Ed.D. diss., Indiana University, 1975.

Child, Brenda J. "A Bitter Lesson: Native Americans and the Government Boarding School Experience, 1890–1940." Ph.D. diss., University of Iowa, 1993.

Lomawaima, K. Tsianina. "Education for Domesticity: Formation of a Standardized Curriculum in B.I.A. Schools." American Society for Ethnohistory. November 13, 1992.

———. "'They Called It Prairie Light': Oral Histories from Chilocco Indian Agricultural Boarding School, 1920–1940." Ph.D. diss., Stanford University, 1987.

Putney, Diane Therese. "Fighting the Scourge: American Indian Morbidity and Federal Indian Policy, 1897–1928." Ph.D. diss., Marquette University, 1980.

INDEX

References to illustrations are printed in italics